Magazine Editing

D1414040

Including comprehensive coverage on both print and online, consumer and free magazines, *Magazine Editing* looks at how magazines work and explains the dual role of the magazine editor. John Morrish and Paul Bradshaw consider the editor both as a journalist, having to provide information and entertainment for readers, and as a manager, expected to lead and supervise successfully the development of a magazine or periodical.

Looking at the current state of the magazine market in the twenty-first century, the third edition explains how this has developed and changed in recent years, with specific attention paid to the explosion of apps, e-zines, online communities and magazine websites. Featuring case studies, interviews with successful editors, examples of covers and spreads, and useful tables and graphs, this book discusses the editor's many roles and details the skills needed to run a publication.

Magazine Editing offers practical guidance on:

- how to create an editorial strategy
- how to lead and manage an editorial team
- researching a market and finding new readers
- dealing with budgets and finance
- working with designers and production staff
- legal, technological and ethical dilemmas
- online distribution, social media and search engine optimisation
- managing information overload
- how to become an editor.

John Morrish is a freelance writer and editor. He is a former editor of *Time Out*, commissioning editor on the *Telegraph Magazine* and sub-editor on *Private Eye*.

Paul Bradshaw is Course Leader of the MA in Online Journalism at Birmingham City University and Visiting Professor in Online Journalism at City University London. In 2010 he was shortlisted for Multimedia Publisher of the Year, was listed on journalism.co.uk's list of leading innovators in media, and the US Poynter Institute's list of the 35 most influential people in social media. In 2011 he was ranked the UK's 7th most influential UK journalist on Twitter by PeerIndex.

Magazine Editing

In print and online

Third edition

John Morrish and Paul Bradshaw

Routledge
Taylor & Francis Group

LONDON AND NEW YORK

First published 2012
by Routledge
2 Park Square, Milton Park, Abingdon, Oxon OX14 4RN

Simultaneously published in the USA and Canada
by Routledge
711 Third Avenue, New York, NY 10017

Routledge is an imprint of the Taylor & Francis Group, an informa business

British Library Cataloguing in Publication Data
A catalogue record for this book is available from the British Library

Library of Congress Cataloging in Publication Data
Morrish, John, 1957-
Magazine editing / John Morrish. — 3rd ed.
       p. cm.
   Includes bibliographical references and index.
   1. Journalism—Editing. I. Title.
   PN4778.M67 2011
070.4´1—dc22   2011009221

ISBN: 978-0-415-60834-3 (hbk)
ISBN: 978-0-415-60835-0 (pbk)
ISBN: 978-0-203-80464-3 (ebk)

Typeset in Goudy Old Style
by HWA Text and Data Management Ltd

Printed and bound in Great Britain by the MPG Books Group

Contents

Illustrations

Figures

Tables

Introduction

Since the last edition of this book was published the media industry has seen enormous changes: digitisation of the way we manage production, publishing and distribution; having to learn to handle increasing amounts of user-generated content; changes in law, and grey areas where no legal precedents exist; and a move from a world where your business was based on advertising and cover sales to one of multiple revenue streams.

Publishers today talk of magazines as 'content propositions': 'Concepts that lead to collections of multimedia content, rather than strictly to the creation of bundles of paper.'[1] Editors with declining print circulations will remain persistently optimistic in public, saying things such as 'The print product is not the only way to reach your target audience, and we are seeing tremendous growth in our readers accessing *Loaded* through online channels,' or 'The *FHM* brand is still in rude health with a website visited by 1.2 million men each month.' Cynicism aside, a printed magazine can come anywhere in a project's development: *The Gadget Show* started on TV, then launched an event, then became a magazine brand too. MyHobbystore launched magazines first, moved online and into events, and finally expanded into e-commerce. To many it's no longer clear exactly what a magazine is; to others the shake-up has opened their eyes to what it always was: something that cannot be reduced to mere paper.

At the same time it is striking how much of the advice in the book is more important than ever. In a period of enormous change it is key to focus on the core skills of magazine editing: clear leadership, effective management, people skills and creative thinking around what exactly it is that your readers are buying into – whether that's printed on paper, pixels on a screen, or something intangible like a sense of community and belonging.

Different parts of the magazine industry have been affected by the rise of online publishing and distribution in different ways. Some sectors – notably teen magazines, and the music and technology sectors – have been hugely disrupted. Big brands with huge reputations built over decades have folded as new audiences found they no longer needed them.

Some titles have thrived – and it is a credit to the leadership behind them that many of these occupy the same sectors. *NME*'s position was as vulnerable as any other in the music magazine scene: for a young music fan it is now possible to listen to new releases on Spotify rather than relying on the judgement of a music journalist, and they can discover new bands by seeing what people with similar tastes are listening to via sites like Last.fm.

But NME.com – launched online well ahead of most publishers in 1997 – has reinvented the magazine's model by focusing on being the place where those fans – and their favourite bands – gather to speak to each other – and then hitching their business to the growing parts of the music industry: live performance, digital single sales, and merchandise.

Other magazines such as *Stuff* and *Kerrang!* have expanded their brand into online television and digital radio, while some have ditched paper entirely as they found the costs of printing and distribution did not justify the benefits. When people say that it is the most exciting time to be working in the industry, they really mean that it is very very scary: but that's no bad thing. Disruption not only creates opportunities for people with the right skills, it also provides an environment where people learn new skills for the right opportunities.

Apart from those areas where changing consumer behaviour has been most keenly felt, the industry has been relatively insulated from media upheaval – indeed, in the decade since the invention of the World Wide Web, consumer spending on magazines actually increased by 48 per cent. Magazines are less reliant on classified advertising than most newspapers, for example, which have suffered more keenly from declining circulation and advertising; and they are used to a more competitive environment than broadcasters have enjoyed.

Indeed, the magazine industry is more accustomed to change generally: it is a rare magazine that can claim to have enjoyed continuous publication for more than a decade. Publishers, editors and, increasingly, journalists are expected to be continually thinking of new fields to launch into: today's fad is tomorrow's charity shop donation, and an emerging market will be overcrowded tomorrow. Culture changes; the 'New Lad' grows up into '4D Man'. We are used to reinventing ourselves to reflect the image communities have of themselves.

And communities lie at the heart of successful magazine publishing – a feature which suits the nature of the web. In 2008, UK Internet users spent on average over three hours every month on community sites, compared with just two minutes on news websites. The web is, for many people, where you go to gather with people like you; people with the same problems, the same aspirations, the same hobbies. This is a huge opportunity for magazine publishers – but one that doesn't come without more competition: what can you offer that a Facebook group cannot? Why didn't you think of launching Mumsnet first?

The other feature of magazines that have insulated them from damage is the product: magazines are, typically, luxury items. Higher resolution than a web page; weighty, satisfying objects to stack on a coffee table for a leisurely flick through. That said, technical qualities have not prevented users abandoning broadcast television in favour of YouTube, and you should be wary of the magazine executive who rests on their laurels because 'You can't read a website in the bath.'

The theme of this book in its previous editions remains its central theme now: that the job of most magazine editors is to find common ground between two rival philosophies. On the one hand, journalism, which aims to provide information, enlightenment and entertainment for a selected group of readers, without much concern for cost. On the other, publishing, which aims to generate profit by creating a magazine whose readers will be attractive to wealthy advertisers. The editor negotiates and translates between the two and makes the whole idea work. Online, the 'Chinese wall' between editorial and commerce is under enormous pressure. Editors can be tempted to 'chase the numbers' in website statistics – but these can be deceptive, as Chapter 2 explains. New technologies bring with them new opportunities but also uncharted ethical, legal and commercial territory. Is it ethical to sell advertising against content created by users? What issues are raised when the magazine takes a cut on all sales of the item you are reviewing? Different readers – and different editors – will have different reactions to the same situation: changing attitudes to privacy are perhaps the best example. Part of the talent in editors in this situation is to get the feel of what is acceptable in these shifting sands.

What the past decade has shown is that the essence of the editor's job is always changing – and your role is to manage that change – but it will not change unduly. Nor will the skills an editor requires. This book describes the job, and enumerates those skills, for the benefit of those becoming editors, contemplating editing, or even just entering the profession with serious ambitions. More experienced editors too may benefit from having a point of reference, a source of ideas and (who knows?) a certain amount of reassurance that they are not alone. The skills of an editor fall into two categories. There are the journalistic skills that get you the job in the first place. Then there are the managerial skills: leading your team, dealing with money, taking responsibility. In the past, many of us had to learn those by trial and error. We went from being 'one of us' to 'one of them' overnight, and it was painful. These days, with increasing numbers of journalists having their own blogs and Twitter accounts, the shift is slightly softened – but it is still a shift.

This book covers the journalistic skills, from the new perspective of editorship: encouraging and managing the way others write and edit. But it concentrates largely on the managerial and leadership aspects of the job. Thinking and talking about money, particularly, doesn't always come easily to journalists. But a wise editor recognises that profitable (or securely funded) publishing is the guarantee of editorial integrity and quality. On the other hand, if profit becomes a publication's only goal, it will fail editorially – and then it will fail commercially. The editor must find the balance and hold on to it.

Knowing our readers and their interests has always been fundamental to editorship. The importance of market research and focus groups has been complemented by ongoing analysis of website usage statistics and interactions with readers across a number of web properties. An editor who does not deign to engage with readers in this way – or allow their journalists to do the same – plays a dangerous game. The playing field has been levelled and competition broadened: if readers have a need, you should be the first to know about it and react to it; if something better is just a click away, you need to be the first to click on it. Often, you will need to link to it too, to serve readers in the best way possible: the website that is afraid to link anywhere else is not worthy of the name. In three centuries, the way magazines have been created and read has changed as radically as society itself. In the eighteenth century, magazines were an adornment to an elite society built on elegant conversation. Printed to be read in coffee houses and learned salons, they developed alongside the City institutions that financed the Empire and the Industrial Revolution. When industrial work brought mass literacy and an advertising industry, magazines came with it. In the twentieth century, the magazine encountered cinema, radio and television and survived.

More recently, desktop publishing and online publishing have opened new opportunities to magazine publishers: lower costs mean the ability to publish to smaller markets; global distribution networks open up new markets entirely. A good editor must have an eye on these opportunities as well as the opportunists who may undermine existing magazines with new offerings. This book starts with a look at the current magazine market, and an explanation of how it has developed. It moves on to discuss the editor's many roles: knowing the reader; building an editorial team; using words, pictures and design; managing money; managing production; and playing a responsible role in the wider world. At its heart is an attempt to explain what editors do and why they are essential in the creation of everything from a parish magazine to a colour supplement. No one ever learned to be an editor from a textbook. No book can replace experience. But a book can offer a modest amount of encouragement and even inspiration, as well as a core of relevant background information. It will help you come to the job better equipped, and ensure you meet fewer nasty surprises. You should be able to speak the language of your new colleagues in management. You will understand the way things have been done in the past. But none of this should stop you doing what every editor has to do – remake the job in the way that best suits your own abilities. Good luck.

1 How magazines work

It is hard to talk of a 'magazine industry'. In truth, there are several magazine industries: magazines are incredibly diverse, in the business models that underpin them, the size of their publishers and the media they use. Combined, these industries are significant. Every year in the UK, 1.5 billion magazines are sold, making it one of the hungriest markets in the world for publishing. The total value of the sector is estimated at £4.88bn – over 60 per cent of which is generated by the consumer sector. This makes it bigger than either the music or film industries.

Like all parts of the media, magazines are having to change to adapt to changing consumer behaviour and the demands of advertisers. While circulation revenue declined by around 5 per cent between 2006 and 2010, print advertising revenue has dropped by around 33 per cent over the same period, and digital advertising increased by 75 per cent. Magazines have moved from high street outlets such as WHSmith to supermarket chains, to websites, mobile phones and tablet devices.

But it remains a massive employer: magazines and journals employ around 114,000 people – not just in editorial, but in advertising, design, web development, finance, marketing, distribution, legal and production. It is a complex business requiring a diverse range of skills.

Willings – the directory of magazines and their publishers – has over 400 pages of business-to-business publications listed, and over 300 pages of consumer magazines. Each of those magazines will have an editor, or will share that editor with a sister title. Few magazines have two editors, for reasons that will become clear: but they do exist. Attempts have occasionally been made to let editors 'job-share': they are usually short-lived. A magazine requires an individual vision, and it needs someone who will take responsibility – the blame, when things go wrong – and two people can't share that. Some magazines, though, have both an editor and an 'editor-in-chief'. This is a tricky situation. If their roles are clearly defined, it can be helpful to both parties. More often, it speaks of a nervousness or an unwillingness to delegate.

If you've never done this, go to a reference library and look at *Willings*, or *British Rate & Data*, universally known as *BRAD*. This is a monthly publication that lists every magazine and newspaper in the UK that accepts advertising (there are many more that don't, of course). You will quickly discover that not only are there a lot of titles needing editors, but also they are extraordinarily varied. And it's not simply a matter of subject matter. They also work in different ways, because they represent business strategies. One way of finding your way through them is to take the advice given to journalists Carl Woodward and Bob Bernstein when they were investigating Watergate: 'follow the money'.

- some magazines depend primarily on money from their readers or users;
- some depend primarily on money from advertisers;
- some depend on money from an outside party with something to promote.

What is interesting is that these strategies developed over time, one after the other. Now, though, they are in operation simultaneously, sometimes on the same magazine.

Reader-funded publishing

The obvious way of publishing a magazine is to get the readers to pay its whole cost. That's how books are published, as well as some scientific periodicals, business newsletters and specialised publications. It is also the way magazines began, as a type of publication that was not a newspaper but which nonetheless appeared regularly.

The first magazine is generally considered to be the German *Erbauliche Monaths-Unterredungen* of 1663, whose title ('Edifying Monthly Discussions') summed up its appeal. It was effectively a literary and philosophical correspondence conducted in public. Similar scholarly periodicals appeared elsewhere in Europe in the following years, but they were usually aimed at the intellectual elite, written by one or two authors at a time, and dedicated to a narrow range of subjects.

The variety in subject matter and authorship that we expect in modern magazines didn't appear until 1672, when the French writer Jean Donneau de Vizé created *Le Mercure Galant*. It was the first miscellany, combining accounts of court life, theatre and books with pieces of verse, and it was widely copied throughout Europe, not least in London. By 1693, London even boasted its first women's magazine, *Ladies' Mercury*.

These publications were not called magazines, of course. That name only arrived with the *Gentleman's Magazine* of 1731. Previously the word, a version of the Arabic term for a storehouse, had been used to describe actual and metaphorical hoards of treasure and, in a literary sense, books containing lots of useful information for sailors, travellers and so on. Edward Cave, creator of the publication, was trying to express the richness, variety and bounty of the new periodicals. The description has never been bettered, but his early issues do little to live up to it. Assembled by pillaging other publications, books and pamphlets, they slightly resemble modern 'press reviews' such as *This Week*, without their scrupulous concern for copyright. Later, though, Cave introduced original writing and began to justify his title.

Cave's recipe was much copied, and magazines benefited from increasing literacy, especially among women, throughout the eighteenth century. But they remained a costly item. In the middle years of the nineteenth century, the first 'family' magazines began to appear, including Dickens's *Household Words*. The formula now included lengthy pieces of serial fiction as well as improving material. Attempts were made to keep prices low. *Household Words* cost 2d, equivalent to about 45p now, and people bought it. Advertising existed, but it was only seen as a modest subsidy to the publishing operation, not least because until 1853 it was subject to a special tax. Even after the tax had been repealed, most respectable publishers recoiled from taking advertisers' money, at least for a while. Elsewhere, the opposition was more trenchant: *Reader's Digest* in the USA did not take advertising until 1955.

Reader-supported magazines continue to thrive. Much academic and scientific publishing operates in this way, the costs of production mostly being borne by libraries. Everyone who joins a club, a society or a campaign and pays a membership fee will probably be paying a significant proportion of the cost of the magazine that the organisation produces, and there are a small number of online communities which support a magazine with a regular fee, or by buying goods and services through the site. Some of these will take advertising, but it is often problematical for them, and it is never the reason for their existence.

Newsletters

Newsletters are basic print publications, usually without advertising, pictures or elaborate graphics. Their editorial proposition is that the unadorned information within is worth the whole cost of production (plus the publisher's profit). This is an extremely difficult act to sustain. In the past, industry newsletters did well by simply presenting a 'digest' of information available from other sources. Readers who considered their time valuable paid for the convenience of having someone else make a selection. All the information was available elsewhere, probably for nothing or on a normal magazine subscription.

But the point of newsletters is that their 'unprofessional' production and appearance provides an aura of authenticity, of 'unvarnished truth', that is attractive to some readers. There is a stigma attached to slickness. Sometimes the editorial skills we cherish – selecting, shaping, projecting, dramatising – are not valued. If we are honest, we will also recognise that there are times when they are not appropriate.

But a newsletter cannot succeed if its content does not convince. A specialist industry newsletter will only justify its price, often wildly beyond its perceived value, if it offers insights gleaned from those working in the field every day. They may need trained and experienced journalists to help them, but they should know their subject matter.

Newsletter publishing is a natural for online treatment, and there are many mailing lists and blogs that do similar jobs. The concept of a regular 'digest' , for example, translates particularly well to a medium based on links: 'linkblogs' perform a similar function, linking to interesting material elsewhere, often accompanied with a key quote, summary, or both. Social bookmarking tools (where you store and share interesting links) such as Delicious and Digg can do this too – and you can cross-publish these to a blog, Twitter account or mailing list through tools such as Twitterfeed and Feedburner.

Advertiser-funded publishing

> Frank Munsey contributed to the journalism of his day the talent of a meat packer, the morals of a money changer and the manner of an undertaker.
>
> (Obituary by William Allen White)[1]

Munsey was a pioneer of American magazine publishing. All he had done to bring down the wrath of White, a fellow editor and publisher, was ruthlessly to exploit an important discovery. He realised at the end of the nineteenth century that magazine publishers could raise so much money from advertisers that they could sell their publications for much less than they cost to produce. It remains the basis of most commercial magazine publishing.

He wasn't the first to come up with the idea, although he may have carried it through most effectively. A fascinating thesis written by David Phillips for his Yale University PhD tells the story.[2] The pioneer was Cyrus Curtis, publisher of the *Ladies' Home Journal*, skilfully edited by his wife Louisa. A spin-off from a local farming paper, the *Journal* was launched in 1883. Full of practical information, with a sprinkling of fashion, it found a readership among ordinary woman at a subscription of 50 cents per year. By the end of its first year, it had 25,000 subscribers; by 1885, 100,000; by 1886, 270,000.

This didn't happen by accident. The Curtises expanded vigorously, using methods that more conventional publishers considered suicidal. They cut the subscription price to drive up circulation, and used that circulation to justify increasing the price of advertising. At the same time, they increased the number of pages, from 8 to 16 and then 32, to accommodate more lucrative advertisements and to give the readers more to read. That, in turn, gave them the justification for raising the price of a subscription.

By 1893, the *Ladies' Home Journal* had become the biggest and most profitable magazine in the USA. It had grown from an eight-page, 25,000-subscriber magazine costing 50 cents a year to a 32-page publication with 700,000 subscribers paying $1 a year each. They were getting twice as much magazine for their money. But the real winners were the Curtises. A page of advertising that had cost $200 in 1883 was now bringing in $4,000.

Frank Munsey, meanwhile, had been publishing, editing and largely writing a fiction magazine for teenagers. Its usual method was to take the stories from British boys' magazines and adapt them with American settings and names. In 1889, he launched a comic weekly, and then in 1891 converted it to a general interest monthly, called *Munsey's Magazine*. Its distinguishing characteristic was that, uniquely, all its illustrations were photographs. But it did not make money until Munsey broke from the established pattern of monthly magazine publishing, which was to sell a modest number of expensive magazines to a wealthy market. He saw the success of the Curtises, and decided to aim squarely at the mass market.

In 1893, he took two radical steps. He slashed the price of a copy from 25 to 10 cents, and he increased both the amount of editorial space and the number of photographs. The fact that these photographs would increasingly feature semi-clothed female statues and paintings from the great museums did him no harm either. His circulation income dropped and his costs rose – but circulation soared. In October 1893, Munsey was selling 20,000 copies. By February 1894, circulation had reached 200,000. By the end of the century, Munsey was able to claim the biggest magazine sales in the world, double that of the combined sales of his three erstwhile rivals, *Harper's*, *Scribners* and *Century*.

With increased sales came increased volumes of advertising sold at higher rates. As Munsey and his rivals moved into the new century, they had come to expect that advertising would account for 80 per cent of their income. (In the UK today, business magazines still expect to earn the majority of their income from advertising.[3] The figure is much lower for consumer magazines, for whom sales to readers are still a dominant concern.)

The new dominance of advertisers had a number of consequences. Publishers had to be able to prove to advertisers that they were distributing as many copies as they claimed, and, after much acrimony, the Audit Bureau of Circulation was created in the USA and UK to do this job. Furthermore, publishers now had to demonstrate that their magazines would work for advertisers, using hard figures. They began to invest heavily in research into their readers' likes, dislikes and spending power. Again, this began earlier than you might think. In 1911, Cyrus Curtis created the first commercial research department to find out what his readers were buying so he could use that information to target advertisers.

The consequences of advertiser-dominated publishing

Beyond all that, there were implications that remain with us today. Magazine publishing became a punishingly expensive business to enter. On the face of it, magazine publishing is a kind of manufacturing operation, producing bundles of paper for sale. But in order to establish a new magazine, publishers must expect to make a loss during the whole period in which circulation is being built. To create bigger, more attractive issues, and print more copies of them, takes more and more money. It only becomes justified when a high circulation is reached and advertising prices can be set high. This has had the effect both of discouraging new entrants to the business and of discouraging innovation.

Without the advertising subsidy, new magazines would theoretically be profitable almost from the start – but readers would expect to pay the full cost of what they read. One of the attractions of the Internet for publishers was that readership could increase all the time without additional production costs. But the Internet presented no significant barrier to new entrants into the market: the expense of creating new print publications is what guarantees the profitability of those that already exist.

In addition, advertisers were unsure what measurement of readers to look for – or how to trust it. This situation improved when the Audit Bureau of Circulations (ABC) expanded into measuring the online 'reach' of some newspapers and magazines – an issue which became particularly important when circulations across print media started to decline. Now an increasing number of publishers present advertisers with 'cross-platform' statistics that compensate for lower print circulations with the invariably rising online ones.

Even so, the situation is more complex for advertisers than it ever was. The metrics (forms of measurement) used by the ABC include:

- How many – the 'audience reach' metric = unique browsers
- How busy – the 'volume' metric = page impressions
- How often – the 'frequency' metric = visits
- What see – the 'opportunity to see' metric = ad impressions
- What they do – the 'response' metric = ad clicks

A further complication is advertising formats, an issue the Internet Advertising Bureau UK (IAB) sought to address when it introduced standardised formats to simplify things for advertisers. The body also produces a range of research and case studies on effective online advertising.

Finally, online advertising is complicated in terms of what advertisers pay for. At first this was simple: the cost of an advert was based on the number of people who saw it. This is often referred to as CPM, or cost per thousand, and is still a major form of advertising online. What has overtaken it, however, is CPC, or cost per click – advertising where advertisers only pay if someone clicks on the advert. This model has been popularised by Google, which utterly dominates online advertising. But you also need to be aware of CPA – cost per action. This is advertising where the advertiser only pays if the user completes a particular action as a result: orders a brochure, books a holiday, registers with a site, and so on. Measurability, it turns out, is not only the biggest selling point of online advertising, but also the biggest point of competition.

Back in print, there's a curious paradox: that the most profitable time for a magazine is when circulation is declining. Advertisements are sold at a price reflecting the previous high sale, but print and production costs are now reduced. Of course, this is a short-term windfall. As soon as the falling circulation figures are revealed, wise advertisers will expect a reduction in the price of advertising.

Meanwhile, there's an important philosophical consequence of the new advertising-led mode of magazine production. It depends on combining commerce and journalism, which is something editors have to learn to appreciate. This, too, emerged very early on. Cyrus Curtis once addressed an audience of advertisers:

> Do you know why we publish the *Ladies' Home Journal*? The editor thinks it is for the benefit of American women. That is an illusion, but a very proper one

for him to have. But I will tell you the real reason, the publisher's reason, is to give you people who manufacture things that American women want and buy a chance to tell them about your products.[4]

Here is the first recognition of the chasm between the publishing and editorial outlooks. When both publisher and editor prosper by selling magazines to readers, their functions are essentially complementary. But the introduction of the advertising-based model of publishing – and some business magazines today have no other source of income – changes that. Editors may continue to see themselves as providing focused, relevant information for readers, but publishers are really supplying a commodity to advertisers. That commodity is the attention of a group of good prospects for them to advertise to. Put bluntly, magazine publishers sell readers to advertisers.

Media theorists have had plenty to say about the consequences of this, particularly in relation to the women's magazine market. Editors, though, know that the way to make the advertising-based model work is to produce compelling independent journalism. Nothing else will produce the degree of commitment and attention in readers that advertisers require in a media-saturated age.

There is a famous story about *Esquire* magazine, which in 1940 published an article praising the guitar as a source of home entertainment. Immediately, piano manufacturers withdrew their advertising, forcing the magazine to issue an apology six months later. Hard times and nervous advertisers always bring similar threats, but editors must withstand them. Independent editorial is the mark of a publication worth advertising in. When important advertisers are upset or offended, publishers may be irritated by the intangible concept of editorial integrity, which stands in the way of harmonious and mutually profitable relationships. Tough – strong editorial is the grit in the oyster. It might be uncomfortable for the oyster, but without it there's nothing worth selling.

For all its flaws, the Curtis–Munsey model of advertising-based publishing dominates the industry today. The usual way of characterising magazine publishing in the UK is to break it up into two parts: business and consumer. Business is dominated by business-to-business titles, which serve those working in a particular industry, but there are also more wide-ranging magazines, dealing with the subject as a whole. Consumer magazines, meanwhile, include both general and specialist titles, some of which – where readers are particularly expert – are referred to as 'prosumer' titles. What they all have in common is an appetite for advertising. Business magazines tend to earn most of their revenue from advertising. Consumer magazines rely more on copy sales. The difference is largely accounted for by the dominance of the 'controlled circulation' model in business publishing, in which readers receive free copies if they demonstrate that they have the kinds of occupations that the advertisers are anxious to address. But some B2B (business-to-business) publishers can charge large amounts to subscribers if the information they provide is financially valuable (such as price information), and some consumer publishers – particularly in the high-end lifestyle market – can rely heavily on advertising revenue. There are no hard and fast rules.

Business-to-business magazines

'Business-to-business' (B2B) magazines used to be called 'trade and technical'. The sector is worth £1.9bn and often the best place to find magazine jobs through traditional job adverts (not to mention the better paid ones). Aside from advertising, they earn a great deal of money from exhibitions, awards, conferences and a whole range of spin-off publications, including directories, apps, sponsored supplements and so on. Many also sell their subscription lists to advertisers. In this way, they have learned to exploit their relationships with their readers to the full without, in many cases, taking any money off them. As an editor of a business title, you will need to learn to love these 'brand extensions', to use the jargon.

There is no such thing as a typical business-to-business magazine, any more than there is a typical business. And there are few industries which do not boast at least one title: there are currently over 100 about agriculture, from *African Farming and Food Processing* to *Soil and Fertiliser Monthly*, and more than 61 clothing titles, from *Bridal Buyer* and *Textile Dyer* to *Knitting International* and Fashion4Media.com. Most will not be stocked on the news-stand – they do not need to be; they can send copies directly to the companies that employ their readers, or to a membership list that has been built over time.

At one end of the scale come glossy general publications aimed at a broad range of people working in business. Titles such as *The Economist* and *Management Today* have more in common with consumer magazines than with much of the business press, and are usually edited by people with wide journalistic experience both within and outside the business market. At the other extreme come technical titles aimed at the specifiers and purchasers of particular items of equipment: *Control & Instrumentation* and *Process Equipment News*. Their editors and journalists will almost invariably have had some experience in the industry.

In between come all the rest. Some magazines are 'industry' orientated, designed to appeal to a range of people within that sector, while others direct themselves at particular professions within an industry or towards particular technical interests. Weeklies will often have a broad appeal within, say, the computing or advertising industry. Monthlies tend to define themselves more narrowly, to particular professional groups.

When paid-for magazines and controlled-circulation (free) titles are battling in the same market, they will have subtly different objectives. Controlled-circulation magazines survive by convincing their advertisers that they are being read. This is no mean feat: those working in fields that advertisers find lucrative are often inundated with free publications. Increasing circulation, which drives paid-for magazines, will not help controlled-circulation magazines. It can only be achieved by altering the qualification criteria and increasing the size of the mailing list: that may simply make the magazine less well targeted and hence less interesting to advertisers.

Paid-for magazines need solid sales, both for circulation income and to keep advertising rates high. One editorial consequence of this is that paid-for magazines aim to be 'journals of record', aiming at longevity and sobriety. They want people to renew their subscriptions automatically, and file copies on the shelves behind the managing director's desk. Controlled-circulation titles, in contrast, need to be picked up, read and remembered, which means they tend to go for hard news and impact. Research must demonstrate to advertisers that these titles are not only seen but read with close attention.

Institutional magazines present a different set of problems. The close relationship with the parent organisation may create difficulties for the editor's freedom of action. Publishing objectives should always be clear, but in this case they may not be. Is the magazine a service for the reader, or a way of making money for the institution, or some combination of both?

The business press' readers can be very demanding. The individual industrial communities served are small, and relationships both with the title and with personalities, can be intense and long-lasting. Editors will be expected to play a role in that community in a way that does not arise for those working in consumer magazines.

One obvious difficulty is that editors will have to publish articles about their advertisers. Inevitably, some of these will be negative. This is a tricky business which will be looked at in more detail later. If your magazine is about chemistry, and chemical companies are your advertisers, you can expect trouble. It helps when advertisers have a more oblique relationship with the subject matter: magazines for family doctors are full of adverts for anti-depressants, but in general the editorial stays off the topic.

In the strictly scientific field, different editorial objectives and procedures operate: papers (academic articles, typically based on research) are subject to searching 'peer review' before being published, to ensure their acceptability, and without exception the journals are edited by those who share the vocabulary and expertise of their readers and writers. Nonetheless, while 'journalistic' values may be inappropriate, editorial skills will always be necessary.

Consumer magazines

Consumer magazines are the more glamorous end of the industry. Where B2B is about work, consumer magazines are about play. They are an accompaniment to leisure – whether that is entertainment, music or games, or fashion, culture, and hobbies. They are highly visible – on the news-stand, under readers' arms and on people's tables – sometimes a badge of identity as much as a source of information.

Editorial technology has made it cheaper and quicker to create new magazines but it is no easier to make them thrive. On one day in November 2001, IPC Media closed six titles, ranging from *Women's Journal*, a 74-year-old magazine that had slowly and inexorably lost its place in the market, to *Your Life*, a women's weekly that was less than a year old. Technology can, however, provide dying print titles with an afterlife on the web: *Sugar* magazine, for instance, stopped printing in 2011 after 17 years, but publisher Hachette Filipacchi said they would continue to focus their efforts on the associated website Sugarscape. On the same day *Elle* –

which looks to offer a '360 degree experience' to readers through complementary web and app content – celebrated its 200,000th follower on Twitter.

Titles that die – and every closure is a kind of death to those involved with it – sometimes succumb to the economic climate. The recession in 2009 hit B2B titles hard, with Haymarket's Rupert Heseltine estimating that a third of the revenue in that sector came from the hard-hit public sector. Before that the collapse of the 'dot-com' Internet economy in 2001 not only affected Internet and computing magazines (many of whose advertisers went bust without having paid for advertising), but also a lot of advertising in more general titles.

But other titles die because of changes in society itself. In the years when house prices slumped, people opted to make the best of what they had, and home interest magazines boomed. When the housing market picked up, people dreamed of new homes, lost interest in decorating, and previously successful magazines such as *Homes & Ideas* and *Garden Inspirations* were quietly put to sleep. Most recently the teenage sector, men's magazines and the technical and gaming press have suffered declines due to consumers spending their time and money online. We may like the idea of magazines that span the centuries, and many titles successfully renew themselves to adapt to changes in society, but publishers and editors are also learning to make the most of short-term enthusiasms. That means accepting that titles will be born, but also that they will die.

In business magazines, the success of a publishing venture reflects entirely the buoyancy of that sector within a nation's economy. New technologies and industries require new magazines. Shrinking industries are less attractive to publishers. Traditionally, business publishing has been practised in large houses offering many titles: as one industry goes into a temporary slump, another enjoys a boom. The titles balance one another out. But increasingly publishers target an industry only while the prospects are good: when it slumps, they turn elsewhere.

In the consumer sector, most of this kind of 'churn' takes place within what is called the 'specialist' area. Consumer magazines are often divided into 'general' and 'specialist' titles. True 'general interest' magazines were the heart of the magazine industry until the 1950s. Titles like *Titbits* or *Picture Post* offered something for everyone: news, features, fiction sometimes, puzzles and games. They ceased to exist when television began providing information and entertainment to a mass family audience. They continue to thrive on the Continent, but here they live on in two pale shadows. The first is the newspaper colour supplement, which, slightly remote from economic pressures, can afford to be interesting but not essential reading. The other is the magazine about television itself: *What's On TV*, *Radio Times* and the rest see the world through the eyes of television, but that does give them broad coverage. For a while these magazines topped the charts, but circulations declined at the end of the first decade of the twenty-first century, perhaps suffering from the rise of the broader celebrity gossip magazines.

Most 'general' consumer magazines are not general at all, but focused on a broad segment of society. They are for women or men in a particular age group and social bracket, or they are for people with a dominant interest in, say, current affairs or popular science. 'Specialist' titles, on the other hand, are for people with sharply defined hobbies and pursuits, often involving the purchase of expensive kit. This is the world inhabited by *Ships Monthly*, *Web User*, *Guitar* and thousands of other magazines: there are fewer than 100 'general' titles. The most successful specialist magazine is currently *Birds* – the magazine sent to members of the RSPB, selling over 600,000 copies. *Gardeners' World* magazine consistently tops the charts of paid-for specialist magazines, at the time of writing selling 260,000 copies – down from 344,000 copies several years ago.

Some specialist pursuits are more short-lived than others. Publishers who know this area, and who can operate at speed, aim to catch enthusiasms before they peak and leave them before they fizzle out. There are plenty of examples: skateboarding, which comes and goes; mountain-biking; particular computer games 'consoles'; TV series. While some specialist areas will always be with us – the major sports, home interests, cars, babies – others will not. So if your career takes you into more volatile areas, you will need to build up solid editorial skills as a backup to your obvious enthusiasm for the subject matter. You have to be adaptable.

The specialist titles are not negligible. About a quarter of the population will read at least one, most months. More to the point, for publishers, the readers tend to be above-average earners and to be relatively untouched by commercial television. Presumably they're working on their cross-stitching, or clearing up after their latest DIY job. They also, according to the publishers' research, read the advertising in their specialist magazines – which makes them a good audience to sell to advertisers. The challenge in the Internet age, however, is that many people in this audience are passionate enough – and knowledgeable enough – to publish online themselves too.

General consumer magazines find their readers from a broader sweep of the population and by more subtle means. If you call your magazine *Fast Ford* and have a picture of a hot motor on the front, no one is going to look inside for relationship advice. But general magazines can't always pull in their target readers so directly. They have to find them and keep them through subtleties of design, balance of content and tone of voice. Readers of women's magazines, while increasingly volatile in their reading habits, will usually settle on a title or group of titles that appeals to them. The editor has to create that appeal and sustain it, month after month, holding on to that group while deterring others who might weaken the sense of community. And yet, in terms of age, income and so on, the readers and non-readers may be exactly the same. All this can be more tricky than producing magazines for people who have kindly defined themselves by their work or leisure interests.

Of course, some editors succeed simply by producing magazines in their own image. It happened with *Private Eye* in the 1960s, and, despite some commercial difficulties, Richard Ingrams did it again with *The Oldie*. James Brown did it with *Loaded* (but failed to repeat his success with *Jack*) and Mark Frith managed it when he turned *Heat* magazine around. Common background, interests and language between editor and readers will always provide a head start. But many editors, if not most, find themselves running titles with which they have no natural empathy. Some consider that to represent true professionalism. But it is always second-best.

In general consumer magazines, especially, editors operate by instinct more than calculation.

Publishing to promote

Another way of publishing a magazine is sell it to an organisation with a message to get across. That message might be commercial, political or moralistic. The magazine is an attractive format for this type of material precisely because it is not often used to put across a single point of view. Instead, a magazine's readers expect to be intrigued, cajoled and persuaded by a variety of voices.

Publications funded by local and national government play a large role here: magazines intended to raise awareness of health issues, for example, or to help people get back into work, or any other government objective (*So British*, launched in 2004 to attract tourists to the UK, had a circulation of 240,000 for example). With increasing pressure on government finances, however, these are falling out of favour, and those projects that are commissioned are increasingly likely to be online-only.

House journals

A house journal is a magazine with no significant advertising or cover price, created by an organisation to communicate with its staff. House journals and in-house publications of all types are often produced by contract publishers, working closely with the management of the organisation concerned. But it is always a good idea for editors and writers to be close to their readers, and while in-house publications produced outside may look more professional, they rarely succeed in providing the necessary sense of an organisation talking to itself (again website news pages and forums play an increasing role).

Communication is one of the great themes of contemporary management. At its worst, the house journal is simply the contemporary equivalent of the threatening message on the notice board or a Tannoy announcement – another form of shouting. Any editor who has worked in this area has horror stories of bundles of staff newspapers delivered to branches on a Friday and returned unopened a week later. Staff must feel the publication belongs to them, even if they're not paying for it. This requires maturity on the part of management, which may not always see the point of paying for a publication that isn't crudely banging the company drum. The challenges for a house journal editor are no different from those facing any editor: you must make the journal read, and the best way of doing that is to make it loved.

Contract publishing and customer magazines

The rise of 'contract publishing' and 'customer magazines' created on behalf of retailers, airlines or membership organisations has been a defining feature of the past decade. Most of the titles dominating the top of the ABC's circulation charts come from this category: Sky's various customer magazines have often headed the list – although it has since scaled publishing down considerably – while the top 20 in 2010 included five separate supermarket glossies, a magazine for customers of a particular bank, and a smattering of publications for members of organisations from the Royal Horticultural Society to the National Trust.

The sector first came to prominence in the 1980s and 1990s, initially as straightforward promotional vehicles for the companies concerned. Since then, however, most have matured to become publishing operations in their own right. In some cases, non-journalistic businesses hire outside publishers to produce the magazines for them. In others, publishers pay for access to the company's customers, whether that is achieved through a mailing list or by direct distribution to their aircraft seat. Now around 79 per cent of the population reads one of these customer magazines.

Companies producing customer magazines have now realised that as well as controlling the editorial messages to their customers, they can sell advertising and in some cases even charge for the publication, just like traditional publishers. If they are retailers, they can give themselves a monopoly at their own checkouts. Or, they can sell the whole operation to an outside concern in return for a fee or a cut.

But the marketing is the point of the exercise. 'It's a chance to sit down one to one with your customer and have half an hour to explain what your company is about,' according to Andrew Hirsch, chief executive of John Brown Media Group, the leading British contract publishing company. 'An ad on TV or on a poster takes just a few minutes or seconds. Research shows that those with a magazine have greater loyalty.'[5] And for that to work, the magazines have increasingly become as creatively slick as the most glamorous bookstall titles.

Publishing and editing

Once editors stood aloof from the commercial aspects of their magazines. The money only mattered in so far as it permitted journalism to take place. They would only take an interest in advertising revenue, distribution and promotion when the money looked like running out. And publishers liked it like that. They thought of editors, and journalists generally, as artistic types who need to be both indulged and sheltered from harsh realities.

But reluctantly at first, and then with increasing enthusiasm, editors have learned to become involved in the publishing process, rather than simply offering editorial services to those whose business is producing magazines. Partly this is a result of tough market conditions, and partly of a new emphasis on teamwork within publishing. It may also reflect the spirit of our age, in which entrepreneurship, management and financial expertise have achieved a new status.

Editors once enjoyed 'gentleman amateur' status, which they felt was compromised by contact with money. Now they must contribute to the commercial well-being of their magazines as well as their editorial quality. All that has left some doubt about where an editor's duty lies, but it need not. An editor's most important relationship is with the readers. But for that to prosper, editors need good working relationships with their publishers.

The word 'publisher' is ambiguous, in that it means both the person or organisation which owns the magazine, or group of magazines, and the individual responsible for the day-to-day management and commercial performance of a particular title. In some organisations publishers and editors work on a basis of broad equality. The publisher organises the advertising strategy and personnel; the editor handles the editorial strategy and the journalists. Both are answerable to a publishing director or managing director. Elsewhere, the publisher is at the top of the chain of responsibility. Editors work opposite an advertising manager.

Historically, publishers have tended to come from an advertising background, while editors have always been journalists. These days, however, it is not uncommon for publishers to have started their careers in journalism before 'crossing over' or 'joining the other side'. What's more, there's less of a cultural divide between commercial and journalistic teams than there once was. Advertising sales people are now likely to have had the same education, and to enjoy the same leisure activities and interests, as their journalistic peers. Both journalism and advertising sales are increasingly graduate-entry careers.

The new generation of publishers are not, then, as remote from editors as was once the case. This is a good thing, but there are dangers. The interests of journalism and publishing are not always identical. This becomes clear when, as is often the case, journalists find themselves writing stories which have an impact on individual advertisers or the wider industries of which they are a part.

A magazine which never has to run stories about its own advertisers is privileged. More often, especially in the business press, the activities of advertisers will be a natural focus for editorial interest. Legitimate journalism will sometimes appear threatening to individual advertisers. Sales executives are protective of relationships built up over years. They will not always see the necessity to print one potentially disruptive story rather than another that would be less troublesome. And, because they work on commission, those relationships have a direct effect on their earnings. In cases of conflict, an appeal is always made to 'the interests of the magazine'. But the interests of the magazine as seen by publishers and editors do not always coincide.

The key phrase here is 'editorial integrity', an expression which has been abused by both parties in the publishing relationship. Editors use it to protect activities they just don't want their publisher to know about. Publishers sometimes use it to cordon off the area in which the editor is permitted to take an interest. An editor who is reassured that a commercial project will not impinge on his or her 'editorial integrity' should beware.

The values of the advertising world are 'hard', represented by columns of figures; those of journalism are 'soft', expressed in terms of 'news value' and 'impact'. Judgements that appear uncontroversial to an editor may not appear so to those less familiar with journalistic practice. Editors have learned the language of money; good publishers must come to terms with editorial values. Some publishers, of course, are former editors. What is striking about them, sometimes, is their 'convert's zeal': in demonstrating their commitment to commercial values, they can prove troublesome to any editors who follow them.

Distribution

Distribution is a key factor in the success of any magazine. No matter how good your publication is, if people cannot buy it then there is little point in producing it. The last ten years have seen big changes in the distribution network. There are 30 per cent more retailers selling magazines now than there were in 1992, with non-traditional outlets growing by over 50 per cent in the past five years. The biggest growth has been in the supermarket sector, which has had a direct impact on magazine formats: the move from monthly to weekly publication is at least in part due to supermarkets' preference for stock with high turnover.

WHSmith, the traditional powerhouse of magazine sales, now accounts for around 5 per cent of all magazine sales compared with the 32 per cent share claimed by grocers in 2009 (up from 26 per cent in 2004). But it does account for 17 per cent of specialist magazine sales, not least because it holds a much wider range of stock: over 2,000 magazines compared with an outlet such as Tesco, which only takes a maximum 700 titles.

The two types of outlets serve very different markets: half of WHSmith's customers are aged over 45, and a quarter of all sales come from just the Sport and Motoring sectors. A quarter of Tesco's magazine sales come from Children's and Women's Interest titles. 40 per cent of shoppers visit WHSmith specifically to buy a magazine; but people go to Tesco to buy groceries.

Negotiations with the various supermarkets, newsagents and high street outlets typically take place through a distributor, such as Comag, Marketforce or Seymour. Distributors will take their own cut of magazine sales but it is in their interests to get your magazine into as many stores as possible. They can also negotiate special display arrangements: most stores will charge you for the most eye-catching spaces, such as at the till, or on the ends of aisles.

Outside of newsagents and grocers an increasing proportion of magazines are sent direct to consumers via subscriptions – these accounted for 18 per cent of sales in 2010. Subscriptions have the obvious appeal of cutting out both distributor and outlet, while guaranteeing sales for six or twelve months ahead and demonstrating to advertisers that you have committed, engaged readers – which is why you often see huge discounts being offered. Recently a number of publishers have teamed up to offer more flexible subscription packages that allow consumers to switch publications or benefit from special deals.

Directories and data

Often a spin-off from business-to-business magazines, directories and data publications can provide anything from raw data in real time to in-depth listings of reviews. This sector has risen in importance of late partly because of the spread of Internet access: a natural platform for delivery as it provides for both timeliness and personalisation; and also because of the sheer amount of information that many businesses have to cope with: paying for a pre-filtered digest, or authenticated data, has real utility in that situation.

Data services often work in conjunction with a magazine and free website: the website brings in potential customers for both the magazine and the data service; the magazine builds on that and drives customers towards the data services too. *ICIS Chemical* from Reed Business Information is just one example: 'data reporters' gather the price data that forms the basis for online price alerts, analysis in print and a range of other journalism.

Digital magazines

Increasingly publishers and – in the case of promotional or in-house magazines – clients are looking to launch digital magazines. These can range from extending existing publications online, or launching an 'app' (read on a mobile phone or tablet such as the iPad), to completely new publications. Many are attracted by the much lower costs; others because they feel it is the fashionable thing to do; and some because they simply recognise that that is where the audience work, rest and play.

Most publishers now have some online-only properties in their stable: Dennis has the gadget magazine *iGizmo* and men's magazine *Monkey*, both of which aim to replicate the physical magazine experience – down to being able to turn the covers of virtual pages – but with video and links embedded right into the page. Future has the likes of *GamesRadar* and *MusicRadar* – more traditional websites based around online communities. Natmags has *Handbag* and *AllAboutYou*, which aggregate content from across their magazines under a separate brand. Some of these have been acquired, and some launched in-house.

While most magazine websites were initially launched as a place to sell more advertising against content that had already been produced, publishers soon discovered that the prices they were used to charging for advertising were unsustainable in this much more competitive environment. As a result, many have changed their strategy towards using their websites as a way to attract new subscribers to print and data services, and as a way to building customer databases. Econsultancy's Craig Hanna says they used their free blog to collect information on 100,000 registered users, to which they then could market events, supplier listings, training and data services. They also use the platform to advertise subscription-only reports, and social media platforms such as Twitter to invite new project ideas.

Almost every magazine is expected to have some online presence, and many will have associated 'apps' – on iPhones, Android and other mobile platforms, or on the iPad and the tablets that have followed. The tablet phenomenon kicked off by the launch of the iPad in 2010 was welcomed by many in the magazine as a potential 'silver bullet' for the woes haunting the industry. The tablets themselves were magazine-sized and Apple's App Store presented a ready-made news-stand where consumers were willing to pay for content. Nicholas Coleridge, managing director of Condé Nast UK, who launched iPad apps for both *Wired* and *Vogue*, predicted that up to 40 per cent of the publisher's sales would one day come from tablets.

But this simplistic vision came up against a number of brutal realities: first, unlike real news-stands, magazines would still have to compete with the limitless free online content that users could access on the iPad – not just magazine websites and blogs, but games, video, books and audio.

Second, not only did Apple take a 30 per cent cut of all sales, but also they held back the valuable data on who was actually buying their apps. For many publishers who relied on being able to tell advertisers who was looking at the adverts, this was a deal-breaker.

And finally, it turned out that most consumers were not willing to regularly pay print prices for a virtual product. *Wired*'s iPad app, for example, famously outsold the print version when 105,000 copies of the first app were downloaded – but three months later sales had dropped to 32,000 per issue. *People* and *Men's Health* only managed downloads equivalent to 1–2 per cent of print sales. ShortList Media's Mike Soutar feels that this is because 'Beyond the novelty of the launch edition, consumers are not happy to pay anything like the same amount that they might pay for the magazine.'

There is also clearly a lack of either creativity or understanding of the medium in many magazines' ventures into apps. One publisher even bragged about the lack of money that they had spent on their iPad app. This is akin to reading out your magazine on the radio: it's a different medium, with different strengths, weaknesses, and consumption behaviour. The *BBC Good Food* app, for example, includes 'videos displaying cooking techniques demonstrated by the *Good Food* Team, and a personalised shopping list to help the user plan their meals throughout the month. The app also includes a glossary of ingredients and techniques, and an easy-to-use search facility for the user to find their favourite dishes.'[6]

It's worth explicitly identifying how these tools play to the strengths of the medium: multimedia, personalisation, links, and search. You could add to that the ability to share with others, live updates, and providing information related to the user's location.

The problems with the tablet platform may be addressed as the technology matures, tablet penetration increases and the offerings become more creative – many consumers complain that iPad versions of magazines offer little different from the print product, for example. But this proliferation brings further problems too – not least having to launch apps into more than just Apple's marketplace using more than their technology. By the time you are reading this, the industry should have learned plenty of lessons about the platform: you should find them, read them and learn from them. A good place to start is the US Association of Magazine Media's web page documenting all the initiatives they are aware of (www.magazine.org/digital/14321.aspx).

The publishing imperative

A journalist who is only interested in making money is not to be trusted. But then, neither is a publisher who is not interested in it. In the commercial sector, making money is the essence of publishing, and provides the validation for the activity. Profit is a measure of how well you are employing people's talents and your company's resources. A profitable magazine is one which is wanted, valued and has earned its right to exist. This is not something to be scorned.

A publisher who is not interested in making money has some other motive. This may be entirely honourable. There are publications which run permanently at a loss because they provide the publisher with rewards that are not financial in nature. They may provide an entrée into a particular social or professional group. They may provide an outlet for the publisher's views, talents and desire to be a patron. Or they may promote a cause. All are types of 'vanity publishing'.

Generally, editors should want their magazines to make a profit. It is a mark of success and the guarantee of independence and longevity. Sometimes long-term financial success makes publishers conservative, but profitability is usually welcome. The alternative, unending financial stringency and uncertainty, will not help you concentrate on editorial excellence.

Publishers work by finding market 'niches' into which they can introduce new magazines. That means finding a group of likely readers with a common interest that is not being served, or finding advertisers wishing to reach a particular type of customer, or some combination of the two. Publishers have to do the sums. The number of readers and their spending power must be sufficient to bring in enough lucrative advertising to make publishing pay. Once the magazine is running, the publisher must keep income high and costs low. Both bring the possibility of conflict with editors. Journalism is costly, and can lead to the loss of income.

According to John Wharton, author of *Managing Magazine Publishing* (1992), 'Editors and journalists must accept that in the tough world of magazine publishing no action should be taken which harms the profit potential of a magazine or a company.' Many editors will find this unacceptable. An editorial attacking, say, the pricing policy of a major advertiser might lead to a drop in income. It might also be necessary to remind the readers that the magazine takes their side. Reviewing several products, and finding one to be preferable to another, is always dangerous, especially in markets where advertisers have come to expect a supine attitude from both magazines and their own customers. But both types of article are valuable. The magazine's long-term prospects depend more on serving its readers than on keeping all its advertisers happy all the time.

Naturally, you must strive for fairness in your dealings with everyone – readers, sources, advertisers and potential advertisers. Favouritism, bias and self-interest will be more damaging than the occasional row with an advertiser, although that can be hard to explain to people who work on commission. Even in the world of controlled circulation, where virtually the entire income of a magazine comes from advertisers, editors must remember that the interest of the readers comes first, followed by that of the advertisers as a group, rather than individually. When advertisers are scarce, and rival publications are both numerous and less fastidious, this is difficult advice to follow. But while theory may say that magazines exist to serve advertisers, it's not a practical or desirable view for an editor to hold. Put the readers first.

The editorial imperative

The language of profit and loss is, on the face of it, unambiguous. Those who use it have the advantage of straightforward objectives and goals in their working lives. But accountancy won't help you edit a magazine. The modern magazine industry is highly commercial, but editors should not lose heart. It only exists because of editors and editorial. And the importance of strong, accurate, independent editorial is likely to grow.

When rival content is a click away, the quality of content and the personality and reputation of its authors are more important than ever – and when readers are your distributors (through pushing you up the search engine rankings by linking to you, and through sharing on social networks), building that is key.

If making a profit is the publishing imperative, what is required from editorial? To tell the truth, some would say, but that's both too much and too little. No publication can ever tell the whole truth, not the Bible, *Ulysses* or the *Encyclopaedia Britannica*. And telling 'nothing but the truth' offers little editorial guidance. For our purposes, the editorial imperative is to seek new and relevant information and entertainment for a particular group of readers, to vouch for its accuracy and to shape it into a useful and approachable form. In the networked age, it is also to connect readers and allow them to communicate with each other.

At heart, editing is creative, but its administrative and managerial aspect must be mastered if the creativity is to come through. A magazine is always more than a collection of parts: it has a personality of its own. The editor works through others, but takes the dominant role in shaping that personality. In discussions about the commercial and managerial aspects of editing, that role should never be forgotten, because it is the one thing no one else can to do.

Beyond the culture clash

The scene would appear set for an epic battle between the representatives of two philosophies: on the one hand, the advertising fraternity, motivated and directed by money; on the other, the editor, righting wrongs, slaying dragons, tilting at windmills and offending advertisers.

Luckily, these are caricatures. The two sides have plenty to learn from each other. It is often the case, for instance, that those who have come through the sales route have better 'people skills' than those in editorial. They know how to negotiate, how to structure a discussion, how to present themselves, and so on, and it can be good for editors to come into contact with this kind of expertise. The detailed information some sales staff keep on their contacts, so they can start each new call with a casual reference to the contact's recent holiday or new car, might usefully be copied by reporters struggling to get to know new sources. At the same time, people from a commercial background are often very good at sorting out the different interests involved in any discussion or negotiation. They know what their clients require from them, they know the service they have to provide and they know its value.

Most editors are less happy in this context, and they lack a guiding philosophy. They are often confused about the web of relationships in which they occupy a central position. How are they to balance the different duties they owe to readers, advertisers and those they write about? As in most business situations, it helps to take the view that 'the customer is always right', and for magazine editors the customer is the reader. The editorial effort of the magazine is directed to finding and keeping each reader. It is to the reader that editors owe their deepest duty and loyalty. Too often readers are seen as an irritant, an unnecessary drag on the smooth running of the publishing machine, a group to be steered, persuaded and bullied but never consulted, engaged in discussion or trusted. This is a mistake – particularly when they have more power than ever to talk back, and organise themselves to make you listen.

This same power can be used for the good of the magazine – as long as that coincides with the good of the readership. It has already been noted how important readers are in online distribution, but you also want readers to come first to you with interesting stories, to contribute video and other media when a project suits it, and to initiate or support campaigns that the magazine pursues.

Some will argue that an editor's loyalty should be to the publisher. Certainly, the act of publishing needs to be a team effort, and the publisher provides the wherewithal to make it happen. But that relationship is not at the heart of the editorial task. Nor is the relationship between you and your advertisers. They are not your customers. Your obligations to advertisers are met through your relationship with your readers.

A compelling magazine will win readers and draw them back time and time again. They will enjoy the magazine, value it, trust it and want to spend time with it. The need for such a relationship comes particularly strongly to the fore when readers do not pay for your content. The launches of free magazines *Shortlist* in 2007 and sister title *Stylist* in 2009 were met with widespread scepticism on this score: 'I suspect that most people who read it only flick through – which makes it less appealing as an advertising prospect,' commented one former men's magazine editor in 2009. But ShortList Media – and its chief executive Mike Soutar – succeeded in convincing advertisers that you could build a strong relationship with readers even when they hadn't paid for the magazine.

The rise of high quality free content online certainly helped, removing some of the poor reputation that 'free' had previously had. But it has also introduced new challenges for publishers.

Magazines have a different type of relationship with their readers – or users – online. Even free printed magazines have some limitations on their market, because they have to choose where to distribute copies, and how many to print. Online, users can come from anywhere and many will be encountering its content for the first and only time – what have been described by some executives as 'window shoppers'. These casual visitors may contribute to impressive visitor numbers, but that may count for nothing if the advertiser wants a specific type of user, rather than lots of them.

If that is the case, you may need to provide evidence of 'engagement' – i.e. that readers are passionately interested in your content rather than encountering it accidentally. Typical ways of measuring this include the time a user spends reading a web page (the longer, the more engaged), the number of pages visited, and the 'bounce rate' (the proportion of visitors who leave the site after looking at only one page). In addition, traffic coming from social networks suggests that people are coming through recommendation, which is another positive sign.

The advertisers pay to join the relationship between reader and magazine, but they do so at a tangent. They want a share of the attention the readers give the magazine, and they want to wrap themselves in the good feeling the magazine gives the readers. They are essential to the magazine's economics. They are the advertising department's customers, and they're also the publisher's. But they're not your responsibility, and they're not your customers.

Publishers tend not to grasp this. From the glossy magazine factories of the West End to the business-to-business houses in new towns and suburbs, editors are increasingly expected to make themselves available to advertisers. Companies which advertise with you will undoubtedly have interesting and useful information and views on the people and the world you are serving. But it is not a sensible use of your skills or time to be paraded before advertisers as a kind of trophy, shoring up the sales staff's efforts to flatter the advertisers into signing up. That said, US editors often have visits to advertisers written into their contracts.

An editor is employed to produce a magazine that will attract the readers that advertisers are keen to reach. Your strategy for reaching those readers, your proposals to improve the quality, integrity and standing of your magazine, may well have some influence on advertisers' intentions. You may well, on occasions, be persuaded that you are the best person to explain to them what you are doing. You may have created special new projects that will appeal to advertisers and may want to talk about them. But you are not, and must not be seen to be, an adjunct to your magazine's advertising team.

The magazine life-cycle

Every magazine starts with a launch, and sometimes editors rather than publishers are the driving force. But that is rare. Sometimes, an editor and publisher or advertising director will leave a magazine together and start a new product, often in competition with their old employer. Most commonly, though, a publisher or would-be publisher will have an idea for a magazine and then go looking for someone to provide its editorial.

By the time you have been recruited, the publisher may already have decided on a paper format and/or online content management system, found printers and created a schedule, acquired premises and computers and, most important of all, conjured up a business plan and raised the finance. But you will have to come up with the editorial strategy to make the title work. You can't do that in a vacuum. You need good information about the supposed advertisers and the readers they want to address. Then you have to find out what you can about those readers and what they need to read.

Planning a launch

In theory, it should be quite cheap to start a magazine, especially now that most production jobs can be done in-house on reasonably cheap equipment. Certainly, you can launch an online magazine with no expenditure at all (although you should at least invest in a memorable web address).

You can immediately put together a paper dummy, which really need be no more than a title, a slogan, some sort of mission statement, and some ideas about the kind of pieces you propose to publish. You can also put together a running order or two and try some flat-planning (all these are discussed in Chapter 7). These will give you, and perhaps your publisher and new editorial colleagues, some idea of what's needed.

For outsiders, you will need a more elaborate 'design dummy', featuring a realistic attempt at your cover style and a couple of laid-out sections using dummy copy. You should also create what book publishers call a 'bulking dummy', with blank pages but giving an idea of the weight and heft of the finished product. All these things are shown to your backers, your printers, your distributors, newsagents and a good cross-section of your potential readers.

In practice, few launches are quite such do-it-yourself affairs. New magazines tend to be expensive, specialist products, carefully targeted so that they don't run headlong into successful mass-market magazines, or 'slow-burner' projects that build an audience online before moving into print (if at all).

There are obvious questions to ask to avoid making basic mistakes. The most obvious one is: where will most of the money come from? Can you justify a high cover price? Are there advertisers desperate to reach this audience? If it is advertising-led then you need to know whether they will be looking for a high circulation, or a targeted audience. Or do they merely want your 'brand values' to rub off on their public image?

It's easy to forget about retailers. Your new magazine idea may tap into an as-yet-unnoticed market, but if that market doesn't fit into the categories that WHSmith uses on its news-stands, then it will be difficult for retailers to stock – and even harder for consumers to find. Equally, if you're launching into an already overcrowded market, retailers may simply decide they do not have any more space for you.

You need to look beyond the first issue and ask how sustainable the magazine is: your idea may be unique, but is the execution better than the rest? Will your competition fight back, and how? How will you respond in turn? How long will your audience buy your magazine? And how long do you need to keep going before you break even? New launches take a very long time to start making money.

Instead, their sales immediately slump after the launch issue. This is called the 'hockeystick curve': it can take anything up to 18 issues before titles return to the level of sales achieved with the first issue. Publishers always have a sales target as part of their preparations. By the end of their first year, most new publications are probably 25 per cent down on that. Some never make it.

Survival

Many magazines are strangled at birth, or shortly afterwards: sales are so disappointing that no one can see any hope in continuing. Magazines that are stealthily launched by being spun off from existing titles are in less danger here. But those that have depended on massive television advertising and cut price offers to get them going may not survive when those artificial aids have to be withdrawn.

The next danger period is after 18 months or so for monthlies or about six months in the case of weeklies. The magazine should by now have survived the hockey-stick period and be showing signs of thriving. The sales should start to grow, and advertising rates will grow with them. If it is not succeeding, however, there needs to be serious discussion about a change of direction. The most famous case here must be EMAP's *Heat*, which was a dead duck despite vast promotional spending: it was only saved when someone had the idea of scrapping its original male target and turning it into a gossip magazine for a new audience who didn't care about European royalty or the stars of ancient sitcoms.

Of course, a change of direction may mean even more promotional spending, as you advertise to undo the image created by your previous campaigns: *Heat* again. Still, if you survive this, and circulation rises, you are into a period of sustained growth. Many magazines find they grow in this way for three or four years, taking the circulation at last up to the target level.

Maturity

A mature magazine can expect its sales to stabilise at about 25 per cent more than it achieved at launch. Its advertising revenue is healthy too. Unfortunately, it is a target for new launches who see it as soft and ready for attack. In order to thrive, it needs to keep sharp editorially, attracting new readers all the time to replace those who drift away, and to spend on promotion.

Decline or institutionalisation

A small proportion of magazines achieve institutional status. They become part of the landscape of British life, which may not be a good thing. It makes it difficult to respond positively to the gentle slipping away of sales. Fear may be the dominant factor in the publishing office, as people shy away from tampering with a formula that has served them well. In the long run, this is a mistake. The true institutions of British magazine life have had to reinvent themselves at intervals in order to thrive. *Radio Times* is a good example, as are *New Statesman* and *Saga*. Those that never find a satisfactory way of responding to changing times are doomed.

Most magazines, though, never achieve that position in the first place. They can expect to see sales decline after seven or eight years, often when the original editor or publisher has moved on or when the publication has been sold to a different organisation with no emotional attachment to it. Relaunches, redesigns and radical changes of editorial stance can achieve temporary improvements, and increasingly publications will continue to publish online, but if other publications have scented weakness and entered the market sector, the end is in sight.

However, the good news is that there are always new launches, even in bad economic times. The death of a magazine, especially a venerable title, is always sad. But as editors we need to be ready to pick ourselves up and start again.

2   Editorial strategy

When you take on an editorship, for the first or tenth time, you are likely to face a number of challenges. Some of these may be technical. Others will be financial. How much do I have to spend? How much do I have to save? But the most prominent will concern relationships. You will have new colleagues, or you will be seeing old colleagues in a new way. The same goes for your boss. You will have to forge new relationships with writers, PR people and photographers, and a clutch of rivals. But your most important relationship is with the reader.

The task ahead

Before you start doing things, however, you need to know what is expected of you. That can be difficult to discover. Employers are not usually enthusiastic about confiding their hopes and fears during interviews, particularly not in the early stages. By the time you agree to take the job, you should know how things stand, but nasty surprises are not unknown. Some editors make a good living by taking on troubled or failing titles; others only discover the true horrors after a month or so. Supplement what you have been told by what you can discover for yourself.

If you are launching a magazine, you, your staff and your publisher will be learning together. More likely, you will inherit a magazine and a market situation and be invited to make things better. You may be asked to increase circulation, and you may have your own editorial ideas for doing that. Remember, however, that non-editorial factors are increasingly important in driving sales: advertising, PR, subscription offers and free gifts. Likewise, the web will be a key low-cost battleground in raising awareness.

You can do nothing to prevent new competitors entering your market. Indeed, some may even launch low-price 'spoilers' aimed mainly at knocking you out of the market (these may not make any profit for the publishers, but by preventing you from competing with them elsewhere, they will protect their profits there). You should also be aware of indirect competition both in print and online: if you publish a niche fashion magazine, for example, watch out when mainstream publications begin to devote regular coverage to that niche. Likewise, your UK audience for Hollywood gossip may find they can get it direct from US websites.

Often you will be asked to do something less obvious than simply improve circulation – or arrest a declining one. You may be asked specifically to persuade your readers to buy the magazine more often. You might be encouraged to find more wealthy readers, or younger readers. Another goal might be enhanced 'authority', particularly if you are producing a business publication. Often your publisher will couple these instructions with stern warnings not to change the magazine's 'brand identity', spend extra money or provoke controversy. Beware of what psychologists call 'double-binds', whereby you are asked to do two entirely contradictory things simultaneously. It is not uncommon for editors to be told to give a magazine fresh contemporary appeal without changing any of the typefaces, or a bright new voice without replacing any of the writers.

Beware also of technology-driven requests to 'launch a social network' or an iPad app simply because everyone else is doing it. These are often perfectly reasonable strategies – but there must be an objective behind them, or it will become easy to spend more than you should, to get mixed results. If you are asked to pursue a project like this, ask what the end result is expected to achieve: is it increased advertising revenue? New revenue streams? Retaining existing readers? This will not only ensure that the project has a clear focus (which may actually mean using a different technology to that originally suggested) but also something against which you can measure success.

The 'POST' strategy proposed by Forrester Research is useful here. This involves identifying:

- People: who are your audience (or intended audience), and what online media (e.g. Facebook, blogs, Twitter, forums, etc.) do they use? Equally important, why do they use it?
- Objectives: what do you want to achieve?
- Strategy: how are you going to achieve that? How will relationships with users change?
- Technology: only when you've explored the first three steps can you decide which technologies to use.

Most editors will have tremendous power to change things, and their colleagues know this. They may not always appreciate it. Change is threatening, and for that reason it should usually be trailed well in advance. You may see a clear need to alter the magazine's direction. But you can't do it on your own, nor should you try. At the very least, you should take the bulk of the readers with you.

On the other hand, change may not be required at all. The usual cliché is 'a steady hand on the tiller'. This can be a gentle introduction to editorship, though in the long term vessels steering an unchanging course tend to collide with immovable obstacles. At some point you may start thinking about a change of direction. But if no one wants that, you may find yourself frustrated.

Alternatively, if the previous editor was not liked, anything you do will be applauded, so long as it is different. Magazines with excitable managements tend to zigzag, changing direction radically as each new editor is appointed. This is exhausting for everyone, notably the readers, who may migrate to find a quieter life elsewhere. Editing by simple reaction – turning things upside down for the sake of it – is a mistake. Change should be based on research and strategy, not a desire to impress: evolution not revolution.

New editors experience two contradictory impulses. The first is to make a mark, quickly, changing enough to show your staff, your colleagues and your professional peers that the magazine is under new management. It is almost a tradition for newly appointed editors to arrive and immediately remake the next cover, after deadline. It's an expensive gesture that may be applauded if performed with sufficient panache. But it won't impress your readers. They will take a long time to notice your changes, and, when the sales figures come in, you may find that they don't like them.

The second impulse is to freeze, to keep everything the same while you struggle with the complications of your new life, from mastering the computer system to learning everyone's name. Your first issues may have little of you in them except the name at the top of the staff box. Those who have appointed you may be disappointed. But they should be patient.

A magazine is a complicated thing, both a product and a human institution. At first, the most important thing you can do is listen. Discover why things are the way they are, observe the complex interaction of personalities, determine the inner workings of the magazine, and then act. It is better to make slow changes than wrong changes. In any case, the only audience which really matters is the one which hands over its money to the newsagent.

That is not a surrender to inertia. Many of your colleagues will have a vested interest in leaving things the way they are. But they won't be held responsible when doing nothing leads the magazine into disaster. You will. Demonstrate, early on, that you have the will and the authority to make the changes you consider necessary. But first make sure they are the right ones.

Prepare for yourself what the military call a 'situation report', establishing how things stand. Even without access to management information – obviously you will get that in due course – you can consider the character of your magazine. Start with the fundamentals, such as publishing strategy, distribution method, frequency and paper format. You should also have a strong understanding of the magazine's place online: what sort of traffic does it get? What Google PageRank does it have (there are various calculators online)? Does it have pages or groups on Facebook? Followers on Twitter, Flickr, YouTube or other platforms?

Is this a magazine that lives by taking money from its readers, or does it depend more on advertisers? Is there any other subsidy in the background, perhaps from a professional organisation? Does it have a strong presence on the bookstall, or are its readers mainly postal subscribers? Or does it go out free, by controlled circulation? Does it have an email distribution list? What consequence have those facts had for the magazine's authority and outlook? How will they affect your freedom to edit?

How does the magazine sit in the workplace? Does it have rivals? How does it perform against them? How is it perceived by those rivals, and by the industry it serves, and by advertisers? What is its corporate situation? It may be one magazine among many similar titles in a giant house. It may be an individual owner's pet project. Its future may depend entirely upon figures in a spreadsheet – or on the changing moods of its owner.

And what is its history? A long and distinguished heritage may help a magazine to hold a place in the current market. On the other hand, history is just as likely to represent a serious obstacle to making it thrive. The example of *Punch* comes to mind. The magazine was founded in 1841, and was still thriving in the mid-twentieth century, with a weekly sale of 175,000 copies as late as the 1940s. In 1969, it was acquired by United Newspapers from the printing firm that had owned it almost from the beginning. United attempted to turn it into a more commercial proposition, packed with glossy upmarket advertising. Then, in 1989, United appointed David Thomas, a young editor from a colour supplement background, with a brief to find younger readers. The changes horrified a vociferous group of traditionalists and former contributors and alarmed long-standing readers – without attracting new readers in sufficient numbers.

This is not unusual when attempts are made to save venerable titles by radical surgery. *Punch* closed in 1992. Then, in 1996, Mohamed Al Fayed reopened the magazine, only to close it again in 2002, when its circulation had dropped to only 6,000.

At the other end of the scale, a new magazine is usually burdened with a terrifying weight of expectation. The average time a magazine has to prove itself is four years. If it is younger than that, a day of reckoning may be approaching. If it is older, it may already be living on borrowed time.

The difference between weeklies and monthlies is another important question. It's not solely a question of publishing rhythm, staffing and topicality. It's also about how the different types of magazine are perceived. A difference of paper format, whether A4 or tabloid/A3 or the A5 'handbag format' popularised by Condé Nast's *Glamour*, will also have effects on working practices and the way the reader is addressed.

Questions of how a magazine presents itself, the approach it makes to its readers, are vital for an editor. You can find out, through research, exactly how the readers feel about it. But you won't usually have that information at hand. You need to sit down and read the magazine afresh, leaving aside everything you know about the struggles involved in magazine publishing and everything your journalistic experience tells you. You must look at it with innocent eyes.

Now, is it friendly, or is it remote? Does it seem to know everything? Is it interested in sharing? Is it authoritative, or just pompous? Is it irreverent, or just facetious? Is it informative, entertaining, or neither? Does it understand its readers, share their concerns? Does it even like them?

Now, broaden your scope a little. Pick up some of the other magazines in the same market and look at how they work. How does your magazine compare with its rivals? Is it upmarket or downmarket of them? Does it lead trends, or does it follow them? Can it be trusted? What do its rivals think of it? What kind of advertisers are drawn to it? Are the ads addressing the same reader as the editorial? If they don't, you'll want to find out why.

Repeat the process online: are there blogs or online communities that serve the same audience? Is there a fan community for the magazine? Or a hate community? Are there magazines from other countries which don't compete on the news-stand, but do online? What about mobile or tablet apps?

Not everything about a magazine is on the surface. It may have a symbolic significance that is at odds with the reality. It may remind your readers of happier times. It may be its owner's first magazine, or favourite magazine. It may be where your publisher learned to sell classified advertising. Certain apparently minor aspects of the magazine – typefaces, running orders, individual columns – may have a significance to other people that is not apparent to you as a newcomer.

Think all these things through, but do so quickly. It is not uncommon for magazines to be left directionless for months while the editorship is touted around. You may arrive to find that the issue in progress consists of little more than the scrapings from various bottom drawers, cobbled together by a resentful and demoralised workforce lacking direction.

Worse, you may be taking on a launch which has everything except a reason to exist. Magazines start with a publishing strategy, created by research, mostly quantitative, which shows how many people in a certain bracket might be interested in purchasing a particular type of magazine, how old they are, where they live, how much money they earn and what they do for a living. Unfortunately, such information does not constitute an idea, and without an idea magazines rarely succeed.

An editor's strategy starts where the publishing strategy stops. It stops talking about groups of people in socio-economic brackets and starts to consider individuals: what type of person will read this magazine? What is he or she like? And then it builds a magazine around those individuals, deciding what to include and what to exclude, how to approach the subject matter and, crucially, how they should be spoken to.

Increasingly, in a multiplatform environment, the readers are part of production, and attracting the vocal users who will drive your forums, comment threads, ratings charts and Facebook groups, is an equally important part of strategy.

Good magazines are edited by their readers.

(Pat Roberts Cairns)[1]

In the case of an existing magazine, your readers are already in position. It is your job to rediscover them, to get to know them, to clean away the patina of assumption and prejudice about them that has been built up over the years. Then the editorial strategy is a matter of tightening, shaping and focusing. You can do research, you can ask questions, but you need a 'feel' for it. Can you summon up a vivid sense of what readers want from your magazine, keep it with you through every last editorial task and communicate it to every member of your editorial team? It is by this process that editors are made.

Building your editorial strategy

The editorial strategy is your contribution to the team effort involved in publishing a magazine. At an early stage, the magazine will have been the subject of a marketing plan which will have explored the size of its potential market and gathered statistics about the people within it. The editorial strategy identifies your readers within that potential market, and explains how you propose to keep them interested. The strategy may be in written form, or it may exist only in your head. Either way, you need instant access to it. You will be expected to talk about it at short notice and with confidence.

Your editorial strategy is tested with every issue. Sales figures for individual issues may not be a reliable guide to how it is working (many other factors are important), but patterns emerge over time. It is not enough to wait for sales to tell you whether you are heading in the right direction: by then, it may well be too late. Your theoretical editorial strategy needs to be tested against the interests, desires and needs of the readers at frequent intervals, and adjusted as necessary.

What the readers want from you

Imagine for a minute that you are a stand-up comedian, or that you have been called upon to make a speech to a packed hall. How can you ensure that you communicate with your audience? It is tempting to say that you must make them like you. But that's hard to achieve when they may be sceptical or even hostile, as audiences tend to be. You don't want to appear needy.

The real answer is to convince them that you like them. If you convince them you know them, understand them, value them, they will like you. It's automatic. And that is what an editor needs to do: to see the world through the reader's eyes. After that, decisions on what to cover, and how to deal with it, should fall into place.

Turning your attention to the readers' interests, desires and needs, and following where they lead, is frequently called 'focus', and is in many ways the most important part of the editor's job. As editor you may be a brilliant manager, an inspiration to staff, a leading prose stylist and a legend within the industry, but if you don't know your readers all that will be wasted.

Some would say you need an 'instinctive' grasp of what the readers want – and, almost as important, what they don't want. And instinct may work for those who edit magazines which cater to their own personal passions or who are lucky enough to be able to produce the magazine they want and hope readers will come to them. Most editors have to develop their focus on the reader through hard work. If you are editing an existing magazine, you have plenty of opportunity to encounter your readers. Are they, for instance, to be judged by the vociferous minority who contribute to the letters page? Or the larger group of people that populate your online forums – but who may not actually buy the magazine? Are they the people you see on the bus, reading your magazine? Or are they the people you meet at trade shows? Or who sign up as fans on your

Facebook page? They are all those, not to mention the vast majority you never hear from.

Website analytics

In addition, you will be able to gain some understanding of your readership by looking at the 'analytics' from your magazine's websites. Website analytics are pieces of information about how people use the website, where they come from, and where they go to. For the purposes of understanding your readers – and website users – the key pieces of information here are the phrases that people search for when finding your website (see Figure 2.1). This gives an indication of which topics are most popular – but also which topics your website ranks best for on Google. Overlooking this last aspect and paying too much heed to these stats can mislead you. It may be, for instance, that if you publish a classic music magazine many of your readers are searching for 'The Beatles' – but they are not arriving at your site because you don't appear highly in search engine results for that term (the solution to this problem – search engine optimisation – is covered in Chapter 7).

You should also be able to see which articles are the most popular, although again this can be misleading: an article can be popular because your readers love it, or because another very popular website has linked to it (not always because they

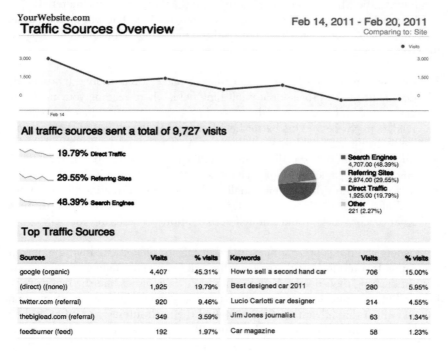

Figure 2.1 Example of a section of a web analytics report

like it). Tracing back where the traffic has come from to 'inbound links' from other websites, emails and social networks will give you more contextual information.

Finally, you'll be able to see what countries your users are accessing your site from, what browsers they are using (i.e. Internet Explorer, Firefox, Safari, etc. – useful information in testing your website), and also more detailed information about how long they spend on each page, how many pages they read, and how frequently they visit – but little of this information is likely to be illuminating other than to suggest possible international opportunities (if you have a lot of users in Spain, for example) or user behaviour (for example, if a significant number of people access your content from mobile phones).

When you do meet readers, get into the habit of asking them about the magazine. Be aware, though, that people do not always tell the truth, either to magazine editors they don't wish to offend or to professional researchers. They may tell you they enjoy articles about careers, when what they really like are pictures of celebrities. Be aware, too, that a simple 'want' expressed in a market research group or in a discussion with an editor is rarely enough to make anyone buy a magazine.

The designer Jan V. White, in his classic *Designing for Magazines*, came up with a useful idea for editors and art directors working on magazine covers. He said they should 'appeal to the reader's self-interest'. But the idea has wider application than that. The reader's self-interest may well be the most useful guide an editor can have to the whole process of selecting and shaping journalistic material.

Look at in this way: what can you give your readers that will give them an advantage over people who have not read the magazine? Typically content splits into three types:

- information that saves the reader time or makes them money (particularly dominant in the professional publishing field, where reading your magazine can provide a competitive advantage, but also in the consumer field, where readers might be seeking better health, more intelligent use of their money, career inspiration, and so on);
- information that is socially valuable (allowing readers to be 'in the know', 'ahead of the game', or simply having something new to talk about);
- and information that is emotionally valuable, or entertaining (for example, real life stories, or 'How to' articles that give the reader satisfaction through what psychologists would call 'self-actualisation', or bettering yourself).

Readers will not support a magazine that fails to offer them anything new or surprising. If you only give them what they ask for, you are failing them: you are not anticipating their needs. And needs, rather than wishes, are the real drive in human life. You must look at the way your readers live to discover the things that will give them that advantage. You must find their self-interest, and that of their families, even when they are unable, or unwilling, to recognise it for themselves.

Sometimes readers buy magazines because they want to read something specific. We design our covers to make that process work. Often, though, they buy a magazine in the expectation that it will be interesting, even without knowing what precisely it contains. This is the basis of the trust between editor and reader: the editor promises to include the kind of material the readers will want and need and to exclude things they don't need, don't want or will find insulting or offensive. This trust relationship is increasingly built online too: if readers come across your brand online they will be looking for signals that you share a worldview.

To make this work, the idea of the reader needs to be a vivid presence in all your editorial discussions and calculations; and not only for you, but for your feature writers and sub-editors too. To create such a presence, you need two things: information and imagination.

Knowing your reader

Somewhere in your magazine's offices, there is a lot of hard numerical information about your readers, or readers the magazine was intended to attract when it was launched. Advertisers do not generally throw money away. To advertise with you, they need to be convinced that you are reaching the right people. So the advertising department will certainly have relevant information.

If you work on one of the larger consumer or business titles, your publisher is likely to subscribe to either the National Readership Survey or the British Business Survey. These constitute valuable research, but they are conducted on behalf of a whole stratum of the industry rather than any individual magazine.

The National Readership Survey (NRS) is intended to find out who reads over 250 publications. The method is 30-minute interviews with people in their homes. In 2010, more than 36,000 people were surveyed in this way. The interviews establish a whole series of useful information, starting with the most basic facts about who has read what over the last year, month or few days. These are extrapolated to give national figures. The 'top-level' figures for the average readership of any given issue of the publications included in the survey are available free on NRS's website, http://www.nrs.co.uk/. They show, for instance, that just over 9 per cent of British women read the average copy of *Take A Break*, and 2 per cent of British men.

That's the free stuff. The survey also acquires a huge amount of information which is for sale to publishers. After asking people about their reading, NRS's interviewers have a few more questions, covering:

- where the reader acquired the magazine;
- what other media the reader uses: television, radio, cinema, teletext, Internet;
- topics of interest;
- age, sex, occupation and marital status of everyone in the household;
- own occupation and that of the 'Chief Income Earner', in detail (used to determine class);
- food spending, mail order spending, housing status;
- personal and professional qualifications;
- holidays and travel;

- ownership of cars, dishwashers, videos, satellite dishes, CD players, computers, etc.;
- future household plans and aspirations (e.g. 'have a baby', 'buy new car');
- credit-card ownership, pension arrangements, income;
- languages spoken;
- willingness to be interviewed again.

The British Business Survey is similar. In 2008, it looked at the business readership of 68 newspapers and business magazines – down considerably on 150 several years previously, and it has not published any research since. The same research company also compiled the European Business Readership Survey, but this hasn't been undertaken for many years now.

All this information is available only to subscribers to the survey, but they invariably extract the maximum commercial value from it. If your publication appears in either the NRS or the British Business Survey, any positive findings about it will be repackaged to form part of the magazine's media pack, the information used to convince advertisers of its value as an advertising medium. *Management Today*, for instance, used the study in its media pack[2] to show that not only is it the best-read monthly magazine, but that its readers were forward-thinking and ambitious.

These surveys are of limited use to anyone whose magazine is not included. In those cases, a publisher will still need hard information to help sell advertising. But the magazine will have to commission its own research. A new magazine from an independent publisher has no alternative. The great advantage of conducting your own survey is that it can also be used for promotional purposes in the wider media. The oft-quoted figure that 'The average wedding costs £20,000', for example, comes from a 2008 reader survey in *You & Your Wedding* magazine which generated huge publicity for the magazine and many media appearances for its editor. (Of course this 'average' only applied to the 1,500 readers of that magazine who took the time to complete the survey, not to the 235,000 couples marrying every year in the UK as a whole, which the media conveniently overlooked. The real, median, 'average' is likely to be half that figure.)

What readership surveys can show

Here are just a selection of statistics from magazine media packs:

- *Sky Magazine* readers spend an average of £187 million on DVD players per year (that's £22 more than the national average).
- 60 per cent of *Sky Magazine* readers have done DIY in the last year, compared with the national average of 55 per cent.
- *Sky Magazine* readers account for more than £1 in every £7 spent on UK groceries.
- *Sky Magazine* readers own 23 per cent of all Blu-Ray players in the UK.
- 67 per cent of all *Sky Magazine* readers own a games console, compared with the national average of 52 per cent.

- 34 per cent of Journalism.co.uk users are freelance; 22 per cent earn £26–40k; 67 per cent are based in the UK.
- Each copy of *Auto Exchange* is read by two people.
- 95 per cent of *Auto Exchange* readers are looking to buy a car in the next six months.
- 73 per cent of *Auto Exchange* readers are prepared to travel up to 60 miles for their car.
- 72 per cent of *Auto Exchange* readers are prepared to spend up to £10,000 on their next car.
- 71 per cent of *Auto Exchange* readers do not pick up or buy another motoring magazine.
- The average personal income of *Financial News* readers is £242,353. The average value of their watch is £2,412, and their car £40,696.
- 1 in 4 readers have bought an item featured in *i-on* magazine.
- 1 in 3 *i-on* readers visit the gym more than twice a week.
- 81 per cent of readers have visited a website in *i-on*.
- More than half of readers have visited a store they've seen in *i-on*.
- 50 per cent of *i-on* readers eat and drink out at least twice a week.
- 54 per cent of *i-on* readers shop in boutique/independent stores more than twice a month.
- *Literary Review* readers purchase almost a million books a year – about 25 books per reader.
- *Literary Review* readers drink the following regularly: wine 98 per cent; malt whisky and whisky 41 per cent; champagne 27 per cent; gin 26 per cent.
- 72 per cent of *Literary Review* readers donated to charity within the last year.
- 35 per cent of *Literary Review* readers bought a work of art within the last year; 23 per cent attended an auction.

Even a cursory glance at this kind of survey demonstrates both its usefulness and its limitations for editorial purposes. Invariably, we learn a great deal about what our readers earn, what they do for a living and what they spend their money on: wine, books, watches. And the reason for that is obvious. These surveys are paid for and designed, in the main, by the commercial parts of the publishing operation. Their purpose is to demonstrate that the magazine's readers are well-off and interested in buying its advertisers' goods and services (particularly when ad sales people are looking for advertisers in areas not obviously related to your subject matter: the *Literary Review* may advertise books, but it would also be selling advertising to wine merchants, auction houses and charities, among others). They also seek to show that readers like the magazine and read it carefully and often. Anything we in the editorial department learn from them is acquired almost by eavesdropping. This research should always be available to us, but it is not intended for our ears. It does not answer the questions we would put to our readers.

What such surveys don't tell us, because they don't know, is anything about the reader's hopes, fears, prejudices, ambitions and so on. Those are for you to work out. What's more, they rarely contain bad news. Research organisations might proclaim their objectivity, but they are human: they want to be asked back. So they are inclined to accentuate the positive. Editors need to know hard truths, but we won't find them in documents commissioned to help sell our magazine to a sceptical world.

The point about those surveys is that they are 'quantitative'. They gather essentially numerical information, using straightforward methods: street interviews, doorstep interviews, telephone interviews, home interviews, and questionnaires distributed by post, email and the Internet. All are rigidly structured, using a set sequence of yes/no questions and checkboxes. If your company does plan such research, you may be invited to add some questions for editorial purposes, but there are limits to what you can expect to achieve. Bear in mind also that 'respondents' – your readers and potential readers – tend to dislike tedious doorstep questioning, telephone interviewing of all sorts, questionnaires that look like junk mail and most kinds of interview that have not been agreed by appointment.

Another option open to you as an editor is an online survey. There are a number of tools that allow you to conduct surveys for free – there will be limitations on numbers but these can be lifted if you pay a very small fee. A problem still remains, however, in that responses will tend to be quantitative and that your sample is self-selecting: you will only find out about readers who a) visit your website and b) like filling in surveys. They are also easily hijacked.

One way of addressing this problem is to use an email survey instead (or an email with a link to an online survey that people could not find by browsing the web). This is more targeted and less open to manipulation, but you should expect no more than 1–2 per cent of people to respond.

For our purposes, we need specific editorial research, but it is more expensive, difficult and troublesome, because it is 'qualitative'. It involves gathering subjective impressions and emotions, most of which are expressed through language and are open to interpretation. The central method here is the 'focus group', in which a number of people are placed in a room in a pseudo-social setting and gently coaxed to provide their thoughts on an issue or a product. Another method is the 'depth interview', where an individual is questioned at some length – although not in a forensic way.

Working with a research consultancy

If you are working on a magazine with some history, ask around and you may be able to find examples of previous research. Be wary of it: it will usually reflect a different era and different market conditions. But review it in conjunction with some examples of the magazine from that era, 'before' and 'after', perhaps, and you may well observe a strange dance taking place. Research discovers that the readers want something, so the magazine provides it. Then the research discovers that they'd really rather have something else, so the magazine provides that. Article lengths go up and headline sizes go down; then the process is reversed.

Many doomed titles first have to endure a period of research-induced vacillation, which generally finishes them off. Research is valuable in helping you create an editorial strategy and carry it through. It is not a replacement for that process. Remember that your readers want you to like them. But they want to be liked by someone confident and steady; they don't want a magazine that panders to their whims and appears desperate.

There are many ways in which research can be abused:

- It is asked to replace direction: 'I'm not telling you to do this: it's what the research says.'
- It is used to discover things that should be blindingly obvious to everyone.
- It is used to support a decision that has already been taken.
- It is ignored, because it conflicts with established prejudices.
- It is not shown to the people who need it.
- It paralyses decision-makers.

For editorial work, you need a consultancy with relevant experience. You also need to be able to relate to the researchers. The way journalists work is rather paradoxical. We are creating an extremely subtle and complex product, but we rarely talk about it in an introspective way. The language of journalism is about action: hit the phones, slap in the copy, bung in those photographs, hurry, hurry, hurry. Market researchers, by and large, are dealing with straightforward relationships between dull consumer products and the people who buy them; but they conjure up great flurries of language during presentations of great length and theatricality.

Research fills a vacuum. It tends to dictate attitudes to a subject, so that all future thoughts have to exist in relation to it. Prepare yourself before any research exercise begins. There must not be a vacuum where your sense of the reader should be. Prepare to learn, to adjust, to gain insight, but do not expect or allow research to create that sense in the first place. It's better to let your instinct and the researchers' findings confront and modify one another.

Many research projects will have both quantitative and qualitative aspects. For instance, a quantitative study of your magazine by your advertising agency suggests that you should concentrate on finding new buyers rather than getting existing buyers to purchase more often. That is followed by qualitative research, focusing on non-buyers and their perceptions of the magazine, looking at value for money, personality, appeal and editorial focus, even descending to the level of discussing reactions to individual articles, layouts, pictures and writers.

You should be interviewed by the research team, either formally or informally, to discuss the direction of the study. Don't skimp this, but it can be a strange experience. Use these pre-research briefings to tell the researchers the specifics of what you want to know, but also what you want the whole exercise to achieve. After that, you must make sure you are helpful to them when they need you; but otherwise stand aside and let them get on with it. In this instance, they are the experts.

Qualitative research will show what readers and non-readers think about your magazine's credibility, its authority, its trustworthiness. Partly these come from the magazine's tone of voice, the address it makes to its readers. Partly they reflect the readers' sense of how well it matches their interests and point of view. Then there are more technical questions about the way the magazine looks, reads and performs.

Before you know it, the interviews will be under way. If you just want to know whether people would like your magazine if they gave it a try, the research might involve superficial questioning of a fairly broad sample. For a consumer magazine, that might mean 'hall tests', in which people who broadly resemble your target audience are taken from the street into a church hall, shown copies of the magazine and questioned. There might instead be telephone interviews, sometimes done in stages so that the readers are interviewed, sent one or more issues of the magazine, and then interviewed again to see whether they like it more or less.

This should tell you whether readers aren't buying your magazine because they just don't encounter it (a distribution issue), or whether they actively dislike it (an editorial or design issue). It might tell you which parts of the magazine they like and which they dislike, but because the survey is carried out through a multiple-choice questionnaire, the results will be numerical rather than anecdotal.

You can also insert a questionnaire into the magazine. A research firm will design this for you, or you can do it yourself. When the results come in, you can let the consultancy make sense of the figures or draw your own conclusions.

Alternatively, you might want a more subtle analysis of your magazine. If its problems are mysterious and deeply embedded, this might be the way to go.

The approach in this case is narrower and more intense. Small groups are created, representing various demographic types, and they may or may not be given the magazine to mull over before being gathered for a group discussion. This will be led by a skilled researcher, and the comments of the group members recorded for later presentation. As editor, you may be invited to watch a video of the proceedings, to peer through a two-way mirror, or even to sit down in the group. This is always disconcerting. You watch as your perceptions and those of your readers slide gently past one another without quite meeting. Features you found witty and pointed might just seem rude. Matters of vital editorial import might simply pass them by. They might be more concerned about the crossword than they are about your award-winning columnist.

Design raises particular problems. What seems sophisticated and clean to you and your designers may appear boring and empty to them. Readers know nothing about the discussions that have made things the way they are. They judge what they see in front of them. If there is a gap between what you intended and the way it is understood, then the design (or the feature, or section, or anything else) is faulty. Misunderstandings are your fault: the customer, however slow or obtuse, is always right.

At the end of the research process comes the presentation. You will attend, along with the rest of the publishing management. Presentations are theatre. You are given a selective gloss on the results, based on what makes a coherent 'story'. Ask for the raw material: the percentages and the interview transcripts. It is important to see the interview subjects for what they are: a tiny sample of your readers or potential readers. Unfortunately, research can give the views of these people a disproportionate influence.

Sometimes what looks like a significant percentage may represent only a tiny number of people. A base survey of 150 people might be used. From that group, 30 say they find your magazine difficult to use and are selected for further analysis. Percentages of their responses are then presented: for instance, 38 per cent of them don't like your contents page. That's a disturbingly high percentage, until you recall that it represents only 11 people out of the original 150. Percentages are nonsensical with such small samples, but they are still used.

'Focus group' research produces a different type of material. Here the findings are often a series of striking phrases, picked up by the interviewer or group leader.

More often, research organisations try to clarify their findings by the use of what are called 'typologies'. This means dividing the mass of your readers into a series of groups with common attitudes, and giving each 'type' a name. You may be told that your readers are divided between 'clubbers', 'stay-at-homes' and 'anoraks'; or 'home-makers', 'careerists' and 'fantasists'; or 'newbies', 'geeks' and 'Alpha geeks'. It's a caricature, of course, but a useful one. It should not be mistaken for the whole story.

Out-of-context reader comments from focus groups can be more damaging. A wounding one-liner from a reader, especially if it touches on a real truth, can come to haunt an editor. And this sort of research can easily provide reinforcement for prejudices. That is why it is important for editors to go into research from a position of confidence: otherwise, research is likely to become one more pressure on you, one more opinion on the right direction for the magazine. Editors thrive by acquiring, or appearing to acquire, a deep intuitive understanding of their readers. Once they have to start asking about them, and inviting others' opinions, some of that mystique is gone.

If you use research, insist on taking part in the selection and briefing of the research team. If you are involved in setting the research's goals, you are less likely to become a victim of its conclusions. If you see names you recognise on the client list, make some informal enquiries about how it went. And reserve your right to cast a sceptical eye on the investigation's research.

Nothing you learn from research will guarantee you a successful editorial direction. It is dangerous to expect that. Publishing history is littered with the corpses of magazines which researched well but failed to sell to real people. On the other hand, research has certainly saved a few magazines that would otherwise have perished. One problem is that research, like training, is a low priority when money is tight. But money tends to be tight in the launch period and when magazines start to fail; and both of those are when research is needed.

A magazine designed solely to meet research criteria will have no centre, no identity and no soul. And a magazine which constantly resorts to research to try to find an identity is treading a dangerous path. Angling your magazine to meet the tastes of a few people you meet in research may lead to your ruining it for everyone else.

How market researchers see magazines

Rob Nathan is formerly head of business development at the market research consultancy Vivid-Interface, whose clients include EMAP, United Business Media, the National Magazine Company, the Informa group, Haymarket and many more.

We'll be called in when a publisher has a magazine in a market that's suffering decline, particularly in the business or technical press. They want to predict future trends that may affect them, and to know what readers are looking for in a technical magazine. In business titles, they want to know how important classified and recruitment advertising is to the magazine. They may find it's the main reason readers buy it.

With consumer magazines, they sometimes don't seem to know exactly what they want from research. A lot of editors and publishers feel, 'Why should we consult research? I know the industry better than anyone else.' But they're too close.

One of our specialities is part-works [magazines where readers 'collect the parts' – normally a cover mount – from issue to issue]. We can predict their likely circulations within 2 or 3 per cent. We could offer advice on the likely circulations of new magazine launches, but usually we are consulted after the horse has bolted. The publishers want to know why the magazine hasn't done so well as they'd hoped.

We did some research on a consumer magazine where they didn't quite get the focus right. It was launched as a homes magazine with a strong craft element. It was a big launch, with television advertising, but sales were lower than they hoped and there was a problem attracting advertising. We conducted a 'brand mapping' exercise, to see where it fitted in the market, speaking to both subscribers and occasional buyers.

We discovered that their perception was that it was a craft magazine with a homes bias. It forced the product into a niche market rather than the mass-market homes sector. The magazine shifted its positioning immediately, and it became profitable. As far as I know it remains profitable to this day.

To get effective research you have to do some quite serious digging; you have to speak to people in depth. Focus groups are incredibly effective for this kind of thing, but we also use telephone interviews and 'hall tests', where people are pulled off the street into a church hall and asked questions. We pride ourselves in getting under the skin of magazines, and that's down to the skill of the research director in finding out the issues. If the salient questions aren't asked, you aren't going to get the right information.

Publishers always want to get opinions from their readers, but how do they get to them? If a magazine sells 100,000, how many people do you have to stop on the street before you find a reader? We go to events and find people. For a gardening magazine, you might hold a focus group at the Chelsea Flower Show. For a trade or technical magazine, you can do it at an exhibition.

Focus groups are sometimes held in special rooms with two-way mirrors, but often there's not the budget for that. Normally it's in a hotel dining suite or something like that. Editors and publishers do sit in, and at the end they can ask questions: but we don't let them interfere with the research and we don't necessarily say exactly who they are. I don't know if it's a British thing, but people are always happy to give their opinions. Sitting in as a client, you do want to stand up and say 'Hang on a minute, you don't understand!' It is incredibly frustrating, but at the same time you find out an enormous amount about the product.

In these focus groups we sometimes walk through magazines with people, asking them what they found relevant, what they used, how they found the layout, how they found the features, how they rated each member of the editorial team. For one client, a motor racing magazine, we took four front covers and asked people which they found best and most appealing. Then we ranked them and the publisher looked at their actual sales. The one the group preferred was the one that sold the most.

In many companies now, the editorial people are the ones pushing the research. They take great pride in the product and they want to know what's going on. A typical thing, in the trade press, is that on the back page there'll be humour. We test out how effective it is. The editors generally think it's great, but we've often found that the readers don't even glance at it.

There are a lot of magazines out there that are struggling and the publishers cannot see it; they can't see that the way they perceive the magazine is different from the way the public sees it. With effective research you can change a struggling product into an effective product in a very short space of time. But publishers never admit that a magazine is struggling: it's always just 'we're giving it a few tweaks'.

If you can't afford to research

The research consultancies will tell you that you can't afford not to research. Well, that's fine if you have the option, but many editors don't. You will be expected to know all about your readers, without being provided with the tools to let you do that job. Don't despair. You have some scope for making your own enquiries, and the good news is that if you do that, you don't have to account for your methods or share your results. You may have your own dark suspicions about what the readers think about the editorial package you are producing: you certainly won't want them raised in public unless you are forewarned.

So why not make your own enquiries? If you are a magazine with subscriptions, you can ask the subscriptions department for some telephone numbers of subscribers – or, perhaps more usefully, lapsed subscribers (you will need to check your data protection policy and whether subscribers have agreed that their data can be used in this way). Ring them and ask them what they think. Try and ask the same questions each time: the point is to get several views on a single issue. And make sure you listen to the answers. These can be revealing, but you should bear in mind that readers cold-called by the editor of a magazine are not likely to tell you the unvarnished truth. It's not scientific, of course, because you won't have time to call more than a tiny number of people. If you want a more representative survey, give someone else a list of questions – a script, almost – and set them on the job.

Another cheap way of testing how your work is received is the reader panel, which professional magazines have sometimes found useful. This is not to be confused with an editorial advisory panel or board, which is often just a way of placing esteemed industry names on your masthead in exchange for an annual lunch. Your reader panel is a small group of readers who promise to read each issue of the magazine, perhaps making notes, so that you can speak to them at regular intervals and ask them what they thought. Of course, these chats aren't only an occasion for them to tell you what they think of the magazine; they can be an opportunity for you to gain a sense of what they need from it. They need to be chosen carefully and changed frequently. Why would they want to do it? Because it flatters them, and makes them feel important. It probably won't cost you much beyond a bottle of something and a card at Christmas.

Insert surveys, meaning questionnaires carried in the magazine, are the other low-cost option. As mentioned above, you can have these professionally designed, analysed and interpreted, and that probably makes sense if you can afford it. But many editors create their own, then tot up the scores and then draw their own conclusions, at a theoretical cost of two pages of editorial space: you need two pages so that the thing folds into an envelope. Actually, the costs will be higher than that. You are likely to need to use a freepost address. You will also want to offer some incentive for people who return the form, although you might be able to persuade an advertiser to give you some sort of prize in return for the publicity. Perhaps if the incentive is good enough the readers will pay their own postage. On the other hand, a good incentive will bring in spurious responses, from people who want the prize but don't care one way or another about the questions on your form.

The response rate is likely to be low, and the sample produced is 'self-selecting', meaning it will include a high proportion of people seeking an audience for their entrenched views. There is also a bias towards the negative, since people who are happy with something rarely feel the need to put pen to paper to tell you so. The same, incidentally, applies to letters pages, which are another obvious way of discovering what the readers think of what you're giving them.

Cunning questionnaire design may help you weed out at a glance those who are not taking the thing seriously, usually by detecting internal contradictions in their answers. But you will always get some bizarre and unexpected results, as you do with most research. If you ask for written comments, you will probably get them. Don't get them out of proportion. However depressing – or flattering – they're just someone's opinion.

Creating the questionnaire is an expert job, but at a pinch you can adapt an old one, working on the basis that at some time in its history it must have been drawn up by people who knew what they were doing. If you are going to do that, look at old results, too, and see if there are any obvious omissions or absurdities. It is easier to see this when you are looking at answers rather than questions.

In-magazine surveys, like most reader research exercises, usually have a commercial purpose. They are there to gather information to help sell advertising – and readers know this, which is why they are usually reluctant to take part. If you're creating the survey, you get the chance to put your journalistic interests first, perhaps by asking topical questions that will help create a news story or a feature. It might be good office politics, however, to let the advertising department supply you with a few questions, especially if it's footing the bill for postage or providing the prize. This is an unusual reversal of the normal way of things, so make the most of it.

Aside from these occasional formal instances of research you should lurk where your readers go online, read their comments on your website and on others. You can set up alerts whenever your magazine or journalists are mentioned in blogs or forums, which will help you head off potential dissatisfaction in your readership (Google News has such alerts, which cover many blogs as well as traditional news websites, and you can subscribe to RSS feeds of search results on specialist search engines such as IceRocket for blogs, Boardreader for forums and search.twitter.com for Twitter). PR companies sometimes offer this service but it is simple enough to do yourself – and important enough to warrant you reacting to some comments as quickly as possible. Quite often the most vociferous critic will become your fiercest ally when you take a minute to listen and respond.

Characterising the reader

You can do all the research in the world, but it won't bring the reader alive to you. To repeat, you need a sense of the reader as a real presence in all your editorial decision making. No amount of consulting figures and graphs or clever typologies will provide you with that. You can only do it by the judicious exercise of your own creative imagination.

Evoking the reader is a creative act, a little bit of magic. We can learn something from the techniques of novelists and dramatists. When they create characters, they do so in immense detail. They know where they went to school, how they felt when they had their first filling, which foods bring them out in a rash, the names of their best friends, what happened on their wedding night and where they would like to be buried. They don't use most of this, but its presence in the background is what brings their characters to life.

We, on the other hand, are able to gather a large amount of factual information about our readers, particularly about their incomes and job descriptions and choice of reading matter. But it's hard to turn that into a person whose interests and concerns we know so well we don't have to think about them. We need to let our imaginations go to work, bolstered all the time by any contacts we have with the real people we are attempting to evoke. This imaginative work is at the centre of our creativity as editors. It is the spark that makes the publishing engine turn over.

You are creating a notional or imaginary reader as a tool for focusing the efforts of the entire editorial team. Sometimes, of course, you will need more than one: some magazines have wildly disparate readerships, so you will end up with something more like the researchers' 'types'. But that doesn't defeat the argument. You are still inventing readers you can think about, discuss, argue with and, above all, speak to. Give these people names, jobs, houses and anything else that helps your characterisation. A notional person may come to embody the spirit of the magazine, long after you have moved on. The famous examples here are 'Cosmo Girl', who later became a woman, and 'the New Lad', forever associated with *Loaded* magazine. More recently Bauer coined the '4D Man' to refer to a man with 'four dimensions'. Unsurprisingly the term hasn't caught on.

Push the characterisation further. What is my reader worried about? What does my reader have on her desk? Where did my reader go to school? What does my reader love about his car? What does my reader hate about her body? Does he have children? Does she have pets? What are they called?

This is useful; it can also be fun. Let other members of the team join in if you like. This is a good example of something where true brainstorming might help: remember, the rules say you must not criticise other people's suggestions. You want strong, accessible evocations of realistic people. Pictures can help, as can props. Novelists find it helps to pin up on the wall photographs of anonymous faces from the newspaper, postcards of locations, anything that 'evokes' the right kind of person. It wouldn't do to push the comparison too far, but the same kind of strategies can work for us.

The point is for you to know exactly who you want your magazine to speak to. Then you can communicate that to your team, so that they don't have to have it explained to them all the time. They have an instantaneous understanding of it, just as you do. 'Is this feature "us"?' Of course not. 'Which cover photograph should we use?' It should be obvious. This is not a device to stop office discussion – it's to make it more purposeful and efficient.

If all this seems too fanciful, take what you know about your readers, from research and surveys, and use that material to play a 'yes/no' game about your reader:

- Is my reader male? Yes.
- Did he go to university? Yes.
- Is he married? No.
- Does he have a job? Yes.
- Is he working towards professional qualifications? No.
- Would he like to be? No.
- Does he own his home? No.

And so on. Obviously not all your readers will be male; not all your readers will be home-renting men with degrees and jobs but no professional aspirations. In your more considered calculations about content and attitude, you can take that into account. These exercises are to sharpen up your editing instincts, and for that you need a simple primary target.

More fun, perhaps, than the checklist approach is to take your lead from the 'in and out' lists that have been a staple of magazine features departments for many years. You know the sort of thing: red is in, black is out; tight is in, baggy is out; and so on. You can try it with your reader. 'Our reader is Marks and Spencer, not Aldi.' 'Our reader is Manchester United, not Manchester City.' 'Our reader is Mini, not Ford Ka.' You need a long list before this starts to work, but it will work as a group project with the editorial team. Many magazines have had a lot of fun with this idea over the years, extending it as far as it will go: 'Our reader is a panther, not a tabby.' People will take considerable warming-up before they get into the idea, and after a while they'll get cynical and sarcastic. Stop well before you reach that point.

A similar technique is the 'You know you're a reader when ...' list. *Red* magazine's 'defining moments of a *Red* woman' give a typical example:

- You buy pressed olive oil instead of Mazola.
- What suits you is more important than what's 'in'.
- You'll only go down the pub if you can sit down.
- You spend money on a holiday where you don't get a tan.
- You know polenta isn't a make of Italian car.
- You're fussy about the coffee you drink.
- You celebrate your birthday with a weekend in the country instead of a night out.

You get the idea.

These ideas have tended to expand your sense of the reader, to build up a rich, evocative mental picture of a person's background, habits and even appearance. But you may also want to see if you can find a way of clarifying the essence of what that person is about.

This is the role played by the magazine's slogan, in its role as a rallying point for the editorial team. Of course, it will usually also appear on the front cover, just below the logotype (sometimes erroneously called the masthead). That means it has to be chosen with care. The way you characterise your readers may not exactly match the way they see themselves.

Slogans tend to fit one of four broad types: what your magazine is; who it's for; what it was; and what it aspires to. The 'what it is' slogan is bluntly descriptive, which makes sense in context. If you are producing *Heat*, a weekly magazine of gossip about celebrities, you might as well have a slogan that says 'This week's hottest celebrity news'. The 'who it's for' slogan can be equally literal: if you are producing a solid, authoritative monthly for dentists, 'The magazine for the dental care team' is fine. *Cycling* magazine's slogan is representative of the hobbyist equivalent: 'For people who love to ride'.

The 'what it was' slogan boasts about the magazine's achievements or history: 'The UK's favourite Internet magazine' (*Web User*); 'The original car weekly'

(*Autocar*); or 'Magazine of the Year' (various). And finally, the 'what it aspires to' slogan is more memorable. *Woman's Weekly* pretends to a long shared history with its 'We've come a long way together'. *Pick Me Up* is similarly inclusive – if generic – with 'We like a bit of everything!' *Shout* insists: 'It's all about you' while *House Beautiful* promises 'All you want from where you live'. These types of slogans were popular a decade ago but have fallen out of favour since.

Over time, slogans do decline in relevance and have to be changed, but that's a good thing: it's an opportunity for you to think about whether it's just your language that needs updating or whether the whole approach needs tweaking. 'For girls in their freedom years', ran *Company* magazine's slogan. Then 'girls' sounded wrong, so it was 'For the freedom years', which might be more palatable but is less effective: it expresses a vague aspiration, but it does not define its readership either for your benefit or for theirs. It has long since gone.

Editorial departments are not the only people in a publishing operation with an interest in characterising their readers. Publishers and advertising teams need to do it, too, but they may come up with a rather different perspective to your own. As always, they will accentuate the positive. Even so, it is worth looking closely at every piece of promotional material that emerges from their discussions. There should be agreement about the basic demographic facts. Here are a few typical pieces of promotional reader characterisation, from *Marie Claire* magazine in the UK, US and Australia (all slightly different markets). Can you imagine this person? Could you write cover lines or a contents page that would interest her? Possibly, but could you edit a feature to intrigue her? And can you guess which is which?[3]

> The Marie Claire reader is fascinated by what the world has to offer, and how she presents herself to that world. She is a woman who likes to be challenged and informed at all levels.
>
> The Marie Claire reader is socially connected and heavily networked.
>
> The Marie Claire reader is smart; stylish; fun; ambitious; and savvy. Aged between 25 and 35, she is a well-educated, urban professional with a wide range of interests and awareness of global issues. She has a high disposable income and is passionate about fashion, shopping and investing in key designer items every season.

Sometimes, the advertising department's wishful thinking about who reads the magazine may seem remote from the reality of your advertisers. Trust the advertisers. They are backing their guesses about your readers with money, and if they weren't getting results they'd stop. Take newspaper colour supplements. They're full of enthusiastic features about the latest youth music sensation, not to mention cutting-edge fashion of the kind you need to be 20 and rail-thin to contemplate. So are the advertisements for similarly 'edgy' products? Not all of them, by any means: they are for stair-lifts, trousers with elasticated waists, and 'collectable' crockery, often featuring paintings of Second World War aircraft.

Some people are deluding themselves, and it seems unlikely to be those advertisers. On the other hand, there may be reasons for the yawning gap between the magazine's real readers and those it seems to be addressing. By pitching the content too young and too radical for the magazines' carpet-slippered readership, the editor may be trying to build for the future: all publications need new readers, and those serving an ageing population need new readers more than most. But it's a dangerous business: old readers are better than no readers.

Of course, no one buys a newspaper supplement, subscribes to it or asks to receive it. The real interests of its current readers may not be that important. Its editorial is calculated, instead, to entice those placing high-value advertisements, and they want their products in a glamorous and forward-looking environment. The publisher calculates that those selling foam rubber shoes for tired feet will always come along for the ride, even if the magazine's editorial shows little sign of admitting that old age or poverty even exist.

Applying what you know

Your research should have given you plenty of ideas about what to do next. In Chapter 3 there are some thoughts about planning and decision making. There will be things you did not expect, but that can be easily remedied. It is quite common for editors to discover that their readers are having trouble coping with their magazine's elegantly small body type, or their designers' liking for reversed-out panels, featuring white type on dark backgrounds. Other readers will complain they can't find anything from the contents page, because you've stylishly placed your folios (page numbers) halfway up the outside margin of each page instead of at the top or bottom. All these things can, and should, be changed.

But that's the easy bit. Your research might also show that readers don't like the magazine's tone of voice, or its perceived attitude to a subject, an issue or even its own readers. They might think you are failing to cover the right things, or missing the story, or getting things wrong. These problems are more difficult to put right. You can't resolve them by tweaking your settings in InDesign.

But your research was never intended to be just an opinion-gathering exercise. You were finding information to help you establish or change your direction. The research tells you whether that direction is feasible, and, if so, whether it's desirable. To take one basic idea, namely the range of your coverage, you should know, from the first day you occupy the editor's chair, the basic recipe for each issue: which regular items, how many features, the balance of long and short, and the range of subject matter they tend to cover. You can work this stuff out as a reader, or prospective editor. When you take the reins, you can start to change it.

Most research will include a basic question about that coverage. It might ask: what do you like to read about? Or: would you like to see less or more about the following subjects? Take this information and compare it with the magazine you see on your desk, and the one you're planning next. There should be a broad similarity between their ideal magazine and yours, at least over a period. But don't make the mistake of thinking that editing a magazine is like doing someone else's shopping, dropping the required features into the wire trolley and ticking them off on the list as you do so. That list of subjects does not account for light and shade, for balance, for topicality, for responsiveness, nor for the element of surprise. Your readers want you to know them and like them well enough to give them things they haven't asked for. Think of the 'outspoken' columnists in the newspapers: we have all heard people say 'She says just what I'm thinking.' Of course, they weren't thinking it, otherwise they'd find the columnist boring; it's the sort of thing they might have thought. Those are the ideas we give our readers.

One of the frustrations of the research companies is that their insights are either ignored or abused in some way: used as a battering ram in office politics. When research is carried out on behalf of your title, you need to sit down quietly with a copy of the detailed report and work out your response. Put something on paper. Don't be unnecessarily negative – most managements want people who bring them solutions rather than problems – and stick to the point. Take this response and sit on it for a bit while you decide what to say to your team.

Research will have an impact on your staff. Even if it is only a question of increasing the type size, someone will have to incorporate it into the design, and someone else will have to cut the average length of a story to make room. Worse, it is not uncommon for research exercises to ask people to grade their appreciation of individual sections, pieces and writers. You simply cannot take such research and circulate it to everyone, or pin it on the wall and invite people to take a look. You need to speak to those individuals first and to reassure them – unless, of course, your intention is quite the opposite.

A research document will influence the mood of an entire team, even if it is largely innocuous. Everyone knows the research is taking place. Until it is discussed, no one will relax. So you must prepare yourself to explain what's going on. Remember that anything coming from you will have twice the impact that it would coming from almost anyone else. If you point out that certain subjects are ill-appreciated, your colleagues will immediately assume you are going to cease covering them. On the other hand, if you are loudly dismissive of the survey, you will find it hard in future even to consider change.

One solution is to present both the research and your response to it. Make it clear that the research is not editing the magazine, you are. But research that is commissioned and then ignored is like a cache of weapons: sooner or later someone's going to dig it up and use it to cause trouble. Better to use research openly and honestly: act on it, or dismiss it. It may tell you unpalatable things, but it's better that you discover them in a focus group than on the newsagents' shelves.

Staying in touch

This period of intense involvement with the readers – finding out what they're like, trying to anticipate what they want to read – tends to come at critical points in the magazine's development: in planning a launch, attacking a market leader or fending off a newcomer, or in staving off a decline. The rest of the time there is a tendency to take the readers for granted. This is understandable, but foolish. The editor–reader relationship is at least as important as that of the editor–publisher or editor–staff.

It used to be thought that all readers wanted from magazines was to buy them, read them and throw them away. These days, few people think like that. All modern managements have discovered that it is cheaper to keep a customer happy than to search for new ones. The magazine industry has a deep-seated belief that its product has a special meaning to its buyers. 'People love their magazines!', according to the title of an elderly but much-quoted piece of research by the advertising agency WCRS:[4] 'The most impressive lesson emerging from current research is that readers enjoy a very close relationship with magazines that they chose to read. It is a relationship that is impossible for other media to replicate.'

But if they have that commitment – and surveys continue to find evidence of it – they should receive some sort of recognition or pay-off for it. At the very least, they deserve to get a sense of belonging and of being recognised. But you can get something from them; guidance on your direction.

There are many straightforward editorial devices for reader involvement. Editorial contact numbers should be clearly displayed and phones promptly and politely answered. It is feasible to give all staff direct lines and to print those numbers in the magazine. A proportion of calls will be from timewasters and cranks, but most will not. Readers should feel able to ring with ideas and suggestions, and, when necessary, with complaints. All should be dealt with courteously.

Email addresses should be printed in the magazine and on your website. Spam filters should be able to deal with most of the junk, but you will need to develop strategies for managing your other email effectively, for example setting up filters so that emails from mailing lists you've subscribed to, from known PR companies, or from people not in your contacts list, go into separate folders that you check less regularly. Spending a little time familiarising yourself with filtering options will save you a lot of time further down the line.

A third point of contact will be social networks. Twitter is a particularly useful one for journalists because of the 140-character limit, which forces people to get to the point when trying to tell you about something. It is also a good way to make contact with other journalists, and an excellent place to spot breaking news. You should include your Twitter name beside your name in the magazine and website – and on your business cards too. You will probably belong to other social networks such as Facebook and LinkedIn but there is no need to link to all of them.

There is an emerging body of scientific research which suggests that our chemical makeup leads us to compulsively check emails and social media, and certainly some journalists find themselves easily distracted by the Sisyphean task of endlessly clearing out their inboxes. One recommended tactic is to allocate set times for checking email – two or three times per day, responding to those that are urgent, deleting others, and leaving the rest for another day. Then once a week or so, you should 'purge' through everything that remains at that time.

Some editors resist publishing their direct line and email, in fear of being deluged, but in reality the volume of calls will be less than you might expect. Most people would prefer to deal with someone lower down the chain: only those with a strong sense of their own importance – lawyers, politicians, captains of industry, other journalists – will insist on going straight to the top. It can pay to deal with such people yourself.

If your magazine's staffing runs to it, the best answer is probably to have some assistance in screening your incoming calls. That way callers are never more than one transfer away from you, which is about the most people should be asked to bear. And if they don't need to speak to you – for instance, PR people making routine checks to see whether you will be using their exciting product releases – they can be politely redirected to the appropriate person. You might also find you need another phone, a direct line separate from the switchboard system, mainly for making outgoing calls and international calls outside switchboard hours, but whose number can be disclosed by you personally to those who really need it. Some people use a mobile for that purpose.

The object here is to elevate reader calls and enquiries from their traditionally low position of importance. You must have a standard procedure for dealing with complaints, which may range from the trivial to the potentially disastrous. Such calls from readers should be logged and investigated, and a follow-up call made. Readers must not be treated as passive consumers of what we, the professionals, see fit to serve them. All promises to readers must be kept.

Magazines increasingly use their readers as editorial sources. Women's magazines are great users of their personal stories and confessions. In such circumstances readers are paid, which reflects the competitiveness of the market. Editors in other markets will normally hope to encourage their readers to share information and experiences without payment. The glory of having their names printed in a national publication will still be enough for many, but only if you deal with them properly.

The letters page and readers' contributions

Every magazine must find room for the views of both the readers and those written about. There should be a letters page, and you should take it seriously. Many letters will need modest copy editing to make them clearer. But avoid the heavy-handed rewriting associated with the tabloid newspapers, where all the letter-writers sound remarkably similar. If you want that effect, make sure you print a warning to letter-writers that their contributions are likely to adjusted. On a business or professional magazine, on the other hand, you will need to discuss major changes with their authors.

Controversy is important on a letters page, although if it is too interesting it should be moved rapidly to the news pages and broadened into a real running story. If you don't have controversy, you can always stir some up by soliciting letters. Other readers should not be able to detect you stirring the pot, but stir it you must.

This is not the same thing, however, as writing your own letters. That is a desperate measure, but it would be a rare editor who has never done it when the postbag suddenly dries up. Let discussions run, but bring them to a close as soon as they become boring.

Letters should have headings, which should entice as well as summarise. Where they make direct requests or factual complaints, they should be answered on the page. Serious problems shouldn't be dealt with through the letters page: they should be answered in private correspondence. Don't feel tempted to add smart replies to everything. It looks smug. If you want to achieve that Punch-and-Judy effect, create a special column elsewhere: that's the way to do it. Otherwise, let the reader have the last word.

The letters page is a perfect place for campaigning on your readers' behalf. If you receive a letter or email highlighting bad practice in your field, for example, you can put it to the culprit and get a heart-warming result. If readers have received bad service, you can often get things sorted for them. This shows that you are firmly on the side of the readers, but don't do it so often that it looks like you're showing off. Use your power wisely.

You might also want to consider having a Letter of the Month, with a prize of some sort (a free subscription is one – but quite often an advertiser can be approached to sponsor a better award; you might also have prizes for all published letters). This might be particularly well written, or helpful, or insightful – but don't pick it for the sake of it or you risk annoying all the other letter writers whose equally worthy missives were not showered in glory.

Longer pieces from readers are a good idea, both as copy and an expression of the magazine's approachability and openness. Either they can be written and sent in or done as 'as told to' interviews with a journalist. If the readers send them, you will be able to assess the strength of the underlying experiences and thoughts. But don't expect your readers to be able to write polished copy for publication. These stories will usually need work by a skilled editor. On the other hand, they may bring you close to a personal or professional experience that you would otherwise miss.

It is also worth having an 'Errata' or 'Corrections' box. Honest mistakes cleared up in that way can prevent trouble later, although seriously aggrieved readers need to be handled in a different way (see Chapter 8). You should also correct online – monitor your comments for users pointing out errors or lazy journalism and thank them for pointing it out. Corrections can make quite entertaining reading: see the *Guardian* for details. Your readers won't mind the fact that you are human. Obviously, if your corrections box turns into a corrections page, or section, you have a few problems.

Competitions

Magazines can always involve their readers through competitions, but the editorial department rarely initiates them. Instead your colleagues in the promotional area will cajole advertisers or PR companies into providing prizes in return for a flattering mention in the accompanying text and liberal use of the benefactor's logo. The questions are always easy, especially for anyone who has read the copy, ensuring that the 'competition' brings in the maximum number of entries, which come in on a coupon cut from the magazine or an online entry form. The winner is usually picked from a hat. The whole operation is of dubious legality.

Keep this kind of thing at arm's length. Read the copy to make sure it is not misleading, and that readers are being treated fairly. But such competitions are best viewed as advertisements that happen to be paid for in kind rather than in cash. They have a value for advertisers and for readers, but they're nothing to do with journalism. Even so, most publishers will count competitions as editorial pages for the purpose of flat-planning and determining the advertising/editorial ratio (see Chapter 7), because they don't bring the magazine any money.

The size and prominence of the coverage should be measured against the value of the prize, but that is for other people to worry about. Companies supplying prizes obviously want the maximum exposure in return for the value of the object. Your publisher will want to extract the best prize in return for space in the magazine. Such on-page promotions are regulated by the Gambling Act of 2005, which does not make things easy. For more detail on the legal aspects, see Chapter 8.

Of course, the editorial department can initiate its own competitions, but they take more work. You can hold writing competitions, photography competitions and contests that in some way challenge the professional skills of your readers. Caption competitions can liven up a flagging diary page. If you can find someone willing to donate a prize in return for a little logo on the page, why not? At least here the competition can have genuine editorial value. Since you are now judging actual skill, every effort must be taken to be fair. Names and addresses must be detached from entries to prevent any sort of prejudice. The basis of the judging should be made clear on the page and online. Experience suggests that a proportion of those who lose will find rejection difficult to take. At that point you must be able to say that everything has been done fairly.

You can of course delegate judging or shortlisting to website users. This is a great way to increase traffic but is also obviously open to abuse: a competition can turn into an election campaign, with candidates cajoling friends into voting for them and smearing their opponents. You will need to decide if such competitiveness is in the spirit of the competition, and plan for various problems, implementing technical protections if necessary (your developers may be able to write scripts that detect rushes of votes from the same location or for the same candidate, for example).

Awards

Awards are much more than a way of keeping in touch with your readers. For many business-to-business publications, they provide another source of income after advertising and circulation. They do provide editorial benefits – enhancing the status of the publication, providing an opportunity to make valuable contacts and links with useful organisations, raising the magazine's profile in the outside world – but they are time consuming. Editors are increasingly pressed to come up with revenue-generating ideas, and awards are among the least irksome.

Some advertisers have found that they can gain kudos and an editorial presence by setting up their own award schemes and bullying editors into promoting them. It is better to take the initiative: devise an award scheme or major competition in conjunction with some professional body or expert organisation, then ask your commercial colleagues to look for an advertiser to sponsor it. That way you retain the initiative.

Any such scheme must be run on fair and transparent lines. If not, the image of the magazine will suffer. Nor should you overdo it.

Increasingly, awards are seen as part of the 'brand' of which the magazine may only be a part – in some cases the event can actually make enough money to support the magazine for the rest of the year.

Meeting the readers

Most magazines will have some sort of 'reader event', but often the connection with editorial is remote. They are organised by the promotional department, or the magazine's name is associated with an event, without any closer involvement. But readers don't see it like that: they expect members of the editorial staff, from the editor down, to be present and visible. Women's magazines hold successful readers' evenings at department stores. They organise conferences and lunches, with speakers from the magazine and elsewhere. Film magazines can arrange reader screenings of new movies with the help of the film distributors. Why not use these opportunities to speak to the readers about the magazine and your plans?

Campaigns

One final area of involvement with the readers is campaigning. A campaign is more than a series of articles on the same subject. At its best, it arises from a reader experience. That is followed by an investigation by the magazine's journalists, opinion surveys and more detailed articles. In the latter stages there should be discussions with public bodies or politicians to make something happen. Readers expect an emotional pay-off, otherwise the campaign will cease to be a source of editorial excitement and become a curse. Think about where it's going to end, even before you get the special campaign logo designed.

The networked age has made it easier for anyone to start and manage a campaign, but magazines still have a large amount of clout that they can wield. Pairing this traditional print authority with the agility and viral nature of the web is a sensible strategy – and you will need to consider how your campaign will play out online as well as across your pages. Chances are that a number of people online have had the same experience you wish to campaign about: they may have blogged about it, set up a Facebook group, or complained on a forum. Or they may simply have tweeted about it. Connecting these people together can form a useful foundation for what follows.

You will also need to work to a different rhythm online, keeping people updated through online channels, and moving the story along more quickly and in more ways than you may anticipate. Flexibility is key. When it works, a campaign binds readers and magazine together, showing that you can identify your readership's concerns and speak up about them.

3   Leader and manager

There is a creativity to writing a feature or designing a page, but also, after time, a certain routine quality: you must work within all kinds of restrictions, from the time you have to the sources you can access. Sometimes these restrictions can make you creative; often, they force you to fall back on 'factory line' methods that you know you can rely on.

The creativity of being an editor is very different. Quite often it is about jolting your team out of their routines, or coming up with innovative new ones. Sometimes it is about providing an opportunity for someone to shine in a way they've never been able to before. Some find this frustrating: you are no longer creating lots of beautiful small things but larger, more complex projects; the process of creation turns into something slow, remote and indirect. But when it is working properly, you achieve something that is not only better than you could do on your own, but better even than the sum of your individual efforts.

It's the best thing about the job. You might call this the spirit of the magazine, and you have to conjure it up and keep it alive. If you are used to being directed in what you do, this can be quite liberating. If you don't like the way things are organised, you can change it.

The word for this feeling is power. It's a strong emotion. Some are corrupted by it. Some find it addictive. Some can handle the rush, but not the come-down afterwards, when they discover that for everything that goes right, several other things may go wrong. But don't feel bad about acknowledging the emotion. Becoming an editor is a great achievement, and you probably wouldn't have made it if you didn't want to experience that moment of god-like command, even if it only happens when everyone else has gone home. Don't disown the emotion: relish it, then put it away for rainy days, of which there will be many.

While feeling powerful may help you lead, it won't help you manage. No one else shares the intensity of your feelings about your magazine – why should they? – and you can't expect them to be driven by your equally strong convictions about the way things should be done. You've got to start talking to them, not giving them instructions on stone tablets. More importantly, you've got to let them speak to you – and you've got to take notice of what they say.

Born to lead, or to manage?

As an editor, are you a leader or a manager? Some writers on management make this distinction. It helps explain some of the problems editors experience. Gerard Blair was a professor of mechanical engineering at Edinburgh University who taught management skills to his graduate students. His writings on the subject are widely available on the web, and they stand out from the field by being concise and well written. He says that leadership is not the same as management, nor superior to it, but a skill managers should learn.[1]

Managers increase the effectiveness of an organisation through organisation, planning, staffing, directing and controlling. Leadership, says Blair, is part of the 'directing' function of the manager. It's not as important as management – some businesses and projects run perfectly well without leaders. Managers have formal authority, because someone appoints them. Managers have to do certain things, and they have to do them the right way

Leaders can take on leadership themselves, because they have the ambition and because other people are prepared to be led. Leadership is the fun part. Leaders can do what they think is right, using their own initiative. Here are a few more characteristics of leaders, as identified in the business books:

- They attract followers and supporters, and acquire loyalty because they can create it.
- They appeal to the emotions rather than reason.
- They take notice of the individuals in their team and appreciate them.
- They apologise for mistakes.
- They celebrate success.

In other words, leaders have exactly what it takes to lead people, whether they are crossing the Andes on foot or producing a new supplement about office equipment.

> Leaders are observant and sensitive people. They know their team and develop mutual confidence within it.
>
> (John Fenton)[2]

The poor old manager, in contrast, gets a poor press. Such managers:

- have only modest ideas for change, not radical plans;
- risk losing the leadership initiative to their subordinates;
- may have become a manager by accident rather than through talent;
- can only hope for people to do what they are told, rather than gain their enthusiastic support.

Magazines need a leader. The leader has the vision of what the magazine should be, based on an understanding of what its readers expect. The leader encourages the team to produce the magazine according to that vision. And the leader gets to decide whether what the team comes up with matches the vision.

However, leadership is not everything. The magazine needs managing, too. Managing is everything that leading is not: making sure things are done properly, that people turn up on time, that deadlines are kept and budgets are observed, that people are hired, trained, appraised, mentored and dismissed in accordance with the law, and so on. The job of a manager in any organisation knows few limits, and a magazine office is no exception. Magazines must have an editorial manager – and often that's the editor.

But the qualities that make someone a good leader don't normally make a good manager. Someone who has a brilliant, intuitive grasp of the world out there, and can convince a room full of cynical journalists about it, is not always so good when it comes to querying expenses or turning down a request for promotion. Perhaps there should be two jobs. Some magazines have tried that. There's the editor, who has the vision, and there's the managing editor, who deals with angry freelances and unhappy staff.

In that situation, the managing editor has all the authority: the keys to the castle, if you like. The editor has the title, and the crown, and a following. But any human being in the managing editor's position is going to be tempted to offer alternative leadership, either on occasion or semi-permanently. What's more, it will come easily, and it will start to feel good – and they won't live happily ever after.

It needs to be one job. But it is two sets of skills, and two sets of problems. The best way of dealing with it is to recognise that, breaking the job down into its component parts and then working hard on mastering them. We have already seen that leadership is the exciting bit so, in time-honoured journalistic fashion, we're going to look at that first.

Leadership

People will tell you that leaders are born, rather than made. But they'll tell you exactly the same thing about writers and editors. Like those things, leadership is something you can learn to do better. But fundamentally it's not up to you. A person gets management authority from above, but becomes a leader when the team agrees to be led. The ability to unite people behind you, and retain their loyalty even when things turn rough, is something managers don't necessarily have. It's certainly not something you acquire while clawing your way up the journalistic ladder. Journalists, especially reporters, are competitive by nature. The arts of praising others, celebrating success and taking blame when necessary don't always come easily.

Leaders must focus the attentions of a mixed group of colleagues so that they can achieve success. They do that by planning, organising work, communicating what they need, and then motivating people to see it through.

Types of leader

By the time we are being measured for the editor's chair, most of us have had the opportunity to experience different types of leadership. You might have come across these:

- The Great Dictator
- The Ditherer
- The People's Friend.

The Great Dictator leads by pushing people forward, and has a clear sense of direction. Unfortunately, this leaves little room for contributions from the team, and all its frustrated energy and ingenuity soon turns into passive resistance or active opposition. But the Great Dictator has some good points. In a crisis, being told what to do is strangely comforting. What's more, the traditions of journalism (the slogan 'Just do it!' was known in a thousand newsrooms before it ever appeared on a box of training shoes) are authoritarian: journalists moan about them, but many prefer them to long discussions and compromises.

The Ditherer sees all points of view, all of the time. Editors with a tendency to indecision hand over control to their colleagues and let them argue it out. If those people are motivated and have a good sense of direction, all may be well. But the Ditherer has relinquished the task of directing the magazine, and will find it hard to insist on standards being maintained. And if the Ditherer's subordinates are not competent and well intentioned, the magazine is in trouble.

The People's Friend, meanwhile, has the best intentions. The idea is to build on the abilities of the team by involving it in every aspect of the job. The drawback is that the magazine turns rapidly into a meeting that never ends, with the process of management taking over entirely from the process of producing a magazine.

Look critically at these leadership models, and others you have known, and see what you can use and what you should discard. In modern management, participation and democracy are favoured. Give your team members objectives, but let them decide how they should be carried through, even letting them carve up the work between themselves.

Management

> The secret of management is to keep the guys who hate you away from the guys who are undecided.
>
> (Casey Stengel)[3]

Leadership is a great thing, but it is secondary to management. The key word is 'responsibility'. A leader inspires, but a manager ensures that the magazine thrives and that everyone involved prospers. When you become a manager, you have the power to control your own work and that of all those around you. But it is daunting. You may think you can essentially remain a journalist, giving your new management tasks the least possible attention. But it won't work. The powers you refuse to exercise will be quickly swallowed by other people, and that may not help you or your team. If you don't manage, you will be condemned for it. If you do manage, you will meet opposition. You are sandwiched between your journalistic colleagues and senior management, forced to uphold the very decisions you would once have attacked. All the time, you must defend your colleagues against those who don't understand why they cost so much and seem to work so haphazardly.

Inevitably you will do things differently from your predecessor, and change is threatening. Place yourself in your colleagues' position for a while and see how threatened you feel. New managers are not only scared, they are scary. Gather information quickly but act slowly. Keep edging forward: gently does it. To help with your own fears, find a mentor, someone outside your immediate working environment but with experience you can draw on. You won't be able to let off steam with your old colleagues: better to find an understanding ear where it can't do any harm.

Your responsibilities

The position is quite clear: editors are legally responsible for every word and image that appear in their magazines, in both editorial and advertising matter. Beyond that, an editor has a moral responsibility for the attitudes and expressions within the magazine, and must be prepared to defend them.

But the editor also has responsibilities as an employer, in terms of the way people are treated and their working conditions. You are their 'line manager', to use the jargon. There must be fairness in employment practice and adherence to good standards of health and safety. And you are also, sometimes, a member of the company's commercial management.

In practice, some of this may not affect you. Editors rarely have much to do with the day-to-day running of the advertising department. In many companies, personnel functions are controlled by a separate department. Even so, you still have to know the rules – the law, in fact – and operate by them. The same goes for health and safety.

On a more general level, you as editor may be held responsible for things you have no power to change. Your circulation may decline, not for editorial reasons, but because other publications have higher promotional budgets and more vigorous promotional teams. If you are to be held responsible for such matters, you must be represented in the management forum which deals with them.

Underlying your dealings with your colleagues must be an awareness of employment law. Unfortunately, that's not what you'd call a neat package, since the laws are drawn from many different sources: common law; British legislation, mostly passed since 1963; and European legislation. On top of that, generations of judges have introduced a mass of case law, modifying and elaborating the written principles.

Companies should have written employment procedures, built on these frameworks and examined by solicitors, but some will not. If these procedures exist, you should know them thoroughly. Trouble can come from many directions: disciplinary procedures; racial and sexual discrimination; maternity rights; safety; holiday entitlements; hours of work; sick leave; the wording of employment contracts; and so on.

This is not the place for a detailed examination of employment law, and you should be aware that the law around employment changes all the time – so all advice given here is subject to change. There are specific books on the subject, such as *Croner's Reference Book for Employers*, and if your company has a human resources (HR) or legal department they may subscribe to a service that provides continuously updated material.

As an editor you should check any employment issues – including recruitment – through with those people to ensure that you avoid problems further down the line. You should also familiarise yourself with online resources such as the Employment section of the Directgov website, and the 'Employment Matters' section of the Department for Business, Innovation and Skills (formerly the Department of Trade and Industry) website.[4] The main thing is to understand the key terms you will come across: the letter of appointment; the contract of employment; sick pay; maternity payments and leave; trade union duties; redundancy; wrongful dismissal; unfair dismissal.

In a small company you may write your own letters of appointment, so you should be aware of their legal significance. The actual 'contract of employment' is made when both sides agree verbally, before anything is put on paper, so it is vital not to offer anything at the interview stage unless you intend to provide it. New employees must receive the following details within two months of starting work:

- their employer's name;
- their job title or a brief job description;
- the date when their employment began;
- their pay rate and when they will be paid;
- their hours of work;
- their holiday entitlement (there are statutory minimums – check the current status of these);
- where they will be working (this may be more than one place);
- sick pay arrangements;
- notice periods;
- information about disciplinary and grievance procedures;
- any collective agreements that affect their employment terms or conditions;
- pensions and pension schemes;
- if they are not a permanent employee, how long the employment is expected to continue, or the date their employment will end.

Once made, the contract can only be changed by mutual agreement.

There is a legal requirement to pay people who are sick, providing they and their period of illness meet the conditions laid down in the regulations. There are also many requirements concerning pregnant women, new fathers and people who adopt, laying down both the payments they receive following the arrival of their child and their right to return to work afterwards in a position that, while not necessarily identical, has terms or conditions that are no worse. Requests to job-share or work part time must be considered fairly. No female employee, however briefly she has been with the company, may be dismissed for being pregnant or giving birth. Such a dismissal is always automatically unfair.

Redundancy is the procedure whereby people are dismissed because the firm no longer requires that type of work. Remember that the job becomes redundant, not the individual. It is emphatically not a way of removing individuals whom you do not want in a particular job, although some employers try to use it in this way. Individuals must be selected for redundancy by a fair and agreed method, given a redundancy payment, plenty of notice and, where possible, the offer of alternative employment. Trade unions, where recognised, must be consulted. Where correct redundancy procedures are breached, the employee will be able to bring a case of 'unfair' dismissal. This should not be confused with 'wrongful' dismissal.

A wrongful dismissal is one in which the employer breaches the contract of employment, either by failing to give sufficient notice of dismissal or by failing to comply with the disciplinary procedures detailed in the contract. Where the employer summarily dismisses the employee because the employee's behaviour constitutes a breach of the contact of employment, no case of wrongful dismissal will be found.

The government's Advisory, Conciliation and Arbitration Service (ACAS) has produced a code of practice on disciplinary procedures,[5] and although this theoretically has no more than advisory status, it would be a brave employer indeed who deviated far from it.

By this point you will be realising how complex an area employment is. If there is one piece of advice to sum it up, it is this: *do not hire or fire without first taking advice from someone who is up to date on employment law.*

Whether that is through a call to in-house lawyers or HR staff with an up-to-date and in-depth knowledge of what your options and requirements are, or having on-call access to an external employment lawyer, you need to seek advice. Any employer that skimps on these resources is pursuing a false economy: defending a case brought by a dismissed employee will wipe out any savings they think they are making, and a former employee who wins their case can also win anything from lost earnings to unlimited damages.

Having a well written employment contract and clear procedures regarding probation periods at the start of employment – and disciplinary procedures and reviews for poor performance or behaviour – will also make your position clearer if a situation deteriorates.

Remember that a dismissal is only fair if:

• it is for redundancy, and all procedures have been followed;
• it is on the grounds of failings in 'skill, aptitude or health', a situation which normally arises at the beginning of an employment;

- it is on the grounds of misconduct: incompetence, negligence, violence, drunkenness, immorality;
- it is on the grounds that the employee can no longer work legally (for instance, if a driver loses his or her licence);
- it is for 'some other substantial reason' which you are prepared to argue before an employment tribunal.

So you must understand what is involved before you even think of dismissing anyone – and unless you are a saint, you will certainly have such thoughts from time to time.

Your approach

When you become an editor, your first job is to work out exactly how to place yourself in the process. You will have had good and bad examples. Some editors spend most of their professional lives away from the editorial department, either in meetings with management colleagues or outside, representing the title, meeting advertisers and so on. The result is that the magazine can appear to run itself, although such magazines invariably have a strong deputy editor. On the other hand, we have all come across editors who never leave their desks and who need to control everything.

Veteran editors will warn you against trying to edit by committee, especially when the pressure is on. Gene Roberts, formerly of the *New York Times,* puts it like this: 'A newspaper ought to be a participatory democracy until 20 minutes before deadline.' Many would say the same for magazines. But editors will achieve little by being autocratic. It makes more sense to communicate your vision to your staff and invite them to share it. We learn to achieve success through the creativity of the people we are leading and managing. One of the best things is when your colleagues surprise you by their commitment and ability. You have to give them the opportunity to do that, even if it means accepting that, on occasions, they will let you down.

Managers today are supposed to be 'facilitators' or 'team coaches', not police officers. Most people will accept your authority. But you must make it worth their while to do so, by succeeding in the task that you have been set. If you listen to what people around you are saying, you will learn a lot. There is something called 'manager's joke syndrome', whereby people laugh twice as hard at a joke told by a superior. It is hard not to be flattered. But the point of the anecdote is that the impact of *anything* you say now will be exaggerated. That includes words of warning and praise.

Those whose work you are required to direct may be friends and close colleagues or complete strangers. In the latter case, meet each member of your new team quickly, and individually. This will give you an opportunity to provide reassurance, even a modicum of flattery, but also to put across your drive and ideas. You must also assess those you are about to work with, making a note of your impressions. At the end of your first week, and then again after a month, look again at what you wrote and reconsider.

Set an example of diligence and enthusiasm, particularly in your dealings with the outside world. You need to impress your vision of the magazine upon your staff, and to project enthusiasm and the confidence that it can be achieved. You need to be decisive, and to take the blame when things go wrong. You mustn't make promises you don't intend to keep or can't keep.

People need to know that you are interested in both their work and their lives. When you praise, it should be in public. It also needs to be specific and detailed if it is to have any effect. Not 'I always enjoy your features' but 'I really liked the moment in your feature on aircraft safety when you …'. Criticism must be tough when necessary, but it should be in private.

Editorially you can expect to be judged as much on the detail of your magazine as on the overall picture, and so your immersion in it has to be almost limitless. While you are setting your standards, you need to be everywhere: reading copy, looking at layouts and web pages, looking at pictures, suggesting headlines, encouraging, cajoling, persuading.

One ideal approach might be to concern yourself with 'nothing except everything'. You should make sure you are not tied to fixed, time-sensitive jobs in the production cycle, so that you can become involved in what needs doing as and when it arises. In that way, you can look at a feature early on and suggest a rewrite, you can see pictures when they come in, you can stand at the sub-editor's shoulder when headlines are being written and you can reassure the lawyer when a controversial piece raises worries. You can also attend the necessary meetings with publishers and other managers without worrying about what you are not doing while you are there.

Delegate important editing and writing tasks to your senior colleagues, if you have them, so that you can remain slightly detached but ready to seize on key details and deal with them. This remoteness may feel difficult, even painful, especially in the early stages. But once you have set a direction and laid down standards, let the team get on with it. You can dedicate your time to planning and organising for the future, and fighting corporate battles on behalf of the editorial team.

The 'nothing except everything' model will not suit everyone's circumstances. Some editors have few real managerial functions. Instead, especially on small titles, they continue to carry out a lot of the journalistic work on an issue. The model here is the 'player manager'.[6] You have to do the job and manage at the same time. This is a growing trend, and not just in journalism but in information technology, law, banking and health. Here you are more leader than manager: it is difficult to exert formal authority, so you must inspire and motivate through the quality of your commitment to work.

Every magazine has its own 'culture', a set of attitudes, procedures and ways of working that may have existed even before the current staff were in their jobs. As an outsider joining an existing magazine you will find yourself under pressure to go with the flow. Although this might feel like a personal defeat, the first task is to get the magazine out. Changes can come later.

There are at least two views of how new editors should act during their first days. One says that immediate decisions must be taken about personnel and appropriate changes made. This can leave you with a reputation for dynamism, but also for impetuousness and unreasonableness. Concentrate on listening and learning in the first days and weeks; then you can act from a position of strength.

Many editors are reluctant to enter a new and potentially hostile environment single-handed, preferring to bring a trusted deputy or assistant. This is only human, but your new staff will think you have consigned them to the outer circle. You will soon need allies if you are to get anything done. Convince people that you are going to make things better for them.

Once things start to improve, opposition will crumble, but until then you need one or two key people to follow your lead. If they happen to include people who really feel they should have your job, so much the better. Their future prospects are likely to be enhanced if they are loyal to you rather than disloyal. In a small team, you may be able to convince everyone at once. That's excellent, because then you are well equipped to face any hostility from outside. Loyalty will only be entrenched once you have some members of staff who owe you their present positions. Appointments and promotions must be your own decisions.

Management textbooks, especially modern ones, are well worth reading.[7] But journalists are creative people, which makes managing them a little bit more tricky. They are generally articulate, sensitive and individualistic. They will question every instruction and are inclined to be distrustful. Don't complain about these qualities: that's why we employ them. But it does mean you can't manage them by barking orders and pretending to know everything. You must let them do their jobs.

Provide the vision, and set the standards. Without a vision that is understood by everyone working on a magazine, the editor is merely overseeing its decline. The vision makes it possible for individuals to act as a team, almost by instinct. If everyone understands who the reader is supposed to be, commissions will be appropriate, the style of writing will be right, and appropriate headlines and standfirsts will present themselves. The vision will run through every page like a watermark. You have created that vision, and now you develop it with your staff. Your enthusiasm must be plain.

But you must also make clear what you expect of people and of the finished magazine. Industrial managers say 'what gets measured gets done'. We can't work like that: we don't keep a tally of individuals' daily keystrokes, although it has been tried, and there are some online editorial jobs which have experimented with payment based in whole or part on the numbers of people viewing a writer's material (the practice does not at the time of writing appear to have been adopted on any wide scale and is inadvisable for at least three reasons: it damages morale; it leads to formulaic writing; and the popularity of material depends on many factors outside the writer's control).

We do, however, assess people's work on quality. How fresh are these ideas? How well are they executed? Journalists need to know that their work is read and appreciated, and that their ambitions and difficulties are matters that can be discussed.

Train yourself to listen. The temptation is to tell people what to do. But you need people to tell you their difficulties and their discoveries. Take what they say seriously and be seen to be doing something about it, otherwise the opportunity is wasted.

On a magazine with a small staff, low pagination and a long production cycle, editors will be involved in every stage of an issue's creation. As the magazine grows, however, that becomes much more difficult. What's the minimum routine involvement you should have in a magazine's production to manage it properly? You certainly need to approve the flat-plan, since the running order and relative lengths of feature material really determine the reader's experience of the magazine. You need not, however, do all the necessary sums and negotiation yourself, providing you have a sensible relationship with your advertising department and a competent deputy or chief sub-editor.

Since you are legally responsible for the entire content of the publication, it is usual to see every finished page. In the days when magazines went to press as pasted-up boards, it was customary for the editor to sign each page last, after a senior editorial figure (perhaps a chief sub-editor or section editor) and the art editor. You must see proofs of each spread as it is sent to the printer.

You won't just be reading pages for typographical errors. Your concern is with the broad picture: are the headlines appropriate? Does the design lead the reader through the material clearly? Are those the correct pictures? It is sometimes a good idea to print a checklist on each proof page, reminding people to tick off each of the elements, particularly picture credits, folios, captions and pull quotes (and headlines – sometimes it is the biggest typo on the page that you miss).

Looking at everything this late has its limitations. Your production schedule should include sufficient time to enable you to change things that are wrong without incurring extra costs. But this is not the moment for recasting a major feature or taking a new line on a news story. There will be no time for significant rewriting and certainly not for extra research.

That is why you must make it your business to insert yourself into the process early on, and not always in a predictable way. Some editors see all the raw copy before it is edited. That can undermine the authority of your team. But you should be able to dip in and read copy at various stages in the process. You may also like to see rough layouts and early picture-edits when they are under construction, rather than wait until a spread is finished before passing comment.

Most editors find that they have regrettably little time to spend on editorial tasks: instead they are trapped in a round of meetings on more managerial and commercial topics. Consequently, you must find ways to make your editorial interventions count, and be seen to be interested in everything that is going on. There is no better way of doing this than wandering around looking at what people are doing: designing pages, sorting out photographs, writing headlines, and so on. This can be infuriating, of course, but people must learn to expect it rather than see it as an imposition.

Management skills

When you first become an editor, you may well have no management skills at all. What will have got you the job will be your aptitude for dealing with people, an ability to make decisions, a certain maturity, added to excellent editorial abilities. But you will need new skills to do the job properly. The most important of these is communication.

Communication

You've spent your whole career using words. But that's not the kind of communication you need now. You need to be able to get your meaning across but, more important, you need to be able to hear people. You must listen both to what people are saying and to what they are not saying. It's easy to hear only what you want to hear.

So when someone asks you for something, or you agree something between you, say it again so you are both sure you understand one another. If it's something that has the capacity to cause trouble in future, write it down: freelance commissions, for instance, and big feature ideas are notorious for 'drifting' after the initial conversation. If they're written down and each party receives a copy, that process is halted. It also makes everyone realise that words do mean something, and differentiates general chat from meaningful discussion.

What about when you have to disagree with someone? There is a useful sequence. Repeat the other person's position so that you know you are arguing about the same thing. Then state your case. Finally propose a way out, preferably using an outcome you thought about before starting the discussion. If you have to criticise someone, get your facts straight, and then do it in a private place. Always concentrate on the work, not on the personality, and push the onus back onto them: 'I'm not very happy with the headings on this page. I think they're a bit uninspired. Are you happy with them?' You can see that this is preferable to that time-honoured journalistic gambit: 'What do you call this rubbish?'

People respond well to your interest in them and their difficulties. By asking people to clarify their own feelings about their work and their problems with it, you avoid a stand-off. At the end, though, you must reassert your authority in unambiguous terms: 'Well, I'd like you to take another look at them before you go on to anything else. Can you bring me a printout of the page at about 11.30? Thank you.' It is important to thank people, even if you really think they are just doing their job.

Meetings

Meetings are an essential part of communication. Unfortunately, most people find them tedious and come expecting to be bored or disruptive. Meetings must not simply happen: they need to be planned, properly run and then followed up. The first question, of course, is whether a meeting should take place at all. If more is achieved by not having it, then don't have it.

You will find that meetings are a nuisance. There will always be meetings with publishers, different departments of management and outside organisations. They should not be allowed to stop you communicating with your editorial staff. This means more meetings, but at least you will be running the show.

Now you can set the timing and the venue, create the agenda, decide on who attends and how long the meeting lasts, and create a record of what the meeting decided. All these things are important.

You need an agenda, however short, to keep the meeting to the point. The list of who attends is important too: people will feel nervous about being 'left out', but it is not always productive for them to attend. Once they know that your meetings are strictly about business they won't feel so excluded. Meetings should have a fixed time-span, to discourage rambling, and they should lead to some resolution, conclusion or policy that can be written down and circulated.

In a small-enough magazine, it could be argued that there is no need for meetings, since everyone is constantly on hand and discussion is the natural state of things. Nonetheless, there are strong arguments for getting people to stop work, put down the telephones and turn their attention to the matter at hand. On a weekly with a strong news content it can be a good idea to start each day with a morning look at the diary and the post, and a discussion of anything that is immediately at hand. Some editors like to see all the incoming post and distribute it at this stage, with an indication as to how important they consider it for the magazine. Such meetings should be short and sharp. More leisured discussion of the magazine in general can take place outside the building and at another time.

On bigger publications it is essential to hold regular meetings to discuss progress. It is often a good idea to do this when the new issue first becomes available, although on a monthly those meetings will be too infrequent to maintain momentum. It is important to review the finished magazine as it first appears, with the intention of doing better in future.

Some offices have what is called a 'whinge copy', where journalists annotate a copy of the issue to indicate where they find mistakes or have points they want to raise. This is a good idea, providing people are prepared to initial their remarks and defend them in the meeting. Journalists are often reluctant to engage in constructive criticism. But it is essential if everyone is to play a part in producing a strong product. Promote the idea by being optimistic, enthusiastic and quicker to praise than to attack.

After the meeting has looked at the current issue, review the state of the coming issue, with contributions by those responsible for the various sections or aspects, reporting any progress or hold-ups and permitting any last-minute suggestions or contributions. Following that, the meeting may wish to move on to future issues and ideas.

Do meetings have any role in creativity? We have all experienced the emptying of the mind that takes place when called upon to produce ideas in a formal meeting. Nonetheless, these editorial meetings may be one of the few opportunities people get to share ideas and develop them. But meetings need work and regular practice to ensure that people feel comfortable. Everyone should be asked to contribute, directly if necessary. But it should be a rule that all ideas will be considered seriously and with courtesy.

This is the trick behind brainstorming. Try it. You must be away from your desks, with no paper in front of you. First you do a dry run, on an amusing topic such as 'uses for a paper-clip'. You, or someone you nominate, writes the ideas on a board or flipchart. The rule is that no one must criticise an idea, and the 'facilitator' must cajole, encourage and wheedle everyone to take part. After the practice, do it again with a real topic: say, ideas for the Christmas issue. When every possible idea is exhausted, you can look at the stuff on the flipchart and evaluate it together. The point is that you separate the process of 'idea creation' from 'idea evaluation'. Many people find this effective – and you can even do it on your own with a blank piece of paper.

It is essential if meetings are not to degenerate that they are seen to lead directly to action. Notes should be taken, and each meeting should include an outline of what action has been taken as a result of the preceding discussion. They should be kept as brief and as pointed as possible. One trick sometimes recommended is to hold them at the end of the day, when people have an incentive to keep things short. Others recommend holding meetings standing up, but you may feel that this is extreme.

Large magazines are much more prone to factional disputes than smaller ones, and you have to navigate through that. Information, who receives it and who doesn't, can be a major weapon in factional disputes, and meetings can make things worse. Stick to the point and tell the truth. A good and noble policy insists upon there being 'no secrets', but if you are following this policy it has to be in concert with your fellow managers. At the very least, you must tell your staff nothing that is capable of being contradicted by other sources.

Because it comes from you, people are inclined to misinterpret or exaggerate what you tell them about your magazine's progress, the rise and fall of circulation and advertising income. An exhortation to belt-tightening can be construed as an announcement of imminent redundancies. If you make reference to pressure from above, people will assume that you are no longer running things.

If something concerns specific individuals, it is right and proper to have them there at the same time and tell them together. For routine meetings, the standard solution is to bring the heads of each department together: chief sub-editor, features editor, web editor, news editor, art editor, community editor, and so on. Those in the meeting must pass on what they learn to those in their departments. You should check that this happens.

The results of meetings need to be transformed into some physical form. After discussions on future issues it is as well to circulate an early running order, showing the state of play on various sections. There are also various wall displays that you can use, usually on purpose-built whiteboards or pinboards. Many magazines these days have a fairly rigid underlying structure that is easily expressed as a type of grid, with issue dates or numbers across the top and the various regular features ('news feature', 'first feature', 'second feature', 'picture feature', 'consumer feature') and regular sections (health, fashion, new products, and so on) running from top to bottom (see, for example, Figure 3.1). For the next issue, each square in the grid will be filled, but as you move across the grid, the picture becomes patchier. It is also a good idea to leave some space on the board to flag up features that are in stock but haven't been allocated to an issue. That way they will sit there as a reminder rather than languish in a drawer and become expensively out of date.

Notice the way the content is less well defined the further you look into the future. This is exactly as it should be: you need to leave room for events and inspiration. It is also essential to create a physical record of the state of the current magazine as it is made. As pages are completed and sent to the typesetters or colour house, reduced proofs should be pinned up in order. It is even useful, from time to time, to lay colour photocopies of the finished feature pages down on the floor and walk around them, before they are sent. It sounds bizarre, but if you have the space it is a good way of assessing editorial shape and pace.

You should leave people, as far as possible, to make their own decisions and organise their own working arrangements within your overall strategy. That will mean encouraging them to have their own meetings, and a well-appointed office should always include a space where this can happen. Features and art staff should work together from the start on complex stories. But you need to be kept informed of what is going on, and you should insist on being given a brief note or email of what was discussed and decided.

Likewise, stories that may require strong web or mobile integration need planning and cooperation. Do you need to invite online contributors early on? Will the topic benefit from a piece of multimedia or interactivity? Do you need to put plans in place to support readers after publication (by, for instance, hosting a live chat or a forum)?

Apart from the routine meetings needed to keep the magazine going, however, there is a strong case for regular 'strategy' meetings about the magazine, its market and its future. These may benefit from the types of analysis beloved of management experts, notably the SWOT technique, in which attention is given in turn to the

	February	March	April	May
Cover story	Drive a bargain	The new Ford	Supercars	Soft-tops
Feature 1	Rover roars back	City car test		
Feature 2	The new Honda	Italian exotica	Budget motors	
News feature	Dangerous parts			

Figure 3.1 Grid or wall chart used to plan content for a monthly magazine

Strengths and Weaknesses of the magazine as it stands and the Opportunities and Threats facing it in the future.

Each of the four terms is taken as the starting point for a wide-ranging discussion. In the case of a magazine in, for instance, the pregnancy market, its strengths might include its specialist nature, the quality of experts used and its good reputation for accuracy. Its weaknesses might be the quality of photography used, low recognition in the market arising from its bi-monthly status, and a lack of interactivity.

The opportunities open to such a title might include the possibility of spinoff products, for instance books and videos, and potential syndication deals. The threats might come from new titles entering an already crowded market, the rise of new online versions, and even the falling birth rate of the country as a whole. To be complete, the SWOT analysis is then turned on your magazine's rivals and competitors in print and online.

Planning

Obviously, you will be planning issues all the time, but there will be times when you will want to get bigger projects moving. It is usually said that planning needs to be a three-stage process. First there comes the planning itself, then a period in which the working of the plan is monitored, and finally an evaluation of the plan.

Start by thinking about what you are trying to achieve, in some detail. Write that target down to keep you on track: it is easy to end up somewhere else. Next, assess how things stand now, before working out how to get from here to where you want to be.

That should lead you towards the creation of a scheme of work. This should be a list of individual tasks, in the correct chronological order and in sufficient detail for someone to start doing them. Work out how long each job will take, and build up from that to create a time-scale for the whole project. After that jobs can be allocated to individuals, making serious efforts to find the right person in each case. All this material should be written down in a project document. It should be just a brief statement of objectives followed by who does what and when.

After that comes monitoring, via a number of review meetings, each of which asks 'Where are we?' When the project is done, assess what has been achieved and then celebrate the success, with a proper acknowledgement of the work that people have done. This is a vital part of the process and one that is easy to forget, especially in the world of journalism, where people are always looking to next week and the next issue. But as editor you must honour these rituals.

Some will argue that a formal approach to planning might do wonders when you are building the Channel Tunnel but is unnecessarily complex for journalism. But some publishing tasks, for instance launching a new section, are complex and do need to be worked through rigorously. They would involve commissioning, flat-planning, design, liaison with the printers, changes to the website and possible setting up of other web presences, copy editing, publicity and promotion – and all those have to be allocated time and resources. Of course, all planning has to take account of money, which is dealt with in Chapter 4.

Delegation

If you don't delegate, you won't be able to manage a team. Delegation means giving responsibility for work to a colleague who can *choose* how to carry it out. You are still responsible for ensuring that the work gets done, but the person you have delegated to has responsibility for deciding how to do it. It is not the same as giving someone a task and telling them to get on with it.

Delegation places a heavy onus on the person delegated to, but it demands a lot from you too. The task should be within the powers of your colleague, but he or she should also be slightly stretched. Explain exactly what you require, indicate any constraints of time or money, and make yourself available should any problems arise. You may also need to walk the person through the task the first time. After that, let them get on with it.

It is very important that you don't go through this whole briefing process only to interfere at every stage. The person you have delegated may, in fact, know how to do the job better than you, because they are closer to it. There may be mistakes – in fact there probably will be – but everyone learns from the process. Your job is checking that the task is done well, rather than doing it. And the time you save can be used for more long-term and tricky jobs.

It is in everybody's interest that you delegate. Your staff will benefit by taking an active part in the whole process, and showing initiative, rather than simply waiting for you to dish work out to them. You will be able to manage the magazine properly.

There are several exceptions to the principle of delegation, however. One is complaints from readers and those written about. These must be dealt with at the highest level, for legal reasons. You must never delegate anything confidential, especially anything personal which has been disclosed to you in confidence. You must retain personnel tasks, including training, motivation, appraisal, salary negotiation and, especially, discipline.

It is not acceptable to delegate those tasks you don't like doing: that will immediately be spotted and will do nothing for your reputation. You must also ensure that you hand over only those tasks you know can be handled by the person to whom you have delegated them. If that person gets into difficulties, that will represent a failure for both of you, but ultimately it is your responsibility for delegating unwisely.

Delegation will help you achieve the goal of most editors, which is to make sure that the production process can carry on without you. In a larger magazine you should ensure that you have a deputy capable of making serious editorial decisions. It is essential that you have appointed or inherited someone who shares your vision of the magazine and its readers.

The crux in delegation comes when you realise that the person to whom you have delegated a task is better at it than you are. Accepting that marks your maturity as a manager. Delegation is the only way to deal with ever-increasing responsibilities. It does not represent a dilution of your power: the people to whom you delegate are still answerable to you. Editors fear that if they delegate too well, their own bosses will wonder what they are there for. This is unrealistic: being unable to delegate is likely to do your career much more harm.

Decision making

An editor's life is full of decisions. Every phone call, every email, is from someone wanting you to make up your mind, usually on the spot, about something. A lot of these messages will be from people who are trying to avoid making decisions themselves, but that won't help.

Convince yourself that it is usually better to make any decision than no decision. Indecision simply postpones the agony. If you decide, you can see how things work out. If it all goes wrong, you learn from it. In any case, you can often remedy the situation later. There is a useful sequence of events that might help you make decisions. It goes like this:

- work out what you are trying to decide;
- gather the information you need;
- list your options;
- weigh up the pros and cons of each option;
- make your decision;
- inform those affected by the decision;
- keep track of what happens as a result of it.

Buried inside this you may discern the most simple technique of all: writing down the 'for and against' of anything you are considering. It is reassuringly effective.

One problem you may have is procrastination. It is always easy to put off a decision, but it's a mistake. Give yourself a deadline and stick to it. In important cases, though, you may find it a good idea to allow yourself pause for reflection between making the decision and putting it into effect. It is no crime to change your mind in private.

Negotiation

Negotiation is becoming more important all the time. In most areas of our lives we are consumers, capable of asking for a better deal or walking away. In work, we expect to discuss what we are required to do and how we should do it. Delegation depends upon it: we are at liberty to refuse delegated responsibilities if they don't benefit us.

Editors will be involved in endless negotiations, formal and informal. You will buy freelance writing and pictures, hire and promote staff, fight for promotional and PR expenditure, struggle to introduce new working practices and systems, and so on. The theory of negotiation has become very important in everything from evolutionary biology to international relations, and has consequently become very complex. But there are a few simple things that will help you.

Most of us instinctively think of negotiation as a battle for scarce resources. If I get more, you get less (this is called a 'zero sum game'). But successful negotiators favour what's called the 'win/win', or collaborative model. This recognises that an individual negotiation is usually part of a long sequence, and that the important thing is to keep the relationship going successfully. If you crush someone in your opening deal, perhaps by paying well below the market rate for a piece of work, that person will feel resentful and may well not want to work for you again. The trick is to find ways in which both parties can win, and that might mean looking beyond the issue on the negotiating table: the price of a photograph or the basic salary of a sub-editor. To pull this off, you need to think of negotiation as a collaborative process. What can we *both* get from this?

First, you need the background. You must know the going rate for a piece of work of this sort, and how much this particular contributor has been paid for similar pieces. It is a good idea, also, to know how much work this person has been doing lately, for your magazine and others.

Now work out how little you would like to pay, and how much you can afford to pay. You also need to think about your 'bottom line'. The jargon for this is BATNA, 'Best Alternative To a Negotiated Agreement', and in our terms it means considering what you will do if you don't reach an agreement. Can you get someone else to do the job as well? Can you fill the hole with something else? If you have a ready alternative, you can afford to take a tougher line in negotiation. After that, you need to think through these figures for the other person. How much would they like? How little would they accept? What's their BATNA: if we don't reach agreement, will they be able to do the work for someone else, or will it all have been a waste of her time?

When you start the negotiations, you will both have a fixed position. You will have one figure, they will have another. Interestingly, the National Union of Journalists advises freelance writers not to suggest a price but to let editors do that.[8] The idea is that the writer's silence will hustle the editor into increasing the offer. Well, it's all part of the game, but if you have worked out your top and bottom prices first, you will always be negotiating within your acceptable range. Anything between those two figures really represents successful negotiation, and the same for the other party. You both go away happy and ready to do business in the future.

But those bargaining positions should be a starting point. Your real interests, and those of the other party, may be quite different. If you allow the discussions to develop, that may become apparent, to your mutual benefit. Your boss may suggest an inadequate figure for your staff budget. In discussion, it may become apparent that the figure could be increased if you showed that increasing staffing would save money elsewhere, perhaps on freelance cover. The fixed position has moved, because you realised that management's interest is in overall costs rather than this one figure.

By being flexible, and moving beyond the fixed battle lines, you can look for alternative solutions. With freelances, it is not all about the rate per word. There are other rights that can be negotiated. Beyond that, think about making a deal for more than one piece: most writers would rather have the security that comes with a short series of features than a high figure for a one-off. But if this goes beyond the rate, you may be able to offer them research help, contacts, generous expenses, or some real involvement with the magazine. Any of these might help unlock an impasse.

Beyond that, both sides should stay relaxed and listen carefully to the discussion. It's not about outsmarting people. It's about coming to an agreement that works for both parties and opens the way for further cooperation.

Time management

Some believe that all management is time management. Most editors find themselves besieged by obligations and demands, leaving little time to think. Things will eat into your time. Worrying is one, procrastination is another.

One of the most useful things you can do at the start is to keep a log of how your time is spent. Log everything, including the time you spend gossiping by the coffee machine. Do it honestly for a week or so, and then work out how much of your time is spent doing your job. That means excluding the time you spend doing other people's work, dealing with things wrongly passed on to you from above or below, adjudicating between other people who really should be able to sort things out for themselves, and so on. Your work is really the stuff that only you can do, and you need to make that your priority.

So be ruthless: skip meetings if they are not necessary, or send someone else. If you find your time is wasted by switching from one activity to another, try and group similar jobs into longer and more productive periods. Allocate time for specific tasks. One of the most useful things you can do with your time is to use it to save time. Five minutes a day spent on organising your diary will certainly be worthwhile.

You must also set aside thinking time, free from interruptions. While it is a noble ideal to say that 'my door is always open' you will have only yourself to blame if people take that as an open invitation to drop in. Invent a way of indicating when you are available for discussion and when not, as simple as leaving your door open or closing it. If you are in an open-plan office, as many of us are, this is harder. You may have to let your attitude to interruption speak for you.

A better idea is to set aside a time each day specifically for brief discussion on subjects close to people's hearts: a surgery, if you like. Obviously this doesn't preclude people calling on you when something flares up, but it may have the effect of discouraging random interruptions. With luck, people will adapt to your routine. You want to be approachable, but you also want to be able to do your job.

If you have an assistant or secretary, even one you share, make the most of the privilege. Your assistant must be entrusted with the bulk of your routine post after the first few weeks, distributing it around the office, filing it or binning it according to a pattern you agree. An assistant can also help you by keeping a diary for you, but you must ensure that your own pocket diary or mobile phone diary is synchronised with the main diary every day. Your diary not only is a record of appointments and meetings: it can also be a device for jogging your memory about ideas and schemes and ensuring that essential routine tasks are done.

You need a good message system. You can get special books, combining a sticky note for your desk with a more permanent record. Or you can improvise your own system. You must not let messages be scribbled on bits of paper and lost. Your incoming calls should be logged, with time, date and caller's name, to ensure you get back to people promptly.

Most time-management systems are about lists. Your time log shows where your time is going. Now extract the necessary engagements and events and, with the help of a diary and calendar, allocate time to them. Many people trust everything to a 'to do' list. This involves starting the day with a list of tasks and allocating them an order of priority, starting with 1 and working down. As one job is done, the priority of the others can be changed. If you persuade someone else to take on one of your jobs, so much the better.

At the end of the day, anything left has to be carried over to tomorrow. The main thing is not to allocate yourself too many things to do in a day: you will be demoralised once you start carrying them over for the second day in succession. Most people find that four or five serious tasks is plenty.

This is such a simple system that it hardly merits further explanation, but you can use a project management website (Basecamp and Huddle are two popular ones but there are also free tools such as Google Calendar) to do the reordering as well as juggling regular appointments and producing a schedule. Avoid creating a pile of To Do lists on paper that you then lose, or lose track of. But also avoid keeping all your schedule in one digital space, such as your computer, phone, or website. Computers can crash and files become corrupt; phones can be lost or stolen; websites can go down, lose your data, or go under. Whatever you use ensure that you have a regular backup copy or that details are 'synced' across multiple devices that can be accessed both online and offline.

Paperwork is another problem. There are many systems for dealing with it. The traditional civil service system, with three trays for 'in', 'out' and 'pending', still has its supporters. Most of us find that the pending tray soon heads skywards. To make this work, you need a rule that nothing stays pending longer than, say, 24 hours. After that it must have been acted on or filed properly.

Another idea you might try is the 'one-touch' system. What this says is that if you pick up a piece of paper, you must do something positive with it. Act on it, file it properly or bin it. It is supposed to remove the clutter from your desk. A variant is to take a red pen and make a mark on the paper each time you pick it up. At the end of the day, examine how many red marks your paperwork has. The paperwork that you have pushed around without tackling will be liberally freckled, and you must do something about it immediately. These are all good systems, but if you are the kind of person who needs them, you are probably the kind of person who won't carry them out. Try them for a regular clean-up, perhaps in that time-management time you allocated. Try to keep a clean desk. You will need a flat surface on which to examine proofs, do flat-plans and all the rest. But it is also a reassuring sight at the start of each day, letting you feel as if you are on top of things.

Email represents a different type of problem, with the temptation to respond instantly. The problem is that responses often simply generate further emails, so many editors only check their emails first thing in the morning, after lunch, and before going home, setting a limit to how long they spend on them. If it helps, you can set your email software to only check for new emails every hour or two. You might set up a separate email address for urgent enquiries, but when people need to get hold of you fast, they are more likely to use a channel such as Twitter, text messaging or the phone – make sure that they know that this is the best way to do so, however.

With email, as with paperwork, read it quickly, then act on it, file it or bin it. And be responsible in your own use of email and the Internet. Don't send emails for the sake of it: make sure you have a good reason, and that email is the best method of communication. People use email to say things they are too cowardly to say on the telephone or in a meeting. This is not good practice in a manager. Don't send or forward 'amusing' web pages. These can easily cause offence, and if they have sexual or racial connotations, there can be serious consequences for your career. Your company should have email and Internet policies, and a social media policy: if not, you ought to think about drawing one up.

Social media policies

A policy need not be particularly restrictive – the key is that everyone is clear what is acceptable (and in some cases, what is encouraged, or 'best practice'), as well as what to do in particular situations (such as when they receive abusive or offensive messages). There are plenty of examples to look at online, including a database of social media policies at socialmediagovernance.com/policies.php – key issues for you as a publication are making all journalists aware of legal risks such as defamation, contempt and copyright (which they might normally otherwise delegate to sub-editors) and professionalism (for example, posting inappropriate images on an account they use for professional purposes).

Also worth considering carefully are the areas of objectivity and impartiality. US publications are a lot more anxious about their journalists being perceived to be anything but completely neutral in all affairs, leading to some policies that would appear draconian to the more opinionated Brits. Neutrality, however, is different to objectivity (which is rather more complicated but comes down to making a judgement based on facts rather than beliefs), and well-informed opinion is a key feature in most magazines. You want to allow your writers to play to their strengths and find their natural 'voice' on social media platforms (institutional voices do not work well here), while also guarding against ill-considered comments that might be used against the publication.

Managing information overload

A magazine editor now has little problem finding information on a range of topics. It is likely that you will have subscribed to email newsletters, RSS feeds, Facebook groups and pages, YouTube channels and various other sources of news and information both in your field and on journalistic or management topics.

There tend to be two fears driving journalists' information consumption: the fear that you will miss out on something because you're not following the right sources; and the fear that you'll miss out on something because you're following *too many* sources. This leads to two broad approaches: people who follow everything of any interest ('follow, then filter'); and people who are very strict about the number of sources of information they follow ('filter, then follow').

A good analogy to use here is of streams versus ponds. A pond is manageable, but predictable. A stream is different every time you step in it, but you can miss things.

As an editor you are in the business of variety: you need to be exposed to a range of different pieces of information, and cannot afford to be caught out. A good strategy for managing your information feeds then, is to follow a wide variety of sources, but to add filters to ensure you don't miss all the best stuff.

If you are using an RSS reader one way to do this is to have specific folders for your 'must-read' feeds. Andrew Dubber, a music industries academic and author of the New Music Strategies blog, recommends choosing ten subjects in your area, and choosing five 'must-read' feeds for each, for example. For email newsletters and other email updates you can adopt a similar strategy: must-reads go into your Inbox; others are filtered into subfolders to be read if you have time.

To create a folder in Google Reader, add a new feed (or select an existing one) and under the heading click on **Fee**d Settings … – then scroll to the bottom and click on New Folder … – this will also add the feed to that folder.

If you are following hundreds or thousands of people on Twitter, use Twitter lists to split them into management channels: 'people I know'; 'journalism'; 'industry'; and so on. To add someone to a list on Twitter, visit their profile page and click on the list button, which will be around the same area as the 'Follow' button.

You can also use websites such as Paper.li to send you a daily email 'newspaper' of the most popular links shared by a particular list of friends every day, so you don't miss out on the most interesting stories.

Social bookmarking: creating an archive and publishing at the same time

Social bookmarking tools like Delicious and Diigo can also be useful in managing web-based resources that you don't have time to read or think might come in useful later. Bookmarking them essentially 'files' each web page so you can access them quickly when you need them (you do this by giving each page a series of relevant tags, e.g. 'dieting', 'research', 'UK', 'Jane Jones'). They also include a raft of other useful features, such as RSS feeds (allowing you to automatically publish selected items to a website, blog, or Twitter or Facebook account), and the ability to see who else has bookmarked the same pages (and what else they have bookmarked, which is likely to be relevant to your interests).

Check the site's Help or FAQ pages to find out how to use them effectively. Typically this will involve adding a button to your browser's links bar (under the web address box) by dragging a link (called 'Bookmark on Delicious' or similar) from the relevant page of the site (look for 'bookmarklets'). Then, whenever you come across a page you want to bookmark, click on that button. A new window will appear with the name and address of the web page, and space for you to add comments (a typical tactic is to paste a key quote from the page here), and tags. Useful things to add as tags include anything that will help you find this later, such as any organisations, locations or people that are mentioned, the author or publisher, and what sort of information is included, such as 'report', 'statistics', 'research', 'case study' and so on.

If installing a button on your browser is too complicated or impractical many of these services also allow you to bookmark a page by sending the URL to a specific email address. Alternatively, you can just copy the URL and log on to the bookmarking site to bookmark it.

Some bookmarking services double up as blogging sites: Tumblr and Stumbleupon are just two. The process is the same as described above, but these services are more intuitively connected with other services such as Twitter and Facebook, so that bookmarked pages are also automatically published on those services too. With one click your research not only forms a useful archive but also becomes an act of publishing and distribution.

Every so often you might want to have a clear out: try diverting mailings and feeds to a folder for a week without looking at them. After seven days, ask which ones, if any, you have missed. You might benefit from unsubscribing and cutting down some information clutter. In general, it may be useful to have background information, but it all occupies your time. Treat such things as you would anything sent to you on paper. If you need it, and it is likely to be difficult to find again, file it or bookmark it. If not, bin it. After a while, you'll find it gets easier.

Management tasks

You can work on your skills, but in the meantime you will already have various management jobs to do. Dealing with money is dealt with in Chapter 4. Most of the other tasks involve handling people.

Building a team

A successful magazine is a team. But a team is more than a loose agglomeration of people. It requires both a careful choice of individuals and a defined structure. Unless you are working on a launch, you will have inherited someone else's idea of what that team should be. In time, you can bring it nearer to your own ideal.

A magazine can be produced by one person, providing it appears infrequently and communicates mainly through text rather than pictures or design work. As the editor of that type of publication, you will commission and process everything you don't write yourself, as well as handling all the administration, perhaps even selling the odd advertisement. House journals, 'fanzines' and professional newsletters are often produced in exactly this fashion, sometimes by people with other day jobs. They depend for their success on simple production and design, a ready supply of material and general enthusiasm.

Newsletter production, however, is very often a two-person job: one to handle administrative matters, including getting in and sending back any photographs and contributions, and the other to edit, but with both involved in final production. Few individuals achieve perfection, however, which is what is required of editors in such a situation.

A typical small monthly will be staffed by an editor, an editorial assistant or administrative assistant, plus an art editor and a sub-editor on either a full- or a part-time basis. In this set-up, the art editor will take responsibility for the acquisition of pictures. Additional freelance sub-editors and designers might well be required during busy parts of the production cycle. Any associated website may have been built to contract, or you may be relying on third party tools such as Wordpress's content management system, and presences on various social networks. The editor, once again, will do all commissioning and any necessary writing, and will share such tasks as headlines with the sub-editor, who must be well-versed in production techniques in order to deal with outside facilities. The administrative assistant will take charge of such tasks as obtaining photographs and issuing payments. Such a lean set-up will work, but makes no allowances for holidays or illness, so it will require a ready supply of reliable freelance help. It needs unanimity of purpose – but that is perhaps easier to achieve in small teams.

As pagination increases, full-time sub-editors and art staff become essential, as does a full-time picture editor. Bigger magazines will also employ more senior editorial staff: a features editor or commissioning editor, for instance. If the magazine has news content, there must be a news editor and/or reporters. If there is an active website there will either be a dedicated web editor, or responsibility for updating the site will belong to the news editor (as the person providing the most time-critical content) or to a range of contributors. Once the size of the editorial staff gets into double figures, the sections have to start running themselves.

Editors of large weeklies can confidently expect their staff to deal with the crises that develop from time to time in the production process. This is not always the case with small magazines, where the editor will usually be expected to know everything. In particular, small magazines rarely allow the luxury of a deputy editor. Nonetheless, someone must be nominated to take production responsibility in the editor's absence. Someone with a sub-editing background is best equipped for this, simply because production matters require the most immediate attention.

Indeed, every editor needs to be able to rely upon the support of good, fast and accurate sub-editors (or copy editors). It is through sub-editing that an editor takes control of a magazine, both in tone of voice and in overall structure, and ensures that it holds its focus over the long term. On-screen page make-up, now universal, has changed sub-editors' jobs. In particular, it has reduced the time and attention they can give to working with words. This is a shame. However, the sub-editors know a magazine's strengths and weaknesses from the inside. And their meticulousness makes all the difference between producing a respected publication and a waste of paper.

The most important appointment an editor has to make, on any magazine with significant visual content, is that of art editor or art director. Editor and art editor should share a design strategy. A good art editor, working to an agreed brief, will have the single greatest influence over the readers' perception of a magazine. Small magazines can thrive without, but must start with a foolproof design.

Beyond that, an editor needs to feel confident that the magazine is being efficiently run on a day-to-day basis. It is possible to put together a single issue of a magazine swiftly and imaginatively from a standing start. But what makes a magazine a magazine is continuity, publishing again and again. That means attention should be paid to finding the right administrative people. Otherwise, problems associated with missing post, lost pictures, lost contributions, unpaid contributors and the rest will bring the magazine to its knees. Ideally, the magazine needs a dedicated administrative assistant or office manager, preferably one with no journalistic ambitions. It is not unknown for people to move from administration into writing, but it is not an easy or fast career path.

Hiring

Ask yourself first whether you need to hire anyone. A departure should not be taken as an immediate signal to seek a direct replacement. It is a chance to think about the way the magazine is developing and to consider whether it might make more sense to share out the responsibilities in a different way. Perhaps this is not really a full-time job? There may be a case for splitting the work between several existing members of staff, or using freelance cover for part of it.

Probably, though, the decision will be taken to replace. Why not consider promoting someone? Some companies and public bodies, especially, insist that vacancies should be publicised and that promotion candidates should compete with outside applicants for the post. This may be reassuring, on all sides, letting the promoted person know they were awarded the job on merit and convincing management that the best person was appointed.

It is, however, an expensive way of arriving at a conclusion that would have cost nothing and may, in the interim, cause a certain amount of discontent. The competitive selection process is unlikely to tell you anything about an existing employee that you didn't already know. There must be an interview, however, if only so that both sides can discuss the job. You can make clear what is required. Applicants can indicate how they intend to proceed.

While it is good for staff to know that promotion is always a possibility, those who have been passed over will need to be handled carefully, to be assured that their time will come and perhaps to be steered in the direction of the extra training or experience that their careers need.

If you decide to make an external appointment, however, several steps must be taken. A new job description should, perhaps, be drawn up. A job description is not a description of the person currently occupying the position concerned. It should not list what that person does, but what they should be doing. It needs to be drawn up with care, because it will be used in later assessments of the new recruit's work.

Many people recommend complementing the formal job description with a 'person specification'. This is a list of the personal attributes that a person would need to bring to the job to be able to carry out the job description. Person specifications usually attempt to assess a person under a set of headings, including physical attributes; qualifications and experience; innate abilities and potential; interests; disposition or personality; and relevant life circumstances.

Physical attributes include such matters as age, health, general appearance and demeanour. University degrees are the norm in journalism today, although it should be remembered that for many years graduates were the exception rather than the rule – and the profession was none the worse for it. You must also consider how closely you need the person's past experience to fit the current job. If you are running a specialist professional journal, for instance, how far does general journalistic experience outweigh specialist knowledge? Would you be better off with a less experienced journalist but one whose limited experience has been in precisely your field? In the 'prosumer' market served by Future magazines, for example, they often recruit experts that they can then train as journalists.

Specialist magazines need a team that balances specialist knowledge and journalistic skills. Ideally you want a person who contributes both, and in this regard it is worth scouring specialist blogs in your sector to see if there is someone already demonstrating that combination of skill and expertise. Indeed, not only is such a person likely to be able to hit the ground running in your publication, but they will also bring an existing audience and status within that community, and an online distribution network to boot (i.e. their ranking on search engines, blog subscribers, Facebook friends and Twitter followers).

In considering innate abilities and potential you should consider both the job now and its future. Will it develop with its new occupant? Or is it likely to prove frustrating? You should not disregard an applicant because of their apparent domestic commitments (or, indeed, lack of them). Instead, you should make the demands of the job clear and let the applicant decide whether they feel it is suitable for them. You will get a feeling at interview whether they are committed.

Many people recruit by word of mouth and personal recommendation, which costs nothing but means you are constantly drawing from the same narrow pool of potential recruits. Word of mouth now has an extra dimension with the opportunity to spread news of a job via social networks such as Facebook, Twitter and LinkedIn, accessing a slightly wider pool. But still, you should advertise the job and actively seek promising candidates.

If you are within a large organisation, you can recruit by using the internal advertising process, but, again, the same applies: you may well know all the likely candidates.

A step up from this is to use the services of headhunters or recruitment agencies. You will need to use an agency which specialises in journalistic appointments. These typically charge between 15 and 20 per cent of a recruit's first-year salary, although if you don't employ any of its candidates you don't normally have to pay.

In most cases, however, you will probably advertise in the media press, mailing lists and recruitment sites. Advertisements must be written with care in order to attract the suitable and deter the unsuitable. Be specific about what you want. Say who you are, and what the job is, in some detail. The job title is not enough, since the responsibilities associated with a title vary widely from company to company. Include both the appealing and the unappealing parts, to deter those who are not serious. You must also mention the qualifications you consider vital, and include a closing date for applications.

There are varying views on whether you should mention the salary. This can cause internal friction, but it tells people whether they are in the appropriate bracket before they apply. Match the style of the advertisement to that of your publication: if yours is a lively, chatty publication don't produce an advertisement that sounds as if it is offering a job with the Inland Revenue. Your advertisements and recruitment procedures must not discriminate on sexual or racial grounds, even inadvertently. That extends even to the notes you may scribble during the interview. What should your advertisement ask for? The curriculum vitae or résumé is the standard requirement, often with a covering letter, but if you are expecting a huge number of applications and you want to compare them directly you can devise some sort of form. Consider, however, how you felt as a job applicant. An application form, packed with impertinent requests for semi-relevant information, can be a serious deterrent even to good candidates. Printed forms don't go well with computers, and all journalists have terrible handwriting, because it is so little used. A curriculum vitae allows candidates to present themselves in their own way, something that does not always work to their advantage.

Depending on the job, there may need to be other requirements. Writers and reporters can legitimately be asked for samples of their writing, or cuttings of their best stories, but a wise editor recognises that work may have been improved in the sub-editing stage. Candidates for writing and editing jobs can be asked for ideas, but care should be taken that these ideas do not escape from the interviewing process into the collective consciousness of the magazine. It will enhance no one's reputation if ideas submitted as part of a job application subsequently appear in the magazine under someone else's by-line. If you like the ideas, but not the candidate, you must either pay for them or leave well alone.

Designers and art directors will, of course, have portfolios of their work. Sub-editors can supply copies of complex editorial spreads they have assembled, or of features where headline, standfirst and so on have been particularly pleasing, but none of this is especially revealing of what a sub-editor is like to work with. Any enclosures that people supply with their applications must, of course, be kept safe and returned unless you specify that they will not be.

Many employers are tempted to 'google' prospective employees but you should be careful about this. The results may include work that is several years out of date, or entries on social media platforms that the applicant is entitled to feel are private, even if they are publicly accessible (an analogy might be stalking your applicant to the pub and listening in to a conversation they are having: the conversation may be in a public place, but the participants have a reasonable expectation that others will not expressly listen in to it). If you discriminate against an applicant on the basis of such information they may be entitled to take some sort of legal action. Likewise, you should not ask interviewees questions about their place of birth, age, marital or parental status – or plans to start a family – religious beliefs, or disabilities. The fact that much of this information is available on applicants' social media profiles adds to the dangers of using them as part of your recruitment process.

The 'person specification' comes into its own in whittling down applications. By comparing your candidates' own self-descriptions with the specification you have drawn up, you can sort them into three piles: rejections, possibles and probables. Decide how many people you want to interview, and then adjust the probable pile accordingly, if necessary adding the best of the possibles. All applicants should receive an acknowledgement immediately. It is safe to send rejection letters to your immediate rejects, but leave the possibles until you are sure you don't need them.

Interviewing needs to be learnt, but it gets better with practice. It is always gruelling. Interviews should be scheduled an hour apart, allowing about 45 or 50 minutes for serious discussion and the rest of the time for a breather in between. Do not attempt to interview more than about four people a day. They will merge into one in your mind, even if you take notes.

You must prepare for the interview, and if there are two interviewers you must discuss how you are going to handle it between you. The interview should attempt to answer all the questions implied by your person specification. At the very least, you need to know what the candidates are doing at the moment, what they did in their previous jobs, why they want this job and what their plans and ambitions are.

If there are obvious holes in their CVs, or strange career moves, this is your opportunity to ask about them. Push harder until you get the information, but nothing is to be gained by being aggressive. It may be that people with unconventional career paths make better journalists than those who travel as if on rails, but it is for your candidates to convince you of that, rather than being vague or dishonest.

On the whole, you should be listening more than talking. This is the candidates' opportunity to tell you what they can do rather than what you can do for them. Make notes as the interview proceeds. At the end, let the candidate ask you questions. This is only partly for the candidates' benefit: these questions should help you to guess how interested or committed they are to the job. Most people will take the opportunity to ask about the salary, but it is disappointing if that's all they ask. Their questions should really be the most important of the interview. As you close the interview, you must indicate what happens next.

Between interviews with different candidates, make a note of your impressions. Some companies use an 'assessment form' that you complete for each candidate, grading them on their qualifications, demeanour and outlook. If two of you are interviewing, you should perhaps have a brief chat about your perceptions before you proceed. Three people is too many interviewers; if more than two people do need to see each candidate they should do it one at a time rather than simultaneously.

If you decide to have a two-stage interviewing process, you must do your homework to ensure that you have something to discuss in the second interview. There may be areas that weren't covered in sufficient depth in the first round. Otherwise, try introducing the candidate to his or her prospective colleagues. Later you can gauge their reactions. All the time, you should try to compare the candidates with the ideal in your person specification rather than with one another.

Interviewing is standard practice, but in journalism there is a case for practical tests of various kinds. No one should employ a sub-editor on the basis of interview alone. It is fairly easy to devise a brief sub-editing test, using some pieces of surplus copy. It should be done there and then: letting people take the work away with them proves nothing. There is also a case for an informal quiz for news reporters: they should certainly know what the big stories of the day are, for instance, and in a specialist area they should understand the subject matter. They should also demonstrate that they are familiar with the publication.

In certain positions it may be possible to invite the candidate to do some freelance 'shifts' with you before you commit yourself. You could even offer a short-term contract. This offers you the opportunity to see how the person works. You risk, however, losing your applicant to a less painstaking employer – and if they already have a permanent position it is going to be difficult for them to justify taking the risk of handing in their notice if there is no guarantee they will be in a job in a few months' time.

These things may help you towards a decision. In consultation with senior colleagues, you must review the candidates and evaluate them against the specification you have drawn up. The person you like best, and see yourself getting along with best, may not actually be the best qualified. You might do better to choose someone who complements your abilities and those of your existing staff rather than anyone too similar. Having made a decision, it is as well to have a fallback position of one or two second-best candidates. Then, when your preferred candidate says 'no thank you', you will not have wasted the whole process. Do take up references.

Now the formalities: appointment and acceptance, over the telephone or in person, must be followed up by a letter of appointment. This forms part of the candidate's contract of employment and must be written carefully, to include the following:

- starting date;
- details of any probationary period;
- salary;
- hours;
- holiday entitlement;
- any other benefits.

A full contract of employment should follow at the end of the probation period and be signed by both sides.

Induction

A surprising number of new employees drop out shortly after joining a new firm. You must help the new employee fit in. Find him or her a desk and a computer and clear out the previous occupant's debris. Staff should also be briefed about the new arrival, and someone, usually the head of the appropriate section, should pass on the basic information about the building layout, the toilets, the photocopier, the coffee machine and all the stuff anyone needs to get through the first days. It would be nice if the person were taken out to lunch, too.

After a couple of days you must ask the newcomer how things are going, and then again, more seriously, after a month. The probationary period for a new employee is often three months, and you will usually expect to review formally the new recruit's performance during that period. If performance is not satisfactory, you need to indicate this to the employee some time before the end of the probation period.

If you decide that a mistake has been made, you must tell the employee of your decision and give him or her time to appeal to a higher authority. But if the appeal fails, you can give notice that the employment will be terminated at the end of the three-month period. You may also choose to pay the employee up to date and let him or her leave early. Otherwise, you might decide that, while not satisfactory, the employee's performance is salvageable, and extend the probationary period. The probationary period is the only chance you get to end someone's employment without entering the complex and tedious world of fair and unfair dismissal, so take it seriously.

Firing

Difficult though it can be, hiring people is at least a generally happy experience. Dismissal offers no such pleasures. It is a failure, both for you as a manager and for the employee concerned. People are supposed to be an asset, after all. You have a duty to make sure that people are happy and working to the best of their capacity.

That said, there are people who do not fulfil their side of the employment bargain. You must be prepared to remove bullies, thieves, frauds, persistent skivers and sexual harassers, without losing sleep. People who fundamentally reject your leadership should be given an opportunity to change their views, but if they don't, they must go too. This is in everyone's interest, although not everyone sees it like that.

Unfortunately, journalism still has a macho culture. It is one of the few areas of industry in which people are fired on the spot, and often for dubious reasons. You can do that, but there is always a cost. Companies that don't mind paying handsome compensation can do what they like. Everyone else, however, must ensure that the disciplinary process leading to the dismissal can be defended before an employment tribunal, which is the employee's first recourse. Sacked journalists used not to use tribunals, fearing damage to their prospects in a small and gossipy industry. That is no longer the case.

All this makes legal dismissal a long and tedious process rather than a sudden and dramatic event. The exception is a case of summary dismissal for 'gross misconduct', which is generally confined to the following:

- theft from either company or colleagues;
- fraudulent behaviour;
- incapacity through drink or drugs;
- arrest or conviction on a serious criminal charge affecting employment;
- violence or destruction of property;
- obscene language and gross insubordination;
- gross negligence or irresponsibility:
- possession of an offensive weapon.

Given the time-consuming nature of the dismissal process, most busy editors would do better to find another way out of the situation. If it is a case of underperformance, perhaps extra training or reassignment to different work might be a better bet. If it is a case of defiant or destructive behaviour, however, these are not options. Frank discussion of the problem usually brings nothing more than protestations of innocence: 'What, me?' In any case, rewarding a nuisance with a great deal of attention, followed by a change of role, sends poor signals to the rest of the staff.

Dismissal is one outcome of a disciplinary process. But the process must not be just a means to that end. It should be a careful sequence of events taking into account all the requirements of current employment law. In the UK, you will need to consult a good book or pay close attention to the ACAS Code of Practice on disciplinary procedures.[9]

All disciplinary procedures, however, involve the same sequence of events: oral warning, followed by first written warning, followed by second written warning, followed by dismissal. Those receiving the warnings must be given some kind of right of appeal. You must act in a reasonable fashion throughout the process. In other words, you must not enter each stage with a preconceived view of the outcome. And since each of these stages needs to take place at least a month apart, you can see that nothing is going to happen very quickly. The only good thing, from your point of view as an exasperated editor determined to dismiss, is that many people get the message once they have received their first written warning and leave before their record is permanently blighted.

The use of the word 'disciplinary' is slightly misleading. While this procedure is used for matters of misconduct, for instance lateness, poor appearance, working for someone else during company time, damaging property and all the rest of it, it can also be used simply for poor work performance. Poor performance or incapacity can lead to a dismissal which will be acceptable to a tribunal, but it is a long and difficult path. Apart from the effects on the individual concerned (and on your own state of mind), there will be effects on the morale of your team.

Those who do no work and take no responsibility represent no threat to anyone and have lots of time on their hands to be everyone's friend. Their dismissal will be resented, although in private people will accept it: indeed, some of those who lead the protests against the sacking may privately have been urging you to get on with it. Such is the editor's lot. Some of these protests will be simply for the sake of form. Often, everyone recognises that something has to be done, but it is you that has to do it.

With new employees, a problem of this sort should really be detected and resolved during the probationary period. With established employees, there are questions which need to be asked. It may be that the person's capabilities have not changed, but the job has. In that case, you must provide retraining and guidance. If you have promoted this person prematurely or unwisely, the problem is yours once again and you have to resolve it by support. And then there are members of staff whose personal problems are getting in the way. Once again, you must support them until they get through it. The law is more forgiving than many employers would be.

If none of these things applies, then dismissal for poor performance is an option. Don't fool yourself about this: it is likely to come as a terrible shock to the person concerned. It is astonishing to discover that individual writers, editors and sub-editors can be seen as a major problem by their employers and workmates without ever being aware of it. As a nation, we hate scenes and confrontations, but not mentioning things is more cruel in the long run. A quiet word early on can bring about changes and halt the whole process, but very often the situation is left so long that either the manager's mind is made up or the member of staff is incapable of changing.

Don't get into that situation. A serious, private discussion should take place early on in which the employee is told, by reference to his or her job description, just what is expected. This need not be a threatening discussion, but it should be clear. It is very common for managers to convince themselves that they have spoken sternly to a team member about matters of performance, only for the team member to have no recollection of any such discussion.

If the necessary improvements are not made, the disciplinary process begins. After one or more informal discussions about performance, an oral warning is given, and a note of what was said attached to the individual's personnel file. A time limit for improvements to be seen should be made and an appointment fixed to discuss them.

If there is radical improvement by that date, you can bring the process to an end, even 'wiping the slate' if you feel sufficiently confident that this is a permanent state of affairs. If there is no improvement, however, a first written warning should be given, indicating that a failure to correct things will lead to further consequences. Again, a date should be set for a further appointment. This warning, too, must be added to the employee's file. If there is no suitable improvement by that date, a final warning should be given. This must state explicitly that the contract of employment will be terminated if there is no improvement.

Dismissal follows if no improvement takes place. It will do no good to back down from the ultimate sanction at this point. The employee will feel that he or she has 'got away with it' and other staff will be bemused. And if you later decide to dismiss after all, your carefully planned disciplinary process will be in tatters, making that later dismissal look like a case of victimisation rather than a necessary response to a difficult situation.

In dismissing the employee, you must, of course, give notice. In practice, though, payment in lieu of notice will be made and the employee will be asked to leave the premises immediately. A letter giving reasons for the dismissal should be despatched, along with any holiday pay and payment in lieu of notice. At that point, the employee will take legal advice while you wait to see if you are going to be taken to a tribunal. There can, of course, be a settlement between your legal advisers and the dismissed employee before the tribunal takes place. Again, you should check ACAS (the Advisory, Conciliation and Arbitration Service) and your company's legal resources for more up-to-date advice.

Appraisal

Information is a prime motivator of people. You must keep your staff informed, but you must also make clear to them what you, and the company, require from them. In the past this information has been provided at their initial interview and never discussed again.

In a well-managed magazine, it should be obvious when someone is having problems and might need help. When dealing with people's performance, there is no room here for gentle hints and subtle ironical remarks. Be straightforward, concentrate on actions and work rather than personalities, and try always to deal with things they are capable of changing. And be constructive.

The time to deal with problems of performance is when they arise, or shortly afterwards. That doesn't mean giving someone a public dressing down because they have missed an important deadline, but it does mean dealing with it before the next formal occasion arises. Point out the problem quietly, the next day, and ask them why it is occurring. Perhaps there is some way you can help: an awkward time conflict, or too many demands at once? If the problem were to happen to anyone in that position, then you would need to sort out that task, rather than the person. Otherwise, ask them for an improvement. If you foresee this becoming a pattern, you might think it a good idea to make a note of what's gone on. The next time, you can give them a written warning and start that whole process, if you are so inclined.

In a small, busy office, it is always hard to find a moment to tell someone how well they are doing, or, alternatively, to point out a few areas of difficulty. A formal appraisal structure ensures that happens. It will also be very useful when salaries are discussed, when training becomes available and when you are thinking about reorganising the editorial structure of the magazine.

You need to timetable an hour for each journalist, in a private place where you won't be disturbed. There should then be a frank discussion of both the employee's work and prospects and the more general picture. You may wish to go to the lengths of working through a formal assessment structure, in which various aspects of the staff member's working life are listed and graded.

For a reporter, for instance, these might include:

- knowledge of the subject matter and area;
- number and usefulness of contacts;
- determination and ingenuity in pursuit of a story;
- attitude and demeanour in public;
- writing style;
- adherence to deadlines;
- accuracy;
- and so on.

For a sub-editor they would be different, including speed, accuracy, creative flair, meticulousness, and so on. It might be a good idea to issue the journalist with a list of the areas to be discussed in advance of the meeting, so that he or she can feel prepared. You should also make sure you find something to praise so that the journalist leaves the appraisal feeling it has been worthwhile.

An hour, every six months, is not much of a commitment on either side, but it is surprising how often these appraisals are skipped or dealt with in a perfunctory way.

The appraisal should be a relaxed and friendly meeting. Invite your colleague to speak first, then give your view on how things are going, and then examine the areas of disagreement before arriving at some programme of improvement, possibly involving formal training. The main thing about this process is that there should be no surprises, but it is quite common for you to discover that the quietest person in the office is nursing deep grievances or suffering from terrible frustrated ambition. Arrange a scheme for monitoring any improvements you expect, make sure both sides sign the document and then keep it securely in your files.

You should always know what your staff would like to be doing and attempt to help them in that direction. Unfortunately, however, their ambitions may not accord either with their aptitudes or with what you require from them. In that case, don't say, 'I'll see what I can do', which will lead only to disappointment. If they want something impossible, it is better that they find out sooner than later.

Motivation

There is a vast literature on the subject of motivation. Those interested in pursuing the subject on an academic level should look into the theories of Abraham Maslow and Frederick Herzberg, to name but two. Another to look at comes from Douglas McGregor, who said that managers operate according two dominant theories, Theory X and Theory Y. Theory X suggests that people dislike work and will only do what is necessary. Theory Y, on the other hand, suggests that work is natural to most people and that they enjoy it. The twist is that the theory you hold as a manager is the one that is likely to prove true for you.

The traditional means of motivating is through incentives, but the work of Herzberg, for example, suggested that removing disincentives is likely to prove more effective. These disincentives are in your hands: they include indifference to people's efforts and unfairness in the distribution of rewards. But the truth is that you can't motivate people; they have to motivate themselves. And what motivates them may not be what motivates you. You really love your work and your magazine: that's why you've made it to editor. You cannot rely on others sharing that enthusiasm. Motivation always depends upon the conduct of the company towards its employees. It will not work if people feel frightened, cowed or put-upon. There are times when every editor has to play the heavy, but fairness should be maintained.

Most people need clear goals. They need an investment in their work. By-lines, where appropriate, recognise that. Designs that bury by-lines in the gutter do no favours to either writers or readers, who like to know whose words they are reading. Sub-editors cannot be motivated in the same way, but editors can show specific appreciation of headlines and standfirsts. On the other hand, problems and complaints arising from copy should be recorded and referred back for explanation. This is particularly the case with inaccuracies, spelling mistakes and proof-reading failures.

It is as well to share your own goals with your staff. The circulation figures are the obvious focus of editorial attention (except on controlled-circulation magazines) and should be discussed when the information comes in. Improving sales is everyone's business, and realistic sales targets and deadlines need to be established. Where a bonus scheme exists, the obvious thing is to tie it to circulation or pageviews. This may seem unfair, when, for instance, advertising income rises but circulation stays the same, but it is the only area in which journalists have a direct influence.

Increasingly, journalists' wages are negotiated individually, which makes it possible for you to motivate in the most direct way. Here your appraisals can be a help. But your freedom of action in this respect will be limited by two factors: the going rate for the job, and the figures in your budget. Creating gross disparities between people doing approximately the same jobs is wrong and can be dangerous if there is a sexual discrimination aspect. Sometimes you will just have to tell people that their salary aspirations are unrealistic. Point out that they will do better through training and promotion. Of course, you may lose the person if your rates are not broadly on a level with those of other employers.

In general, pay only motivates when it forms part of a structured system of grades linked to a rigid system of appraisal. This is fine for the civil service, but less practical in a small publishing office. However, what will demotivate people is unfairness. A bonus system can offer a short-term motivational boost, but only if its basis is entirely transparent. 'Merit money' handed over for mysterious reasons will demotivate not only those who don't receive it but some of those who do, who will feel guilty.

There are few opportunities for direct incentives, based on competition, in journalism. Where they can be invented, they work well but only for a short period. It is better to concentrate on solid long-term improvements in people's working circumstances. People need to feel that the job is worthwhile and that they are achieving something.

But if goals are to motivate they must come about by discussion rather than diktat. Here, too, there is a useful acronym: SMARTER. That means goals should be:

- Specific
- Measurable
- Acceptable
- Realistic
- Timely
- Extending
- Rewarding.

These are self-explanatory, with the possible exception of 'extending', which means they must stretch the employee's capabilities. Aside from clear goals, all employees will benefit from access to training and the possibility of promotion.

Security is another motivating factor. There are still editors who believe in motivating by fear, but at best that will work only for a short time. People need to feel confident that the future is bright and that their leaders know what they are doing. If you have worries about the future, you should keep them to yourself.

To motivate the team, rather than individuals, do what you can to create both a group identity and an aggressive outlook towards rivals. Everyone on your magazine should believe that it is the best in its market. Groups bond by the rituals of celebration: so when things go well, buy a few drinks.

Training

Training used to be something that came at the start of journalists' careers, if at all. That's no longer the case. Formal training is now available at every stage of a journalist's career, up to editorship and beyond.

It is important to let people see the link between training and personal success. It is very motivating for people to see their colleagues first trained and then promoted. People sometimes need training when they are not performing as well as they might. They also need it when they have been earmarked for promotion. Never let people develop the idea that training is a punishment. It should be more of a treat.

It is important to establish a learning culture in your magazine, even if there is no budget for formal training. We all learn every day, and we should also teach. External training is expensive: you have both to pay for the training itself and to make up for the loss of the staff member concerned while the training is going on. This is difficult for small magazines.

Before embarking on staff training, think about what it is intended to achieve, both for the magazine and for the individual journalists. You need to know that all the essential skills are contained within your team, so that a sudden absence doesn't leave you in the lurch. But training should only go to those who are willing and able to benefit from it, something that should become clear in appraisals.

Much training, especially for junior staff, still takes the traditional form known as 'sitting by Nellie', or 'learning by doing'. The official name for this is 'supervised practice', and it is popular because it costs nothing, and keeps the trainee productive throughout. It does, however, require a lot from the trainee's colleagues, who may be excellent at their jobs but less so at explaining how they are done. These colleagues may not be open to question and may be more interested in correcting the trainee's work to use it than in showing how to make it better. This form of training also tends only to ingrain the habits, good and bad, of a particular magazine.

In a larger organisation these problems can be somewhat reduced by moving trainees around between publications. This may, indeed, be the only way of allowing them to acquire the necessary range of skills. Staff who are exchanged in this way should be properly briefed and equipped, and arrangements must be made to ensure that the trainees are properly monitored during the attachment.

More formal in-house training, in which work stops for the duration of the course rather than being combined with it, can also be beneficial. You should expect to take some role in the training of your own staff, whether in a formal session or in individual supervision and coaching. But you should also extend this coaching ethos down through your team. It should be natural for people to share their skills and insights with their junior colleagues. But such training needs planning if it is not to be merely a cut-price substitute for the real thing.

External training, either at an outside consultancy's premises or using their trainers, can be expensive, but it has many advantages. An atmosphere of learning is created, with no interruptions and distractions. Professional training organisations will have suitable premises and equipment. They can introduce a wider range of ideas and techniques than are often found in-house, where inspiration tends to be drawn from the same pool. In an outside training setting, beginners especially will be freer to experiment and make mistakes.

The Periodicals Training Council accredits a number of courses relating to magazine production, and their parent organisation, the PPA (Professional Publishers Association), delivers many too. Check their website[10] for the latest information – but remember that there may be areas that they do not cover, or which are better covered by other providers. Ask others about their experiences.

At the same time, outside trainers can say what they really think about a trainee's work without having to worry about the effects of the discussion on normal working life. But you must ensure that there is a good match between the training offered and what you feel is required. In particular, you should use only specialised editorial training companies and ask searching questions about the qualifications and experience of the trainers. Trainers depend, however, on receiving good information from you about your candidates and what you expect them to learn. After any training, the trainee should be asked to evaluate the experience.

Work experience, placements and internships

Parts of the magazine industry have become increasingly reliant on the free labour of students on work experience, and some are downright exploitative. There is an ongoing debate over the role of work experience in the media industry: some feel that it reduces diversity by limiting access to people on degree courses, or those wealthy enough to be able to support themselves in an expensive city like London for weeks on end without earning any money. Others see it as a good way to provide an insight into the workings of the industry for aspiring journalists. The reality depends on the publication and how they manage work experience.

A good placement is a mutually beneficial experience. It should not be used to cover staff absence, nor should it be a role where the student spends all their time doing non-journalistic jobs. But expectations should be realistic on both parts: you should not expect every placement to hit the ground running without support; and they should not expect to be interviewing that week's cover star. You should find out what parts of the job they are most interested in and try to provide a varied experience for them, shadowing others at first before moving onto more and more demanding work as they gain your trust and respect.

Both the NUJ and the PTC produce guidelines for publishers on using work experience students which are worth reading. They recommend a minimum placement period of at least two weeks, and a maximum of four if the position is unpaid.

The placement student should report to a specific person within your team, who will most likely also allocate them tasks and provide some guidance and support. They will probably also have to write a brief report afterwards for the student's university or college. You should also have a 'deputy' identified in case that person is ill or has to leave the office.

You should not see a work experience placement as 'free labour': supporting the student will cost staff time, and this needs to be discussed with the person responsible to ensure that it does not detract from the job of putting out the magazine. You should also cover the student's expenses and, if any of their work is used in print, pay them for their work in the same way as you would any freelance (and, of course, give them a by-line). If they have impressed, make provisions to give them a small gift at the end of their stay to say 'Thanks'. There may come a time when you are competing with another employer to hire that person.

Finally, you need to be aware of the legal situation regarding work experience. Work experience placements are covered by minimum wage regulations: you must pay the minimum wage unless you have a letter from the student's college confirming that the work placement is of benefit to the student. Even in that situation, if the student carries out work normally done by an employee, or if they have a contract, you are required to pay them a wage under Working Time Regulations.

Health and safety

There is one further aspect to your role as a manager of people, and that is your responsibility in matters of health and safety at work. You are directly responsible for the well-being of those who work under you while they are at work, as well as any visitors and freelances working in your offices. Under the 1974 Health and Safety at Work Act, any firm with more than five employees must have a written health and safety policy, which may allocate you certain duties. You should know who is your department's first-aider, where the first-aid box is kept, and procedures in the event of fires and accidents.

As the supervisor of people working on-screen you need to pay particular attention to the equipment they are using and the way they are using it. There is a detailed government directive, under the Health and Safety at Work Act, on what is quaintly called 'display screen equipment', but adherence to that alone is not enough to stop people falling prey to pains in the arms, hands and neck associated with working on computers.

Usually called 'repetitive strain injury' or 'upper limb disorder', this can have a variety of causes and outcomes: in serious cases it can be crippling. The condition seems to be directly related to stress. Staff should be regularly reminded about posture and the need to take frequent breaks, getting up from the keyboard at least once every 30 minutes. These seem to be the best ways yet devised of preventing RSI from becoming a problem. The approved posture requires the person typing to sit with feet flat on the ground and thighs and forearms parallel to the floor. Chairs should be fully adjustable to make this possible.

Anyone complaining of pains of the sort above should be advised to seek medical advice at the earliest opportunity. They should certainly not be ignored or ridiculed. Ensuring they seek early treatment is the company's best policy to avoid more serious and expensive problems later on. Appropriately, the Internet is a particularly rich source of information on the subject of RSI and other upper limb disorders.[11]

Your health and safety obligations extend to the risks undertaken by your staff and freelances as part of their work, for instance news reporters who have to bang on doors late at night or attend violent demonstrations. Your duty of 'reasonable care' may include making a risk assessment. That includes:

- ensuring that the right person is sent on the job;
- ensuring that that person has the right training and equipment;
- identifying what problems might arise;
- planning what to do in the event of problems;
- deciding whether any precautions are adequate before the work starts.

This sort of risk assessment is widely practised in broadcasting. Now that magazine journalists may also be working in a studio or recording on location, similar processes should be followed: for example, are there any dangerous areas nearby, such as open water? Could a member of the public have an accident as a result on your activity (for example, by tripping over trailing cables)? Is there a risk that equipment may be stolen?

There are useful pieces of advice in the Health and Safety Executive's leaflet 'Five Steps to Risk Assessment'.[12]

4 Money matters

When you become an editor you will be expected, perhaps for the first time in your career, to give detailed attention to the financial aspects of your work. It is easy to be overwhelmed by this, especially given that most of your new colleagues in management will have more experience in such matters.

Don't panic. No one is employing you to be a financial expert. No editor ever gained a reader or won an award by keeping to a budget. Money is just the tool you have to use to achieve your editorial ends: for you it is not an end in itself. Nonetheless, financial control is one aspect of power, and the way you use it is symbolic of your general editorial style. Colleagues need to be encouraged to be aware of budgetary considerations too – not as a straitjacket but as a factor to consider in the creativity of journalistic production. Some of the most creative acts take place with extreme constraints – while being able to financially justify an occasional big splurge is an equally useful talent.

The delegation of responsibility must include the delegation of financial responsibilities. If individual sections and section editors are to use their initiative, they must also help to draw up and manage their own budgets.

Publishing companies vary in the way they approach the question of budgeting, and in what they expect from their editors. Some editors will be part of the company's overall management, brought into the annual budgeting process and invited to estimate their costs for the coming year. In others they will be given a sum for freelance contributions and told not to exceed it. In some cases, the editor will be left completely in the dark: the first you will know about your budget is when you learn you have exceeded it. This might have superficial attractions to a busy editor but it is a cop-out.

Publication budgets

The editorial budget forms only a small part of the whole budgeting system of the magazine, and editors should make an effort to understand all the budgets they are allowed to see, asking for advice from the management's accountant where necessary.

Technically, a 'budget' is a statement of allocated income and expenditure for any given period. A statement of projected income and expenditure is properly known as a 'budget forecast'. In practice, people use the word budget for both. A budget forecast includes both revenue, which means income earned, and expenses, which means costs incurred. In both cases, these are recorded when the purchase or sale is made, rather than when the money changes hands.

A 'cash-flow' forecast, on the other hand, is built around income received, which means cash coming in, and costs paid, which means cash going out. It is linked to the bank balance. Superficially, however, a cash-flow forecast and a budget forecast will look the same. When you're given these forecasts on a sheet of paper, there will be a series of columns side by side across the page, one for each month. And there will be a series of rows, down the page, detailing each significant area of expenditure or income.

A budget forecast is used for:

- establishing and subsequently monitoring spending limits;
- working out the level of sales that will cover overheads;
- estimating profitability;
- analysing the relationship between revenue and expenditure;
- identifying areas for cost reduction;

and so on. A cash-flow forecast is used for more immediate purposes, for instance ensuring that cash covers expenditure, and planning borrowing.

Since yours is a department which does not generate income, you will normally have what is called a 'costs-only' budget, which will show how much you will be spending and when during the year ahead. Its purpose is to allow you to compare your actual spending with that predicted so you don't exceed what you've been allocated in the company's overall budget.

The magazine's overall budgets are drawn up early, on the basis of projected sales, both of copies and advertising, and an assessment of the strength of the market. Individual departments submit their forecasts, making their own assessments of what they are likely to earn or spend each month, and these are then consolidated into the overall budget, with some adjustments. Eventually each department gets a final budget with definite targets for each month's earnings or expenditure. Throughout the year, any 'variance' from those targets will be recorded.

It is good for editors to know how the full-scale budgets work before grappling with their own costs. The process starts with the publication's original marketing plan, which dictates such matters as frequency, quality of paper, binding method, website, other web presences, staffing, likely income and editorial costs. Drawing up a budget usually starts with revenue. Calculating advertising revenue is complicated by such matters as series discounts (when a string of advertisements are bought), but eventually an average 'yield' per page of display or classified advertising is arrived at, and this is multiplied by the number of advertising pages expected in each issue. If the magazine is weekly, this information has to be considered in conjunction with a calendar, since some months will include five issues and others only four.

From this, the crucial advertising : editorial ratio is drawn up. The ratio is designed to give maximum profit for the publisher without destroying the magazine's value to readers. It can either be left as a ratio (for instance 60:40, meaning that a 100-page issue will contain 60 advertising pages and 40 editorial pages) or turned into a percentage: 60 per cent in this case. When the number of projected advertising pages is combined with the ratio, it gives an approximate issue size. But not all issue sizes are possible: the number of pages in an issue must always be divisible by four, because of the binding process, and sometimes the constraints are more complicated (it is even cheaper to print in bundles of 16 pages, for example). Your printer will have explained which are the economical sizes to produce. You will certainly need a minimum number of editorial pages if the magazine is to be worthwhile.

The ratio need not be observed in every issue, but over the year it should average out. You will need to know the projected advertising : editorial ratio and your likely number of editorial pages in a year in order to calculate staffing and freelance costs.

Added to this will be revenue from online advertising and sponsorship, events, and affiliate sales. Depending on the size of the company, some of these streams may be managed separately or centrally – for example, by a dedicated events or commercial partnerships division.

The budget forecast's assessment of revenue will also include an estimate of circulation, which will be multiplied by income per copy (not cover price – you must deduct distribution and retailer costs) to produce a figure for circulation revenue: obviously any unsold returns and free copies will be deducted from that. You might also have an estimate of revenue from syndication of content, from online subscriptions and purchases, merchandise, and membership fees (for special clubs or members-only areas of a website). These may be small revenue streams but could have strategic importance as the publishing landscape shifts.

Then there are costs. 'Overhead' costs (or 'indirect' costs) are those which are not directly related to the magazine's production. They include rent, rates, heating, lighting, water, equipment maintenance and the wages of any staff not directly on the magazine's payroll. In multi-title publishing houses, these do not appear in detail on an individual magazine's accounts because they are not under the control of the individual publisher. They are not normally taken into account when an individual magazine's profitability is being assessed. Increasingly, however, the vogue for 'internal accounting' has seen these costs being allocated to individual magazines and appearing on accounts, usually as a single line to be deducted from the gross profit figure.

More relevant, in most cases, are the 'fixed' direct costs: these are incurred in the magazine production process but are not intimately related to the number of issues produced. They include:

- salaries;
- national insurance and employer's pension contributions;

Table 4.1 Extract from overall magazine budget forecast, showing income, expenses and anticipated profit

	March	April	May
Variable costs	19002	21788	20644
Fixed costs	80474	81576	81576
Central costs	10000	10000	10000
Revenue	112200	142350	132850
Profit	2724	28986	20630

- travel and entertaining;
- motor car costs;
- recruitment and training;
- the costs of administration, including stationery, telephones, computer costs and the purchase of newspapers and magazines;
- website hosting costs.

'Variable' direct costs are those which increase as circulation increases and pagination goes up, or as visits to the website increase – particularly if this involves thousands of people downloading or streaming large media files: if you produce no issues or websites, there are no 'variable' direct costs. They include:

- colour-house origination, any typesetting;
- printing, binding and finishing;
- distribution costs, especially for subscription copies;
- editorial contributions, casual sub-editing, photographs and illustrations;
- streaming or bandwidth costs, for instance of self-hosted video content.

Once revenue and costs are assessed, the calculations begin. Table 4.1 shows part of a publication's budget forecast for three months.

The 'gross margin' is the difference between revenue and variable costs in a given period. When fixed costs are subtracted, a figure called 'gross publication profit' is determined, and it is that which usually determines the health or otherwise of the magazine. If overheads are subtracted, some kind of net profit figure becomes available, but here the figures are often only notional because of the arbitrary way in which overheads are divided among a group of magazines.

The editorial budget

If no previous budget exists, the task of drawing up an editorial budget from scratch is rather daunting, particularly for editors with no previous financial or business experience. Even if someone else has done it in previous years, it can still be worth taking a blank sheet of paper (a computer spreadsheet, in practice) and going through the process from scratch.

Your starting point needs to be staff, since this is where most of your spending will take place. A look at the calendar for the year ahead is a start: is yours a seasonal magazine, shrinking back to nothing in the summer? Are there major events that have to be covered in detail? The question is whether these variations are best accommodated by the hire of temporary freelance help or whether they can be built into your staffing arrangements.

The tendency is for magazines to be run on the bare minimum of staff, with the bulk of editorial provided by freelances. The idea is that freelances can be taken on and dropped at will, with no complications. But there are disadvantages. Freelances are often skilful and enthusiastic, but they are not part of your team. It is wrong to expect deep loyalty from them. They will do their work, probably very well, but cannot make a contribution beyond that. It is wrong to expect them to play a part in your long-term planning.

They can also be costly, especially if you are hoping to use their work in other ways, for instance online. Staff receive many benefits beyond security, and in return they forfeit copyright. Freelances retain copyright unless you make them surrender it in writing, and attempts are likely to meet fierce objections, as happened when Bauer Media insisted that all freelances sign over the right to sell stories or photos without reference to the writers, photographers or the subjects of the work because, the company argued: 'Bauer Media needs to be firmly placed to take advantage of new revenue streams and opportunities as they arise.'

Assessing the staffing of a magazine is not simple. The output of creative individuals cannot be measured like that of machinery. Start by working out the number of pages required and working backwards. Look at other magazines in your market to see how many staff they use and how many pages they process between them. Divide editorial pages by journalists and you get a crude idea of their output per person. Divide that into your projected number of editorial pages and you can get an idea of staffing.

But you must compare like with like. Your publication may be intended to be more serious and authoritative, led by news and investigations, which demand experienced and expensive staff. The crude page-per-journalist ratio is more useful for assessing your magazine's cost-effectiveness over a period. Teams have a tendency to grow, and that ratio is one way of keeping track.

You must make allowances for staff absence. Your magazine may run perfectly on minimal staffing, but each member of staff will take holidays, have time for training and fall ill. Individuals can be replaced by freelances, but it is never as efficient as having enough staff to cover for foreseeable events. In drawing up your ideal staffing plan you need to include wage levels, by keeping track of the going rate. After a period, annual increases and merit awards to individuals may push your salaries out of alignment with what is paid in the wider world, but the market should be your guide.

Bear in mind, also, that wages are not your only staff cost. Pension contributions to staff will also have to be included in your budget document, as well as any bonuses. Expenses incurred by your staff will be your responsibility and must be both genuine and reasonable. Expect travel costs to show seasonal variation, especially if your magazine has a 'conference' season. You will also be expected to make an assessment of likely training and recruitment costs. Training organisations will supply you with prices.

After fixed costs come variable costs. At the top of the list here are contributors' payments. An assessment of the rates paid by rival publishers will suggest what you will need to pay per 1,000 words, but it is worth talking to your chosen freelances to see that this is in line with their expectations. Your designer will give you word counts for various types of feature, enabling you to draw up an estimated word count per issue and hence per page. The final result should be a cost per page for words, which can be multiplied back up to give you costs per issue, per month and per year.

The same process can be undertaken with photography and illustration. Picture libraries will quote for stock material, depending on your projected circulation and the size at which you are using it. If you plan to use commissioned photography – and you probably will – you need to discuss prices with the type of photographers you are likely to be using. Then you can work out the likely balance of commissioned and stock photography in an average issue and arrive, once again, at a cost per page for visual material. Remember that you will also need visual material for your website. This will be lower resolution (72 dots per inch) and so cheaper.

If you are taking charge of an established magazine, of course, all this material should be at hand. There may be priced issues, with the costs of individual features and photographs marked in. There may be breakdowns of spending on freelance material arranged by issue. At the very least, there will be the individual writers' and photographers' invoices. From now on you will need more accessible records of your spending, starting with an issue-by-issue breakdown of what was spent and where it went.

Some magazines will place variable costs associated with production on the editor's budget, which can make sense. But in general you should only be accountable for spending you definitely influence. Certain production costs come into that category. Making economical and sensible use of your printers is one example. Some editorial initiatives may have production-cost implications: additional ink colours in cover printing, for instance, or the inclusion of inserts or extra supplements. Any such luxuries must be budgeted for. Reducing paper weight can save money, too.

Website hosting costs tend to cover a certain level of demand but you can incur extra charges if the site becomes unusually popular – particularly if that involves large numbers of users using high-bandwidth material such as video or audio (this does not apply if the material is hosted elsewhere, such as YouTube, and simply 'embedded' on your web page). You should also plan for special projects – such as online databases – or functionality – such as the ability for users to share material.

Third party tools or custom-built?

When it comes to online publishing you will frequently face a choice between paying for custom-built websites and using free or marginal cost 'third-party' services. Both have their advantages and disadvantages: low cost is the most obvious advantage of third party services; control the most obvious advantage of building something in-house. But there are also other considerations, such as whether your users would actually choose a custom-built service over one that they – and more importantly, their friends – already use. This is known as 'network effects': it doesn't matter if you build your own social network identical to Facebook; if all your users are already on Facebook, they are unlikely to switch because their friends are on there, and not on your service.

Quality is another factor, and is not guaranteed if you build something yourself. The free content management system Wordpress, for example, is used by a number of major publishers because they found it to be more flexible than the commercial alternatives. This is largely because there is an active community around Wordpress developing the technology.

Multimedia hosting presents similar issues. Some publishers insist on hosting their own video to ensure that readers visit their website to view it, rather than using a video hosting service such as YouTube. This brings with it major disadvantages, however: it incurs extra costs in website development; it incurs extra costs in hosting bandwidth; it generally results in a poorer user experience (because your video controls will be more limited than YouTube's); and it is harder for users to find the video in question.

This last point is worth fleshing out: more searches are conducted using YouTube than any other website apart from google.com. That makes it bigger than Yahoo! search and Bing search, for example. Hosting your video on YouTube (and embedding on your own site) makes it much more likely to attract an audience.

YouTube also offers a number of other attractions, such as the ability for people to embed videos on their own pages (if you choose to allow it). This spreads your content further and – if you include any – your advertising too.

That said, you should always have contingency plans for when those services encounter problems. If you rely on Twitter, for example, what happens when the Fail Whale appears (i.e. the service is overloaded)? Or if it changes its terms and conditions? In the service's early days, for example, users could receive text alerts for free, which some publishers used as an easy way to deliver content – but the service was withdrawn for all countries apart from the US and India (where phone customers pay to receive texts) at short notice, leaving many publishers and customers frustrated.

Third party advertising

Advertising can also be sold and displayed through third parties. The best-known example of this is Google AdSense, which allows anyone to display adverts on their website and make money from them. Many large publishers use Google AdSense to fill empty inventory (that is, ad space that they cannot sell themselves) but the actual money generated is marginal at best – although some larger publishers have managed to negotiate better deals with Google.

Aside from the marginal gains in revenue, you need to consider the implications of handing over control of the advertising that appears on your site. Google's technology displays adverts based on the content of the page, which can produce some embarrassing juxtapositions – such as adverts for wills being shown alongside a report of a death. AdSense is not the only such technology – there are others which will link particular words to a related advert, for example. This also carries the risk of potentially offensive juxtapositions, as well as frustrating users who might expect the word 'report' to link to the report that is referred to, rather than a company selling commercial reports. The world of online advertising is riddled with similar conflicts between a positive user experience, and making enough money to provide any experience at all.

A related issue is that of 'linkspam': links being sold for money. This comes in many forms, from companies offering to pay for certain words to be linked to their web pages, to writers offering free content that turns out to contain such links. Linkspam is not illegal, but it is unethical, because its purpose is not to attract potential customers, but to artificially boost the ranking of the linked web page in search engine rankings. In other words, it is fooling a search engine into thinking that you have linked to this site because you think it is worth linking to, rather than because someone paid you to.

The obvious analogy is between editorial and advertorial: advertorial must be clearly labelled as having been paid for. The technical equivalent of such a label is called a 'nofollow' tag. This tells search engines to ignore the link. Even if the links look like an advert, they should include this tag (search engines cannot see, of course). Talk to your web designer and make sure they read up on this if they don't know about it already.

Not including a nofollow tag on such a link can lead to penalties from search engines, who can decide to reduce your site's ranking significantly as a result, knocking you out of prominent search result rankings and losing you significant amounts of site traffic.

The budget grid

Once you have established with your publisher precisely which items you will be responsible for, it is just a question of drawing up a basic budget grid. The months of the year run across the page, your individual cost items run down. If your magazine is a weekly, some months will include more issues than others, so you can't just drop in the same figure for each month. Remember: you are predicting when costs will be incurred, not when the bills will be paid. Any seasonal differences must be accounted for: for instance, if you always produce a summer special at the start of the holiday season, the costs for that must be included in the appropriate month. If you need extra freelance sub-editors to produce your Christmas double issue, that must be included too. If you expect an across-the-board pay settlement in

Table 4.2 Notional editorial cost budget for a monthly magazine

	March	April	May	June	July
Casual help	0	2318	1097	704	1913
Freelance writing costs	14613	15182	15282	14018	12652
Photography and illustration	2724	2295	2533	2583	1969
Salaries (includes pensions, NI)	80474	81576	81576	81576	81576
Travel and entertaining	1665	1993	1732	1581	1270

Photography is not separated from illustration, or travel from entertaining costs.
Salary info includes pension contributions and NI.
Bonuses for editorial staff are generally paid once a year, so most months have no bonus payments
Web hosting, training and recruitment costs are carried centrally.

April, subsequent salary figures will need to be increased, and the same goes for contributors' payments.

Table 4.2 shows five months' worth of a typical costs-only editorial budget forecast. Note the effect of months in which staff tend to take holidays (Easter and summer). A budget might also make provision for a spend of £2,000 in recruitment expenses in May. There is, of course, no way of knowing when someone is going to leave, but it is a certainty that it will happen at least once during the year. (Note to aspiring publishers: these figures are not intended to represent the real sums of money involved.)

The process is that you submit your budget forecast to higher management, and it returns, usually with some amendments, as an actual budget with allotted spending limits. From now on, keep track of your expenditure and compare it with the budget you have been allocated.

Editorial costs in more detail

Wages/bonuses/expenses

The arrival of a new editor is often seen as a signal for members of staff to ask for more money. You must resist this initial onslaught. Until you see how people work, you have no way of knowing who is worth more.

When setting salary levels, several factors must be taken into account. The first, and most important, is what the company can afford. If you are given responsibility for setting your journalists' pay levels you should be given guidance on the constraints within which such awards can be made. The wage bill will be included within the year's budget. In most magazines, it is the second biggest cost after printing and paper.

You should also consider the going rate for the job in the outside world. It is foolish to pay much below the market rate unless you are sure that opportunities outside are strictly limited or unless you want to provoke the existing staff into leaving. But you shouldn't pay too much either. You can find what other people are paying by studying advertisements, consulting employment agencies or headhunters, or simply by asking other editors.

You should study the job market. If a new publication is entering your area, you will want to pay people enough to stop them making a dash for the cash. Of course, some will go, for the challenge, and you should wish them luck. Particular skills are also in demand at times: we saw this first with people who knew Quark and Photoshop, then again with people who knew HTML and Dreamweaver, and most recently we've seen it with those who possess social media skills. In due course this is likely to happen again, but it is not something we can predict. The best we can do is to keep an eye on technological changes and train our own people to be ready for them. There is always a 'training lag': the technology always comes into effect long before the industry has found enough people to operate it, and then those who are ahead of things can cash in. We have little choice but to applaud them.

Pay is a factor in motivation, but also in demotivation. Pay increases should generally be used to recognise initiative and the taking of greater responsibility, rather than to reward long service. Annual increments reward loyalty, but they also reward inertia. Exceptions might be made for long-serving news editors or chief sub-editors whose experience benefits the magazine. But that should really express itself in taking new responsibilities, perhaps in training or planning new publications.

Take into account fringe benefits, from the provision of free tea and coffee to bonus schemes, share options, pension contributions and private health cover. It is naive to assume, though, that fringe benefits will compensate for a poor basic salary. Journalists tend to measure themselves by their salaries: fringe benefits are rarely considered, especially by those changing jobs.

When you join a new organisation, you must get to grips with the expenses culture. In some organisations, claims are rigorously checked. In others, a certain laxness is traditional, and you will earn nothing but resentment when you try to ascertain whether certain examples of entertaining did in fact take place. Make your expectations clear at the beginning and apply them consistently. All claims should be correctly detailed, on the right form, and accompanied by appropriate receipts. Point out to your staff that the tax authorities will treat anything not fully documented as taxable. Nor are journalists immune to accusations of fraud.

Editorial contributions

The purchase of copyright material, whether written, photographic or illustrative, has become an increasingly contentious issue. In the past, negotiations between editors and freelances rarely involved more than a brief chat about the price and the delivery date. The standard right acquired in those circumstances is 'first British serial right'. This allows the publisher the first use of that item in magazine form within the UK (including Northern Ireland). If you are publishing in Eire, as is common, that must be made clear. If the piece has already appeared, the normal agreement for republication is called 'one use'.

These days publishers want more. They want to reuse material in different editions, in book form, or online versions, and to sell the material on to other publishers. Even when they have no plans to do anything of the sort, it is common practice to demand those rights. What's more, they usually want them for nothing.

If you want to buy anything other than single-use rights, the writer or photographer must sign a contract to that effect. If you want to buy out their ownership in the item, in its entirety, the usual phrase is 'all rights'. Many freelances will baulk at this, before raising their price or declining to do business at all. A marginally less aggressive approach is to buy a more extensive licence, including the exclusive right to publish anywhere in any medium and to syndicate the work to other publishers. This was traditionally the writer's perk: now you will probably offer them a portion of the proceeds, say 50 per cent. Technically this leaves copyright in the hands of the creator, and approaches the standard for acceptable negotiation: that both sides gain something and want to do business again.

Some editors decline to discuss this question at the commissioning stage, letting the writer find out about it when the commissioning form arrives or, more reprehensibly, once the work has been done. Sometimes, writers receive a cheque with a wording on the back which they are expected to sign before payment is issued. The signature assigns their copyright. They don't have to sign, of course, but the cheque tells them they won't get paid unless they do so. Since they have already done the work, most will submit. But it is a shoddy practice. All told, fighting endless battles to acquire rights you have no intention of using is a dispiriting waste of an editor's time, but you will probably have to follow company policy.

Editors should ensure that they have an infallible system for ensuring that freelances are paid on time. There should be a commissioning form, with copies going to the writer and the magazine's accounts department as well as staying with the commissioning editor.

Other costs

Magazines save money at start-up by using sensible paper formats and arranging to be printed at the printers' convenience. That means any failures in editorial production will have cost implications. Late pages, missing elements, wrongly configured disks, font problems, and inaccurate flat-planning can all cause production delays and hence increase costs.

Beyond that, your attitude to costs needs to be the same as that of any modern manager: you must always be looking for ways to keep them to a minimum, whether through a regime of sensible telephone use, care with stationery or the most minute scrutiny of expenses claims. Try to spend money on the things that the readers will appreciate: better photography and writing.

Revenue

Editorial is usually seen as a cost to the publisher: your budget is a 'cost only' budget, for instance. But you do have opportunities to help bring in money for the magazine and you will be expected to make the most of them.

News-stand and subscription initiatives

The most obvious way you can play a part in this process is by participating enthusiastically in circulation-building and subscription-building exercises. No editor tries to produce unpopular covers, but there are times when creating an attention-grabbing cover package, with an appealing picture and straightforward cover-lines, gets pushed down your list of priorities. This must not happen. Strong bookstall sales will guarantee you the respect and independence you need to achieve your other aims. If your department is expected to produce posters and press advertisements to promote your issues, make them good.

Subscriptions are not central to the British way of selling magazines, but they are becoming increasingly important, and can make a big difference to income: newsagent chains and distributors typically take a large chunk of your cover price – subscriptions cut them out of the equation. And they can be encouraged by special offers. These should be bold, and in keeping with the magazine's image. A price reduction is the most obvious approach, but other magazines offer free gifts of various sorts. It is essential that any gifts are in keeping with your idea of the readers, both for effectiveness and for their effect on the magazine's image.

You should also be aware of some of the legal and practical issues around cover-mounts and free gifts. The PPA publish best practice guidelines on these which are worth checking in full, but some key points to look out for are making sure that any media carries appropriate age guidance, that toys meet BSI Kitemark regulations, and food (such as free sweets) does not have a sell-by date that expires within the on-sale period. The Waste Electrical and Electronic Equipment (WEEE) Regulations 2004 also means that if a free gift is electric or electronic the retailer may be responsible for collecting unwanted or waste products – and you'll need to discuss that with them.

Advertising

Most magazine publishing is underpinned by the sale of advertising. That makes the advertising department important and influential. But there are limits to that influence, and it is for editors to stress those when they take on the job. A certain distance is desirable if the independence and integrity of the editorial department is to be maintained.

It is a question of you using your skills to the best advantage of the magazine. You should be producing the best possible magazine for people to advertise in. You should not be involved in persuading people to advertise in that magazine. Some supplements or new editorial products might need a bit of help from you on the commercial side, and you should discuss that at the start. But you should not be a part of the *routine* process of selling advertising.

To advertisers spending large sums of money it can seem terribly harsh when their generosity is not reciprocated in terms of editorial coverage, or when the editorial coverage they receive seems unfavourable. Your advertising colleagues may even encourage advertisers to believe that they have some influence over the magazine's editorial content. They should be disabused of that notion, but gently. It is better to be on good terms. They may travel around more, see more of the world than you and your staff do. They may even bring in genuine stories and ideas. But you must be wary of 'puffs' designed to please advertisers.

Watch out for editorial staff who show signs of obliging the requests of the advertising department. When commercial organisations receive repeated mentions in editorial matter – or, conversely, are missing when perhaps they ought to appear – you should ask yourself whether honest editorial decisions are being made.

Few editors will go many years without receiving a threat of the removal of advertising for some editorial offence, whether real or imagined. Treat the advertiser the same as anyone who is written about and is aggrieved. Ensure, in the first instance, that there is no dishonesty or malice in your journalists' work. The story concerned must be fair and accurate, and it must have been published for good reasons. An advertiser that has been criticised should, of course, get the chance to state its case in your pages, just like anyone else.

If there is a complaint following publication, the normal remedies should apply: publication of a letter, factual corrections, and so on. Beyond that, the advertiser must be left to think it over and your advertising department to try its own powers of persuasion. Hurt feelings aside, companies' advertising strategies are based on hard calculation of your usefulness. If that is unchanged, the lost advertising will eventually be restored. But your advertising colleagues may not take the long view. Remember that they have a personal stake – a financial stake, too – in relationships that are peripheral to you and your team. Expect a bumpy ride until normal service is resumed.

Sophisticated advertisers have a powerful place in their industries and in publishing. They have better ways of influencing you than threats. At various times, you will be offered all manner of self-serving 'exclusives'. Judge them on their own merits. Their source does not make them unusable, but neither does it make them as essential as the advertiser or, more likely, its PR company, might think.

Advertorials

Advertorials, also known as advertising features, are advertisements designed to look like the editorial matter of the publications within which they appear. Exactly how closely they should mimic a magazine's editorial style is the subject of lively debate.

Many editors take the view that they should look nothing like genuine editorial matter. Others object to the aesthetic damage that inappropriately designed and written advertorials can do to the magazine within which they are placed. Some publishing houses have a policy of preparing advertorials in-house, using a separate design and writing team. But the problem of producing advertorial material that is of high quality and 'in keeping with' the surrounding editorial without its actually resembling that editorial has never been resolved.

Advertorials are extremely popular with advertisers, however, particularly in the consumer press, because research has shown that they are very well read. They also work. Research shows that readers somehow assume that they are a 'joint effort' between the advertiser and the magazine's editorial team, and that you are endorsing the product. They know that they are reading an advertisement, but they also see it as an article, which gives it a certain added value.

> The readers assume the editor has been involved in the selection of the product shown in the advertisement feature, and this implies researching the products and choosing the one that's best for readers. The more closely the advertorial matches the magazine's own style the stronger the assumption that the editor has written it, and thus the stronger the endorsement. The magazine's own brand values feed into the advertorial, and they in turn feed into the readers' perception of the product. Advertorials are perceived as generally useful and informative, which encourages an overall positive feeling about them among readers. [1]

All of which means you must keep an eye on them. They can be written by the advertisers themselves or by either the advertising or the editorial staff of the magazine, but this must not form part of a normal journalist's workload. It should be a useful bit of work after hours.

The Professional Publishers Association (PPA) has guidelines about advertorials. In particular, advertorials must not make any claims that would not be allowed in ordinary advertising. Advertorials must be clearly labelled so that readers are in no doubt about the provenance of what they are reading. The words 'advertisement', 'advertisement feature' or 'advertising promotion' are to be used, rather than 'advertorial', which is ambiguous for people outside the industry. Staff writers' by-lines may not appear in advertorials. Finally, the size and number of advertorial features should not be such as to compromise the credibility of the titles within which they appear. It is for others to say how well that particular requirement is being observed in some areas of the British magazine industry. Advertorial and advertising features must also comply with the Trades Descriptions Act, whereas editorial features need not.

Creative media sales

'Creative media sales' is a catch-all category that refers to non-traditional promotions and marketing campaigns, including advertorials but increasingly spreading into cross-platform offerings that take in events, websites, and anything else that can communicate the message the advertiser is trying to get across. For a time this allowed some advertisers to get around some of the regulatory limitations of print advertising, but these have since been tightened with the extension of the Advertising Standards Authority to cover websites and social networking pages too (see Chapter 8).

Special features, supplements and sponsorship

One area in which editors have been expected to be directly useful to advertising departments is the provision of 'special features', usually labelled 'focus', 'monitor', 'survey' or suchlike. In-house these are known as 'ad-get' features, which exactly describes their function.

The process is this. A list of potentially lucrative subject areas is discussed between editor and advertising director. Details of subjects and dates are then distributed to advertisers and suitable feature material commissioned. The material is true editorial matter: the 'ad-get' feature must not be confused with 'advertorial' features. Nonetheless, it is hard to avoid the impression in some cases that this material would not have made it into the magazine on its own merits. That is bad editorship: the section or feature may have been designed for the purpose of generating revenue, but that doesn't mean it can be weak. Used properly, this type of feature can be a useful way of giving new writers experience and building up contacts in industry.

Advertisers will also seek ways of 'partnership' with magazines that give them more prominence and hence better value than simple advertising. These may take the form of additional sponsored 'supplements', sometimes of dubious editorial merit, or competitions and award schemes.

Since these are not going away, it is essential that editors take charge. Far better to find a subject that you would like to cover in a supplement form and then seek an advertiser to back it, than vice versa. This can be a creative area: the connection between the supplement's subject matter and the advertisers need not be close. The advertisers want exposure for their brand, but they also want some of the glamour of the subject to rub off.

The same considerations operate when an advertiser seeks to sponsor a competition or award scheme. But there are an ever-increasing number of awards, and not all of them are credible. Organising a proper competition or award scheme is expensive and difficult. A farcical outcome can be disastrous to a magazine's reputation for excellence. The advertiser may simply expect endless editorial support for a scheme that the editor has had little or nothing to do with organising. And the proliferation of such events, competitions, exhibitions, and so on, may damage the supply of paid-for advertising. Consequently, such approaches need to be treated with caution. But the rewards are high, and as publishers search for new business models in an uncertain environment, experiments proliferate. In 2010, Hearst's Seventeen.com partnered with JCPenney on a virtual dressing room and Time Inc.'s *Instyle* experimented with allowing users to buy goods on their site; in 2011, *Esquire* magazine launched Clad, the 'largest online retail store for men' in partnership with one of America's largest retailers. Editor-in-Chief David Granger said 'Magazines have already done one essential thing – we've made people want things, whether it's a better life or better shoes ... But for the hundreds of years that magazines have been around, magazines have stopped short on delivering that desire.'

The PPA has laid down guidelines on the use of 'sponsored editorial' and 'sponsored competitions' in magazines. Broadly, they state that material and events of this kind should be clearly identified as sponsored, and that the editor should retain control over them. The developing grey area of online mobile content, games and e-commerce will inevitably provide experience for similar guidelines in the future.

Colour separations

At one time some publishers of 'product books' (magazines based on promoting new products and services) would ask those supplying press releases to pay for their inclusion. The demand would be disguised as a request to pay the cost of printing their images in colour. Theoretically, those who did not oblige would have their photographs used but in monochrome. Most coughed up. This technique occasionally recurs in other guises, such as paying for special finishes, paper or extra colours.

Licensing and exports

There is not just one *Cosmopolitan*, or even two: there are in fact 59, spread across dozens of countries, languages, cultures – and publishers. This is a feature of international licensing: allowing a publisher in another country to translate and adapt your magazine for a different market. Other widely licensed titles include *Maxim*, *FHM* and *Glamour*.

Exports, on the other hand, are the transportation of a single magazine to other countries. The biggest markets for UK magazines, for example, are the US, Canada, New Zealand and Australia (for the obvious reason of a shared language and similar culture), and Spain (where many UK citizens retire or take holidays).

Licensing can actually be more lucrative than export. Although the partner publisher takes much of the money from sales, the 'brand owner' saves on transportation costs. The risks inherent in any new venture are also spread – but contracts will have to be negotiated and signed as to whether the content is licensed as well as the brand, or whether local staff will write all material.

Both exports and licensing – as well as overseas expansion and acquisition – are growing areas for publishers, not least because they insulate the core business by spreading risk. If advertising and readership is suffering in the UK, for example, they may be booming in India or China.

Making money online

For online-only magazines, or websites that accompany printed publications, all of the above sources of revenue can also apply, with some key differences. Advertising, for example, is traditionally less lucrative, and advertisers can afford to be more demanding, only paying when someone clicks on an advert, for example (known as pay per click, or PPC), or completes an action such as ordering a brochure or creating an account (known as pay per action, or PPA). This is a problem for businesses that still have to pay print costs, but online-only operations which do not have to pay for printing and distribution can – and do – make a business from the traditional advertising model. Online-only publisher Gawker Media was said to be turning a profit as early as 2006, and by 2009 was estimated to be worth $300m. Sugar Inc – publisher of female-focused blogs on topics ranging from fitness to gossip – has raised over $40m in a number of rounds of funding based on expectations of healthy revenue. And on the smaller scale, Young House Love is a DIY blog run by a husband and wife in Richmond, Surrey, which, after a couple of years, was generating enough advertising revenue to support their family.

Licensing and syndication has been an option for some online publishers – but does not look to be one with a future, as potential customers can choose instead to simply link to you. In addition, not providing open feeds to your content can make for a frustrating experience for readers, while restricting your distribution possibilities.

Charging for content can be problematic for similar reasons: charging 'micropayments' for individual articles can be prohibitively costly for the company to process, and frustrating for users who don't know what they're paying for until they've bought it.

Establishing 'paywalls' that only allow users to read content if they pay for a subscription needs careful thought: any revenue from online subscriptions will need to be offset against the losses in advertising revenue as website visits inevitably plunge (previous paywalls have resulted in readership declines of between 30 and 90 per cent). There's also the distribution issue: so many people stopped linking to *Variety* magazine when it set up a paywall that the magazine subsequently launched a blog outside the paywall with an explicit plea that users link to it. People are unlikely to link to your content if they know their friends will not be able to access it – and this will affect your search engine ranking too.

Paywalls are often more about protecting the print product than establishing an online revenue stream. Eighteen months after Emap put up paywalls around all of its business-to-business titles in 2009, the company boasted that print subscription rates had increased by 25 per cent. That is helpful in difficult economic conditions (the decision was taken in the context of low online advertising rates) but doesn't, however, solve the longer term problem of defending your market against online-only competitors, or being ready for changing consumption patterns among readers.

Notably the publisher softened their stance from charging for all content to varying their strategy across titles. *Nursing Times*, for example, gave away a lot of its content for free as it 'suited the needs of the market', reported *Press Gazette*, while *Screen International* adopted a web-first strategy because its readers demanded it, with the print magazine moved from weekly to monthly publication. For most titles Emap also provides free feeds of headlines through RSS and email newsletters, and uses Google's First Click service to give casual visitors access to five stories each month for free.

Events, merchandise and e-commerce are more important sources of revenue online than they are for the typical print operation. *Esquire*'s online shop is just one example, but online-only examples include satirical magazine *The Onion*,

IPC's goodtoknow portal, Sugar Inc's ShopStyle platform, technology blog AllThingsD and the music magazine *NME*. News magazine *The Atlantic*, meanwhile, experienced a surprising move into profit in 2010 based on online advertising and events. (An annual conference was said by the *New York Times* to draw 1,200 people who paid $2,700 for a four-day pass.)

Those events do not even have to take place in a physical space: Reed Business Information is just one of a number of publishers charging for 'virtual conferences' ('webinars' – online seminars – are a similar option). Like physical events, these also offer sponsorship opportunities in addition to charging attendees.

Finally, there are the opportunities to launch stand-alone products and services. Instead of simply launching a generic *Marie Claire* app based around content, for example, publisher IPC created the branded Beauty Genius app, featuring how-to videos shot with leading make-up artists. The app has been hugely successful as a one-off purchase, but also offers in-app videos that users can buy too. Other examples include *Women's Health* and *Men's Health*'s workouts-based iPhone apps, and *FHM*, which decided to focus on images and video of attractive women for its iPhone app. Finally, a number of publishers are experimenting with games publishing, including *Esquire* and *GamePro* magazine. For the latter, reported *Wired* magazine, becoming a games publisher was a way of 'differentiating itself in the overcrowded world of gaming journalism'.

Like so much else on the web, it is becoming difficult to see where content ends and commerce begins. The concept of a 'magazine' blurs when, online, it can also be a shop, a game, or a tool. It helps to think of how the business model of magazines has traditionally worked: gathering a community of people in the same place (on your pages) where companies can then advertise their products and services. The same principle applies now, but the barriers to selling products and services yourself have been significantly lowered, just as the barriers to publishing content have been significantly lowered for those companies whose advertising used to fund print publishing. Integrity is no less important in this context: users will desert your website if your content is only concerned with selling them your products, just as they will desert if your events are badly organised, your merchandise poor quality, or your service shoddy. Publishers increasingly talk of a 'brand experience' of which the content is just one part. In many ways this makes the reader – as they also become a consumer – more powerful, and the advertiser less so. Your insights into what they are talking and reading about may be of increasing interest to those who are searching for new revenue streams.

Ancillary activities

Speaking in 2010, Trinity Mirror's Paul Hood noted how the uncertain environment introduced by a networked world had made 'publishing' a much more diverse business – even for newspapers:

> Ten years ago, Mirror Group had four or five revenue streams. At last count, Mirrorfootball and 3am had 32. Not all of them will turn out to be the big

businesses we hope, but we're working them all, hard, in the knowledge that our future depends on it.

As publishers explore dozens of potential 'revenue streams' in the coming decades it is likely that you will be asked to be involved with these – or to head them up. Some of these are not new to the industry, such as premium rate or sponsored telephone lines; books; reader offers; meetings, lunches, holidays and study tours; and conferences, seminars, exhibitions and touring shows. Others have arrived with the world wide web: e-commerce; affiliate schemes (where a reader can click through to buy the book on Amazon, eBay, or another online retailer, but you take a cut); alerts; apps for phones and tablets; live updates; virtual conferences; members-only website areas; and 'freemium' offerings (where most people get a basic service for free, but a small proportion pay for added features).

The Internet also hosts a number of services which make it easier for smaller publishers to enter areas traditionally only explored by bigger brands. Tools such as Eventbrite and Meetup make it easy to organise events and take payments from attendees. 'Print on demand' services such as Lulu and Blurb allow you to print books only when someone orders them. Moo.com, Spreadshirt and CafePress.com provide platforms for selling merchandise ranging from t-shirts and mugs to greetings cards and stickers. And of course you can easily set up virtual stores on sites like Amazon and eBay.

All of these require editorial input or supervision if they are not to damage the standing of the magazine – but you should also ensure that you do not see them as merely an inconvenience. As management consultant Peter Drucker puts it in *Management: Tasks, Responsibilities, Practices* (1999):

> It is the customer who determines what a business is. It is the customer alone whose willingness to pay for a good or for a service converts economic resources into wealth, things into goods. What the business thinks it produces is not of first importance – especially not to the future of the business and to its success. What the customer thinks he is buying, what he considers value, is decisive – it determines what a business is, what it produces, and whether it will prosper. And what the customer buys and considers value is never a product. It is always utility, that is, what a product or service does for him.

In some cases these extra sources of revenue may end up underwriting the magazine: in some specialist areas such as information for the chemicals industry, the function of the magazine is to attract potential customers for more lucrative online services such as price alerts.

The key across all of this is to understand the strengths – both editorial and commercial – in each source of revenue and try to make them all work together. Your reporters may be required to gather specific material for these, for example, or spot potential commercial opportunities. But there are only so many hours in the day, and editors will invariably have to consider the magazine itself as their priority.

5 The right words

Hand-holding, fostering, pruning, snipping, squelching and encouraging have always been the true functions of the editor.

(Ernst Jacobi)[1]

The job of an editor is primarily to create compelling content by harnessing the creativity of a team. The managerial aspects are secondary. The trick is to release the skills and ingenuity of those around you, while ensuring that the magazine retains a strong central identity.

Vision

After all the efforts you have made to understand your readers, you should have a strong idea of the subjects that interest them. You may even have arrived at a set of 'musts' to be included in each individual issue, or distributed across a series of them. The more frequently you publish, the less comprehensive your coverage has to be. Weeklies can maintain a balance of subject matter across several issues, whereas monthlies or quarterlies need to ensure that each issue covers the most significant topics for their readership.

Interest in a subject, on its own, may not be enough. The real art lies in assessing how close that interest comes towards being a 'need'. Sometimes the facts of people's lives and careers may be a better guide to that than what they say in surveys. Think again about the reader's self-interest: what am I going to find in this magazine that will give me and my family (or my firm, or my department) an advantage over those who have not read it? Remember that an 'advantage' can be as concrete as advice that will help their career or as vague as having something new to chat about.

Broadly speaking, magazine content – indeed, all editorial content – fits one of three types: the financially valuable information that saves the reader money or time; emotionally valuable material that the reader finds entertaining, fascinating or stimulating; and socially valuable information that the reader can use to forge new relationships or strengthen existing ones.

How many people, for example, read about celebrities because they want to be able to participate in water-cooler conversations? Or keep up to date with fashion or culture so as not to be seen as out of touch?

Give people what is new and useful: they don't need to hear things they already know. That's the 'so what?' factor, and you can run into it when your professional journal reports stories a week or a month late, or when your women's magazine gives readers fashion or health advice they have seen elsewhere. If your focus is celebrity gossip, the 'so what?' factor can quickly drive you off the streets.

Every aspect of your magazine must focus on the reader: at best, readers should feel that each article could really only appear in your magazine. That is asking a lot. In practice, you must satisfy yourself that everything you include offers some new insight. It should also be accurate, fair, complete and easy to read. When dealing with ideas and copy, you may like to keep a mental checklist of qualities.

- Is it new?
- Is it relevant?
- Is it accurate?
- Is it well written?
- Is it right for this magazine?

Creating a balanced magazine is not simply a question of selecting subjects: it is also a matter of the way subjects are handled, and the tone of voice in which they are written about. Your magazine needs a range of different approaches and ways of speaking.

If you are taking over an existing magazine, it is a worthwhile exercise to analyse the subject balance of each issue and compare that with what you know of the prevailing interests of the readership.

You might start by listing the subjects your magazine covers both in print and online. Then count the pages devoted to each subject in, say, six issues (and the same period online). Divide that number of pages into your total number of editorial pages over the period and you will arrive at a percentage for your coverage of each subject (keep print and online separate, as the audiences – and therefore content – will differ). Now how does that compare with what you know about your readers?

This is particularly relevant in the case of business-to-business magazines, whose readers have a wide spectrum of different job functions and work in different areas of the market. Their own specific interests may be extremely specialised, but they may also need a general sense of what is going on across their industry.

General interest business magazines are difficult to produce. Even magazines for particular professions have often found it difficult to arrive at a suitable balance. If you are producing a magazine for engineers, how much common ground is there between those working in the motor industry and those working in power generation? If your coverage is skewed towards the former and your readership towards the latter you will be in trouble. The same goes for magazines which attempt to cater for a range of job types within a single industry, say property developers, estate agents and property users. Consider how much of your content is directly relevant to each group, and compare that with what you know of your readership. This is particularly important in the case of controlled-circulation magazines, where it is not as easy to discover how happy your readers are as it is on the bookstall, where you can watch sales rise and fall.

Statistics around usage of the website – 'analytics', or metrics – can also shed light on the most and least popular content, not just in terms of how many times a particular page is viewed ('page impressions') but also how long the users spend on it (sometimes called 'stickiness'), what they click on, and where they came from to get to it. Don't assume that those figures are directly applicable to your print publication, however. Some web pages may be more popular because another website – or someone with a large following on Twitter or Facebook – linked to it; or because that page appears very prominently in a group of search engine results for a particular term.

Your online userbase may be different to the print readership, too – not limited as the latter will be by either geographical location or ability to pay. Your analytics should tell you this information too, allowing you to shape your online content strategy accordingly depending which audiences you want to attract online.

Another way of getting at the underlying interests of your readers is to look at the sources of your advertising and analyse these in the same way. Advertisers generally only put their money where they get results. This can be quite revealing. If you are producing a magazine for the parents of young children, you may be convinced that most of your readers have toddlers; but your advertising may come largely from the manufacturers of baby milk. Clearly, something is amiss.

The range of subjects that you need to cover and the balance between them may help you to devise a kind of template for your own use: a recipe for a typical issue. In the case of a men's magazine, for instance, this might translate into:

- an interview with an attractive woman;
- an interview with an admirable man;
- a 'yarn' or piece of sustained narrative;
- a picture feature;
- an argumentative piece;
- a humorous piece;
- something on sport or adventure; and so on.

In the case of a professional magazine, it might mean

- an interview with a significant industrial figure;
- a case study of some particularly successful enterprise;
- something on a new technological development;
- something on a change in the law or professional regulation; and so on.

Readers like to know where they are: they want a magazine to stay identifiably the same from issue to issue. But it must not become predictable. Any such 'recipe' must be a rough guide to categories of material, rather than a list of specifics. And you will want to ensure that familiar subjects are constantly treated in new ways. Nor should your recipe be unchangeable. The world is changing all the time, and your magazine must too.

Standards

The task of finding the right balance of subject matter and tone of voice forms one end of the span of editorial tasks. But in some ways it is as important to look at the other end, the detail. The reason for this is simple: nothing destroys a magazine's claims to authority more swiftly and comprehensively than spelling mistakes – particularly in people's names – grammatical ineptitude and sub-editing errors.

You will be encouraging your staff to show their own ingenuity, to use their own resources and to take responsibility. But for that to work you have to lay down unambiguous standards of what is and is not acceptable. It's a critical part of producing a strong magazine. The only sensible policy is 'zero tolerance'. You must make it clear from the outset, by sending back unacceptable work for correction, that you will not accept compromises. It is the editor's lot to be a stickler, a perfectionist and a pedant, and to appoint people who share those concerns.

Accuracy, fairness, clarity

While we strive for truth, the minimum we must achieve is accuracy. There is a simple rule: anything that can be checked should be checked. Newcomers to journalism find this a difficult concept to grasp, while experienced staff may cut corners and neglect it. It should, however, be thoroughly drummed into your writers and production staff.

All spellings, figures and other factual statements must be checked against reliable sources: you must ensure that a small reference library is established and kept up to date. The Internet can be a helpful source of additional information but it must be used intelligently and critically.

Wikipedia, for example, is an excellent starting point for checking on types of information not covered by traditional encyclopedias – but it should be a starting point, not the end point. Follow up on references given for facts (if no reference is given, you will need to track it down yourself, and if you cannot track it down, then it is not credible), read the 'Edit history' and 'Discussion' tabs that accompany every page on Wikipedia – these show how pages have been changed over time, by whom (be sceptical if an entry has only been edited by one person), and why. Most importantly, edit Wikipedia entries yourself if you find any extra information or references – and especially if you find anything that is incorrect or out of date. Becoming an active contributor to Wikipedia is the best way of understanding its strengths and weaknesses.

Of course, just as Google is not the only search engine, Wikipedia is not the only reference work online, and you will find different resources more useful, or reliable, for different queries. Print reference books such as the *Oxford English Dictionary*, *Dictionary of National Bibliography*, and *Reference Collection* are also available online through most libraries. You need not even leave your office: often you can access such resources via your library's website by typing in your library card number.

More generally you should be wary of falling for hoax web pages and online rumours. A good approach to adopt here revolves around looking at three C's: content, context, and code. In terms of content, ask yourself if the style matches who it purports to be from, and whether the story is too good to be true: might it be bait that you're swallowing? Can you cross-check it with information elsewhere, ideally via a phone call?

In terms of context, look at what other web pages link to this one (you can use the advanced search feature in search engines such as Google to check this), or which other people are friends or followers of the source of the information.

And in terms of code, look at the web address: if it ends in .gov.uk, for example, then it is a governmental site. Those ending in .org.uk may be a charity – but not always; likewise .ac.uk is no guarantee that it is a reputable academic institution. Use a 'Whois' service to find out who has registered the web address. And look at the raw HTML of the page for further clues. More generally, read about online hoaxes and familiarise yourself with the techniques that are used to fool gullible journalists.

Quotes, as well as facts, must be accurate. With new reporters, it is worth asking to see their notebooks from time to time to ensure that entries are correctly dated and labelled and that the notes within bear a clear relationship with the quotes that appear in the magazine. Most interviewing for anything beyond simple news stories will probably be recorded. Insist that such recordings are transcribed honestly and stored carefully.

Sometimes you might want to put the original audio recording on your blog or publish a short snippet of audio to add something extra to the website – but make sure that you have the interviewee's permission (either recorded at the start of the interview or in writing – for instance, in an email). Many interviewees will welcome this as a way of ensuring their words are not misrepresented (it is best explained in this way) – and some will want to put it on their own websites too.

Beyond simple accuracy, you must encourage fairness in your journalists. When things appear in print, they require a much higher level of both accuracy and fairness than is normal in day-to-day gossip and chit-chat, where it is quite acceptable to say things that are not true and are certainly not fair. The distinction between everyday life and professional duty is something inexperienced journalists sometimes find hard to grasp.

It is important that people your magazine writes about are treated straightforwardly, honestly and even-handedly. In particular, no one on your staff should be operating with any concealed motive. Journalists in the Western world aim at objectivity, at least in news stories. This means reporters leave themselves out of the story, and do not let their attitudes colour the way it is told. Of course, no human being can be truly objective, but it is a stance which most of us expect in news writing. It means we strive to include relevant facts even if they threaten the narrative simplicity of the story, and we don't take sides.

Much ink has been spilled in the past about whether the general obligation towards objectivity requires reporters to be objective between 'right and wrong'. It doesn't. Personal morality is not negotiable. But a story is not a speech for the prosecution. It is closer to the judge's summing up. It is a device for revealing the facts of a situation, even-handedly, and inviting the readers to make up their own minds.

Those criticised in a story, for instance, should be given the opportunity to state their side of the dispute. This is not simply an ethical matter: it is also about self-interest, since most readers will find balanced and objective news writing more involving and more respectful of their intelligence than selective reporting mixed with opinionated rhetoric. Newcomers to professional journalism find this difficult, but they must learn it.

Feature writing and personal columns, on the other hand, allow more subjectivity and opinion. But they should still be based on accurate facts, not least for legal reasons.

Online there is a move towards *transparency* rather than objectivity. This simply means that you should link to any sources you have used in pulling together your story. If you assert a fact – or mention a report, or quote something someone has said publicly – then the user should be able to click to the original source and question it accordingly. Not doing so suggests you have something to hide.

Twinned with this is a desire for *accountability* in online publishing: users should be able to post a comment to highlight mistakes or information that needs updating. This is a sign of strength rather than weakness – it shows that you are confident enough in your material to accept comments on it, and also that you respect your readers enough to listen when they point out mistakes or omissions. You will also often find that you discover genuine experts in your readership who prove indispensable when you need to check facts in future.

It is one of the virtues of journalistic writing that it strives for simplicity and clarity. At the same time, some areas of magazine writing permit greater flair and stylistic experimentation than is common in the daily newspapers. There is a balance to be struck, but most editors will opt for clarity. Writing simply, so that everything can be understood at first glance, is a great skill and must not be undervalued.

House style

One obvious distinction between a high-quality publication and a lesser one is consistency. A magazine which refers to 11 January on one page and January 11th on another, or to the BBC on one page and the B.B.C. on another, is hardly likely to build a reputation for authority. Most offices have a style book or style sheet, although in many cases it may only be a few pieces of paper to supplement some agreed work of reference. The *Oxford Dictionary for Writers & Editors* is often used as a starting point (others include *The Economist* and *Guardian's Style Guides*, both of which are available online), but all editors have their prejudices and variants. If your magazine covers a particular professional area, you will need to work out your own style rulings on that industry's technical language.

Your style sheet should also include examples of grammatical howlers and solecisms to be avoided, the favoured terms of address ('Mr Jones' or just 'Jones'?), the correct spellings of regularly used proper names, a list of registered trademarks that must be used properly or not at all, appropriate rulings on units of measurement, a ruling on whether collective nouns (government, for instance) are singular or plural, and so on.

You should also make it your practice to issue directives on words, idioms, clichés, headlines and standfirst ideas that have become hackneyed and thus should not be used: 'natch', 'kiddies', 'But hey!', 'Just why … ?' and so on. This may seem no more than the exercise of prejudice, but it is part of defining the way in which your magazine speaks to its readers.

You should also ensure that the magazine uses only one basic dictionary, supplemented by necessary technical and foreign language dictionaries, and that your sub-editors have access to reference books. The task of compiling a style book or sheet is one you can delegate to someone else, probably the chief sub-editor, and you should take the opportunity of talking it through with your sub-editors. They will appreciate the attention, and will act as your 'style police' in the future. If they don't share your views on usage and abusage, they should at least understand and recognise them.

Working with writers

Most editors continue to write. They will usually want to write an editorial, and they may do the odd feature. Assigning yourself to do an interview can even open doors which might otherwise be closed. It can be flattering for the interviewee, especially if it is a rare event rather than a habitual one caused by under-staffing. It is also seen as a mark of respect. You must ensure that your performance is up to scratch and that you clamp down on any self-indulgence.

Otherwise, however, you will be assigning writers to jobs, briefing them, nursing them through the process and editing their copy once it arrives. These are all demanding tasks.

Staff writers

There are many times when it is better to use staff, if you have them, rather than freelances. News is a good example. It involves a lot of research for a small amount of printed copy (and typically regular copy for the website), and really needs the resources of an office: post, telephones, fast Internet, faxes, and other people to answer the phone at times to ensure important contacts aren't left stranded.

Freelances are generally paid on the basis of what they produce: usually per 1,000 words. News is one of those types of article that is hardly viable for freelances to produce on such a basis. It is not fair to ask them to do it, although you might pay them a day rate to come into the office and produce what they can in the time available. The same goes for most research-heavy features. For a staff writer, the necessary research can fit around other jobs, in spare time, and the feature can be assembled over a long period.

It is also sensible to use staff for secret tasks, those which are meant to surprise readers and competitors. Freelances are loyal to your magazine while they are working for it: their commitment cannot be expected to go beyond that. Don't expect to bind them to silence about your future plans. But staff should have only one loyalty.

Experimental features, which may or may not work, and those which require the daily involvement of senior staff including yourself, are also better kept in-house. One of the central tasks of the commissioning editor is to avoid paying for unused work. But you are paying your staff anyway, and it makes sense to experiment with their time rather than with the expensive time of a freelance.

Even staff writers need proper briefing. Like freelances, they should be given clear instructions and an appropriate deadline. How much detail you give them is up to you. They can always ask you, although that might not be the most efficient use of your time.

When staff writers hand in their work, especially if they are inexperienced, it is only fair to give it the level of attention a freelance's copy would get. This is a time for gentle guidance and encouragement.

The writing process

Some find writing difficult all the time, and all of us find it difficult some of the time. You may occasionally need to nurse and cajole your staff writers through a difficult job. It sometimes helps to think of writing as a three-stage process: planning, writing and revising. Of these, the initial writing might well be the quickest, so encourage your writers to take planning seriously. They need to remind themselves about who the piece is for, and what it is intended to achieve.

If that can be turned into a simple heading or standfirst, so much the better. Let them refer to that both in the research and writing stages. The point is to be focused. It is very easy these days, given the easy availability of background material on the Internet, to over-research a piece and lose track of its point. It is not about what the writer finds interesting: it is about what the reader needs.

First drafts should be quick and fluent. Most people find a brief outline of the shape of the piece helps, but it is wrong to be dogmatic about these issues. It can also help to take a break between finishing researching and starting writing. A walk around the block will help the important points percolate to the surface. If the point is based on a long interview, the points you can remember may well be more important than those you only unearth when you read back the notes or your transcript.

Now the time comes to revise. Stress simplicity and directness, and hope to find an argument flowing through the piece. Typically your piece will benefit from removing the first paragraph or two, where you may be 'warming up' to the real focus of the piece. Another tip is to look for the one element in the piece which will interest the least people – and chop everything about that out.

Some pieces are overstretched and based on inadequate material. There is a helpful saying: 'If you're short of wood, build a smaller boat.' Others are over-long and over-complex, something that can usually be resolved by renewed attention to the central questions: who am I writing for? what am I trying to say to them?

If your first or second draft is too long, and is only cut for reasons of space rather than quality, consider putting that version online where space is not an issue, and directing print readers online for the 'web version' or 'blogger's cut' (conversely, direct online readers to the print edition for a shorter or more succinct version). This is not an excuse for bloated copy, but only for occasions where you feel you have had to cut genuinely useful information.

Freelance writers

Working successfully with freelance writers means mastering commissioning. It is a straightforward process, but it benefits from experience. You are negotiating to buy someone's services as a writer: everything else flows from that. The first essential is that those given the authority to commission, which could be just you or several of your staff, know the constraints under which they are operating. The sums available per issue will have been worked out during the budgeting process (see Chapter 4).

A commissioning editor must operate within these figures. And every month you must compare actual spending on commissions with the agreed budget figure. There will be some variance from month to month, because the issues will be different. Some will have more pages than were budgeted for, some fewer. Some will contain a greater proportion of freelance material, perhaps because of staff illness or the nature of the subjects chosen. In some months, excess material will have been commissioned and held over or, on unavoidable occasions, simply discarded.

You need a more manageable figure to work with. Take an issue, count the pages written by freelances, and divide that number into the freelance budget to determine a budget per page. Then look at some layouts and work out the average number of words per page across a series of features. Divide that into the budget per page to produce a figure for your likely cost per word and per 1,000 words. You shouldn't normally pay that, since it includes the wastage mentioned above. But it is there as a guide.

A minimum rate should be calculated for quoting to freelances. Any commissioning editor must have leeway to increase that rate for more experienced writers and for more difficult, time-consuming tasks. Commission with two figures in mind: the minimum, and the high figure you calculated. Sometimes it may be more logical to pay on a different basis: perhaps a fee per day, although this must still be arrived at by using the page budget.

This is the background for discussions between commissioning editors and freelance writers. It is not, however, the starting point for those discussions. First you need to give the writer a brief: a short but adequate explanation of what you want written. It should certainly not extend beyond a single page of A4. It should include an account of the subject, the approach you want taken, specific questions you want answered, people you would like interviewed (or excluded), and details of any extra material – boxes, panels, and so on – apart from the main piece. It should also state if the writer is required to collect any pictures or other visual material, or any material for online publication, such as links.

Then you have to set a deadline. This must obviously allow you enough time to edit the material and arrange any illustration. It is not always wise to tell the writer when you expect to publish, though most will want to know, especially if your company's policy is to pay '30 days after publication' rather than on receipt of an invoice. Obviously, if you are not sure about the writer you will need an early deadline.

Next you specify a number of words. Some types of layout are very much denser than others. If the piece is to fit a specified slot you can be very precise about the number of words required. Otherwise, you need to work out an average that will enable you to fill the number of pages required. You might find it handy to draw up a little chart showing how various types of layout work in terms of words. A single-page feature might be about 1,000 words, but a double-page spread on a similar grid will only work out at about 1,800. It is likely that your writers will overwrite. Most do. But the fee is a fixed figure based on the commission. If you ask for 1,000 words and the writer produces 1,500 the fee remains the same. The extra words are free, in a sense, but they will actually cost you money because someone has to reduce them to fit the specified slot. This foible can sometimes be used to advantage. If your writer habitually overwrites, you can under-commission appropriately and save money.

Some magazines also ask writers to spell out that their work is original, not previously published, their own property, factually true and not defamatory. You will, of course, be making your own decisions about what is defamatory or not, and should not expect to shift responsibility to anyone else.

What remains to be discussed is the crucial question of what 'rights' you wish to purchase. All literary and artistic work is 'copyright', which means that it cannot be reproduced without the permission of the copyright owner. The owner of the copyright in freelance material is the freelance writer or photographer. Editors usually acquire a 'licence' to print this material.

The position was complicated by the 1988 Copyright Act, which provided for the first time certain 'moral rights' for the authors of copyright material. These include the right to be identified as the author of the material and the right not to have the work subjected to 'derogatory treatment', meaning addition, deletion, alteration and adaptation, where these have the effect of distorting the work or damaging the reputation of the author. Note that the Act specifically excludes work made for the purposes of publication in any 'newspaper, magazine or similar periodical'.

You may occasionally meet freelances who have read far enough into the Act to hear about these 'moral rights' but not far enough to realise that they don't apply to magazine work. They should be gently advised on the subject. The exclusion even applies to book extracts and other pieces of work made for other media. Once they are made available to you as an editor of a magazine, with the consent of the author, moral rights no longer apply.

Some editors like to spell out, in their commissioning letters, that they require the unlimited right to cut, amend, add to and generally edit the text. The author is required to sign his or her acceptance of these terms. You may feel, however, that there is no point in spelling out the custom and practice of the trade and creating an air of suspicion where none need exist.

'Moral rights' are, however, a side issue. The real issue is the right to publish, and that is still contentious. When no other agreement is reached writers sell a licence called first British serial rights. This means the right of first publication, once only, in a magazine or newspaper circulating in the UK. Extra rights, for instance to syndicate the article outside the UK or to use it in a book, have to be negotiated separately.

Publishers today often want more comprehensive rights, ostensibly for online and other multi-platform publication. Some want the freelance to 'assign' copyright, which is to say sell it. Others prefer an 'unlimited licence' giving them 'all rights' in every country and medium, whether invented yet or not. Sometimes this has been accompanied by the demand that all future commissions by that freelance be undertaken on the same basis.

You can see the point: if the idea is to reuse material – particularly as the industry evolves new products and strategies across new platforms – publishers don't want that process to be dependent on the agreement of every one of the original authors. But 'all rights' and 'assignment' contracts are very threatening to freelances. They may be helpful to the magazine buying the rights, but they prevent the freelance reusing his or her own work after initial publication.

And the demand for more rights has rarely been accompanied by generous offers of more money. The result is often an unnecessary stand-off, with editors in the middle. Surrendering copyright is distasteful to writers, though few have ever earned much by retaining it. Nonetheless, the potential is there – which is why publishers want it. These disputes are likely to continue. Staff writers, of course, have no copyright over their material so the problem does not arise.

In practice, all these matters – brief, terms, deadline and fee – should be embodied in a printed form. At least two copies are required, one to go to the writer and one for the commissioning editor. If you require the author's written agreement, which you must have if you want to acquire copyright or an extended licence, two forms must be sent out so that one can be returned, signed, to the office.

That's the mechanical part of commissioning. The creative part comes in matching writers to ideas. Obviously the safest way to handle commissioning is to deal with a tiny number of trusted writers, who can be briefed in a moment and who never quibble about what is done to their copy or what they are paid. However, this can lead to a certain stagnation. A commissioning editor should always be looking for new voices. Most will be inundated with letters from hopefuls, but you may find it more productive to approach people whose writing you have enjoyed in other fields.

The path of commissioning strangers is fraught and there are no shortcuts. There are various freelance directories, online as well as on paper, but they are rarely used. Freelances may speak convincingly and offer appealing ideas, but that does not prove they can write. If you are trying someone new, give them something small to do. That way, even if the exercise is a complete write-off, the loss is small.

The commissioning editor's task does not end with signing the commissioning letter or form and sending it on its way. The piece itself must be shepherded into print. Every editor discovers, before very long, what it is to receive a completely unusable piece of work. First the piece should be compared with the brief. If it is unsalvageable, though still competent, some kind of payment should be offered to bring the contract to a close. This is often referred to as a kill fee, although technically that term should be used for a commission which is stopped before anything is written. If the piece is not of professional quality you may feel justified in refusing to pay for it. This would leave you open to proceedings in the small-claims court, where you should be prepared to defend your action.

When the piece is acceptable, but not right, the author should be contacted, the deficiencies listed and a rewrite requested. You can demand at least one rewrite under the terms of the original commission. However, once you've asked for a rewrite, you are committed to paying the full price for the piece even if you do not use it. If it is still not right, your staff should rewrite as necessary, thereby salvaging something from the debacle. It is common in magazines for writers to be shown the rewritten versions of their stories and the changes discussed. In newspapers, where time provides an excuse, this happens much less. It is not practical or cost effective to discuss the adjustment of individual items of punctuation, but where the changes are so obvious that the writer would notice, good manners insist that the writer be shown the finished version. In such cases, the author may not wish to have a by-line.

Given the difficulty in securing a commission, some freelances, especially the inexperienced ones, may attempt to sell you material 'on spec'. If someone calls you and offers you a piece like that, proceed carefully. If you agree to 'take a look' at a piece, some writers, especially those from a local newspaper background, will claim that you have 'ordered' the piece and so must pay for it. So, if you agree to read a speculatively written piece, make it clear that you won't be paying for it unless it is used.

With the rise of the commissioning editor, the whole business of working with freelance writers has become time consuming and complicated. Detailed briefing is supposed to prevent misunderstanding and ensure a high success rate, but if you are not careful it can stultify what should be a creative process. Most writers will agree that some of their best pieces have been the result of two-minute conversations, not lengthy commissioning documents. I treasure the words of one veteran writer, who said that the only brief that counted consisted of two words: 'enthral me'.

The other thing that remains to be said is that it never hurts to show your appreciation. Most writers are insecure people, and being freelance is a particularly lonely and isolated existence. A call when you've read and enjoyed a piece will be much appreciated, as will a prompt response to calls and ideas put forward. But a word of thanks is perhaps the most appreciated.

What writers want from an editor

In my experience, the words any writer least likes to hear from an editor are 'it's fine'. I've been struggling all day and half the night, shaping, polishing and refining and it's just 'fine'? 'Fine' is the ultimate damnation by faint praise, suggesting the editor couldn't give a toss what you've written and probably hasn't read it properly anyway. 'Fine' suggests the editor isn't interested or engaged by the piece at all. I'd rather a constructive and reasoned demolition with suggestions about how the piece could be improved than 'it's fine …'.

The best editors, in my experience, seek to strike a balance between respecting the voice of the writer and getting to the truth of the piece. They will be able to bring an overall perspective to the piece which the writer, intimately acquainted with the subject and immersed in fine detail, might not have. They will be able to corral the writer's worst conceits and affectations (a bit pretentious, old boy …) while recognising that it's the writer, not the editor, who's supposed to be writing the story. The worst editors tend to be frustrated writers who think that whatever's delivered they could have written it better themselves.

What do writers want from editors? Lots of encouragement, obviously. Enthusiasm. A clear idea of the strengths and weaknesses of a story. A clear briefing at the outset. There are few things more frustrating than to be told, 'oh but you haven't mentioned … a, b and c' when it was never discussed in the first place.

Minor and major irritations? A particularly well-honed phrase or sentence being chopped and changed simply because the editor thinks they can write it better. Things being changed without consultation. (It's the writer's name that goes on the piece, not the editor's; they have to live with the fall-out.) Sloppy editing: deleting the first reference to that central character in the story, so that the reader meets them five pars down without having a clue who they are … At its best, this is a truly collaborative process. Writing is, by definition, a solitary business, but one of its great pleasures can be sitting down with an editor and working on a piece together, making it the best it can be.

Mick Brown, *Telegraph Magazine*

News

News is where journalism began. It's also where many journalists start, as trainees or on college courses. News is central to many versions of magazine publishing. Most of us are concerned with giving our readers information and ideas they have not heard before. Many of those topics, whether they are stories or product reviews or gossip, are news. And most areas of content work better when they are subjected to the disciplines of news: topicality, relevance, accuracy.

It is important that all your journalists, not just the news team, should recognise what makes news for your publication. Despite formal journalistic training, most people learn their 'news values' by watching how more experienced colleagues react to a 'story', a 'yarn' or a 'tale', all of which are ways of saying the same thing.

Ideas about what makes news have been passed down over the years, but most have their roots in the 'yellow journalism' of the USA in the nineteenth century, the era recalled in *Citizen Kane*. At the head of the list comes a famous observation, 'When a dog bites a man, that is not news. When a man bites a dog, that is news.' It is usually attributed either to John B. Bogart, city editor (news editor, in our terms) of the *New York Sun*, or to his editor, Charles A. Dana. The point of the aphorism is that news should concern itself with the unexpected. Or, in another famous phrase, sometimes attributed to Lord Northcliffe, founder of the *Daily Mail*, 'News is anything out of the ordinary.'

Another famous aphorism is variously attributed to William Randolph Hearst, founder of the Hearst newspaper and magazine empire in the USA, and to Northcliffe again: 'News is what someone doesn't want you to print. Everything else is advertising.'

Finally, a different, less confrontational definition from Dana: 'News is something which interests a large part of the community and has never been brought to their attention.'

This usefully combines two important ideas. It reminds us that news is not something new, necessarily, but something your readers have not heard before. And news has to serve a particular community. In the newspaper world in which these ideas began, that community was a town or a city. In the online world they can be 'hyperlocal' – at the level of a street or village.[2]

But our titles have communities too: they may be a business sector, a professional group, followers of a hobby or a socio-economic group. And again, in the online sphere these can be ultra-niche communities. But stories are either relevant to them or they're not. Get it wrong and your readers will drift away.

Try to identify what constitutes a story for your readership. At the very least it must be:

- new to your readers;
- relevant: it has to affect them, be close to them, or be made to seem so;
- simple: or easily grasped;
- finite: it should be an event, not a permanent condition;
- surprising: which may be the most important quality of all.

News is not about information for its own sake. It's about information that stimulates the reader. It need not be entertaining, in the narrow sense, but it will appeal to readers and make them want to read on. That's the difference between your news pages and the raw handouts and press releases you use to create them. It helps if the story has an emotional impact: dramatic action is useful (such as conflict), but so are large sums of money and frightening diseases. As always, the news has to be right for your readership. Dramatic events involving children and animals will be very useful in some types of women's magazine, but a journal for accountants would be more interested in an unexpected ruling in a tax appeal. In business-to-business publishing, 'angle' – your readers' particular interest – is everything.

That said, people are usually important in news. Most publications, however dry, will have a cast of relevant individuals whose prominence makes their activities and pronouncements newsworthy. Local newspapers turn every story into a 'people' story. But this is not an approach that works for all magazines. Some business magazines like to personalise all conflicts and illustrate every story with dramatic-looking pictures of the protagonists. But readers of many professional magazines have a morbid fear of anything sensationalist. In those circumstances, presenting stories in a dramatic, human way might be the worst thing you could do.

Magazine editors worry about topicality. Stories they send to press on Monday may be out of date by the time the magazine appears on Wednesday or Friday. It is no consolation to know that similar doubts affect the editors of daily newspapers, fated to follow in the wake of television. The print media must play to their strengths. Even a weekly magazine cannot stay on top of a breaking story of national significance. By the time it has appeared, things will have moved on and its readers will have read more recent material in their daily newspapers.

The Internet, however, levels the playing field. TV, radio and newspapers all increasingly begin their reporting online. This is called a 'web first' strategy and has its advantages and disadvantages. Clearly the major advantage is 'owning' the story. If you are the first to report it online then you are likely to dominate the search engine results when people look for that story. This is turn is likely to drive readers – and potential subscribers – to your main product (whether that is print or online).

The major fear that publishers have with 'web-first' strategies is losing their exclusives to rivals. This, however, is to misunderstand the complexities of multi-platform publishing which should involve playing to the strengths of each medium you publish in. Some publishers, for example, will supply video interviews to broadcasters (and online) just ahead of the publication of the print version of their story. This helps attract interest from people who might not normally buy your publication, without 'giving away' the print version of the story itself.

A good example of how *not* to do this comes from *Rolling Stone* magazine's profile of top US commander General Stanley McChrystal. The general was quoted making negative remarks about the vice president and key members of the US cabinet and the publication of these remarks in print led to his dismissal.

The dismissal, of course, increased interest in – and awareness of – the profile piece substantially – but the magazine failed to react to this interest on its website. As the website Talking Points Memo reported in a piece entitled 'How *Rolling Stone* Won The News Cycle And Lost The Story':[3]

> Rolling Stone didn't even bother putting [the story] online before they rolled it out [in print]. In fact, despite the fact that everyone else's website led the profile, Rolling Stone's site led with Lady Gaga … all day and didn't even put the story online until 11:00.

Nieman Journalism Lab explained why this cost them:[4]

> The story made its way across the web anyway. Politico posted a PDF of the story and the Associated Press ran a thorough summary. Rolling Stone didn't get much in the way of traffic out of it … After the piece ran [on Rolling Stone's website], it started picking up incoming links, presumably driving tremendous traffic to the site. I checked in on the story today, exactly 24 hours later, to find that, despite the story completely dominating the news cycle – TV, blogosphere, Twitter, newspapers – only 16 comments had been posted to the story.
>
> Why? Of course the late posting was a factor. National security reporter Spencer Ackerman's first [blog] post on the general's apology, which went up several hours before *Rolling Stone* published, attracted 47 comments on his personal blog. Politico's defense reporter Laura Rozen's blog post on the AP's summary of the story, which went up at 10:46 p.m. the night before the story appeared, has about twice as many comments as the *Rolling Stone* story itself. Twitter was buzzing with comments all day. There was nowhere to discuss at *Rolling Stone*, so the conversation naturally happened elsewhere.

Another approach is to play to the community-based strengths of online publishing, by seeding an online debate with the main points of your exclusive, and using the best parts of that online discussion to flesh out the publication in print of your full exclusive.

In other words, do not fall into the trap of overvaluing the 'exclusive' at the expense of actual readers. If your objective is to attract the largest number of readers – online and in print – then be strategic in how you publish different parts of your story across different platforms. Can you involve online users at an early stage? Can you produce video or audio that bloggers and broadcasters might want to distribute? How can you give it the richest treatment in print that could not be duplicated in a broadcast or web treatment? And, once published, how can you ensure that discussion of the exclusive takes place on – or directs traffic to – your site? All of these elements require thought at the outset of any newsgathering operation.

A magazine has its own strengths it should play to. Instead of trailing behind newspapers and television – whose space and time is more limited, and news cycle more tempestuous – it can provide analytical coverage, based on its trusted relationships within the industry and in-house expertise. It can also focus its treatment more specifically than the mass media will – as a newspaper with a broader audience will not be able to assume much prior knowledge on their part.

Some editors, usually of weekly magazines, take the view that monthlies shouldn't try to compete in the news area. They should simply use the space for something else. This is defeatist, and overlooks the role of the website in providing news updates as they occur. The slower pace of a monthly should mean that it can unearth and research genuinely exclusive stories. That way it will lead everybody else, which is good for morale and sales. It can certainly go deeper, using the sources it has had time to cultivate.

If you are going to do news in a monthly, you must consider the issue of the exclusivity of your stories and whether you wish to lead with the story in print or online. Given the increasing ability of sources to publish themselves (via a company or individual blog, for example – or even Facebook), or the likelihood that someone else might do the same, obtaining cooperation and silence while you wait for the next monthly print run to roll around is becoming increasingly difficult.

Ultimately you must ask yourself where the value lies: in the exclusivity, or in the treatment and distribution of that information? Do people buy your magazine purely for the exclusive news – or largely for other content? Is it better to publish part of the exclusive online, establishing 'ownership' of it and promoting further revelations or analysis in print (while also attracting new readers who come across your publication when a link is sent to them)?

Publishing a part of an exclusive online – and holding the remainder back for print publication – is a strategy often adopted by publishers. Your own decision will depend in large part upon where your funding comes from, where you are trying to attract it, what sort of people read your publication, and how.

More and more publishers are going for this 'web-first' strategy, playing to the strengths of each medium: speed, findability and social distribution online; and analysis and depth in print. It can also increase the life of a story from a single issue to a couple of weeks online, through printing, and back online with further reaction.

Building a relationship with sources often rests on the authority of your magazine and yourself, and the serious treatment you can give to their story. They will have to balance that against the control that they will have if they publish the story themselves, online. One factor that may be worth raising is that 'exclusivity' often attracts more interest from those who missed the exclusive, than a source-published story which all journalists can see at the same time. The founder of Wikileaks understood this when breaking the various 'Warlogs' stories – instead of publishing the logs online as they had with previous leaks, the organisation partnered with individual news organisations in three different countries, attracting wider coverage of the documents not just in those newspapers but also in jealous rivals.

The bulk of your coverage will not be exclusive. Use the focusing power of news design to achieve the right balance. You can give great prominence and projection to your exclusive stories, while covering the stuff most readers may have seen in a round-up box or column of news 'briefs'.

Aside from the news that makes the printed magazine, a monthly news team tends to produce a continuously updated news page as part of the website. This may include one or more individual, team, or subject-based blogs, and a daily or weekly email update.

Your own news feeds may be syndicated to other news sites and blogs, adding to your publication's reach. Typically a magazine website's news section will have an RSS feed of its latest stories; increasingly, they will have a number of RSS feeds for news about different parts of their field.

RSS feeds have enormous flexibility and potential for various uses. If someone uses an RSS reader on their computer or phone, they can read your feeds there; if they publish a blog they can 'pull' your feed to show your latest headlines (when clicked, the user will be taken to your site). You can also use RSS feeds to cross-publish your latest headlines to a Twitter account, a Facebook page, and various other places.

RSS feeds can be full (showing the entire story) or partial (showing only a first paragraph – the user then has to click through to the full story on your site – although this introduces an extra step that can reduce readership and create a frustrating user experience), and they can include advertising and multimedia. They are, in effect, one of the delivery vans of Internet distribution.

The news team

News gathering – spotting stories, putting them together quickly, checking their accuracy – is something that should be encouraged throughout your journalistic team. Set an example by bringing something back from your forays into the outside world, whether it is a tip-off picked up over lunch or a potential lead you spotted in a local paper. You should also do your best to start the week with news ideas found in the weekend's newspapers and broadcasting.

If you are working on a news-oriented weekly, each day can start with a simple news meeting. What's come in the post, via email and social networks, who's working on what, what stories will we be able to place on the page today, has anyone heard any good tips? It gives the morning a sense of purpose. If not, begin with a brisk session of searching the newspapers and feeds and cutting out or printing anything relevant. If you have enough staff, the papers can be divided between them; it should be stressed that this is not an opportunity to look at the horoscopes and sports pages but a job of work. The City and business pages are increasingly relevant for all of us. The average broadsheet newspaper will generally supply several business magazine ideas for stories, although it is important to use this material to trigger new ideas and thoughts rather than to reproduce it slavishly a week or a month after its original appearance. If you are working in a virtual office you may want to use a free bookmarking service like Delicious.com to share links between you.

Your news editor and news reporters need a meticulous and comprehensive approach to news gathering. They must pursue news: it is not enough to open the post or wait for tip-offs. The key tool for news work is the office diary. This should include the dates of all relevant forthcoming events in your field, including meetings of professional organisations, important court cases, publication of reports, press conferences, the opening and closing dates of enquiries, and so on. But there are many things you can add yourself. If people say they can't give you an answer for a month, make a note to ring them back in three weeks. Keep a note of the appropriate dates for 'follow-ups' arising from your own stories. All stories need to be followed through to the bitter end: there is nothing more frustrating for a reader than to read that there will be an enquiry into some incident, only to find that no one has bothered to find out about it. Even promises made by prominent people should be recorded and followed up at some suitable date. You can also provide a diary as a useful resource for readers by using online resources like Google Calendar and Meetup (you can mark public and private diary items separately).

It is important to think through how you will cover important events before they arise. The classic case for most professional magazines is the Budget. You know that the Budget will affect your readers: it is foolhardy to wait until the details are announced before thinking about how to cover them. Better to contact your experts beforehand and discuss possibilities in advance. This is particularly important when you are dealing with events that fall on or around your press day. In extreme cases, say that of a crucial court case with a verdict due on press day, you might prepare two stories, one for guilty and one for not guilty. You can hold them, complete with headlines and even layouts, and drop in the right one when you discover the verdict. Just make sure you use the right version.

A well-kept office diary is one key to successful news gathering. Sometimes 'diary' is used as a disparaging term. So-called 'off-diary' stories, handed to you over a drink or by a social network or telephone tip-off, are more prized. But 'off-diary' calls only come from the painstaking work of building up contacts, and that means careful use of the diary. List the key people in each area of your coverage. Go back to them, regularly.

Why do people talk to journalists? On the face of it, it is likely to bring them nothing but trouble. It may be that they have some grievance, or that they like attention. More often, it is just that they like talking to you. It might make them feel a bit important, or give them a bit of excitement: you would be surprised to find that journalism is still glamorous to many people. The result is that people who are spoken to regularly, in a friendly and good-humoured fashion, rapidly turn into valuable sources who will offer you extra guidance and information.

Social networking services are particularly valuable in this respect, as they allow you to maintain closer relationships with more people than would otherwise be the case, and make it easier for people to contact you if they have useful information. You should have profiles on any social networks that your audience are likely to use so that it is as easy as possible for them to find you, and communicate as much as is possible without that being to the detriment of your job overall. But you should not treat these channels as mere platforms for you to 'broadcast' material and calls for help: followers will soon tire of a 'spammy' stream of self-promotion.

If your relationship with a source is completely secret, however, you will obviously want to avoid connecting with them publicly, and as most companies are able to monitor their employees' email you should be careful of using their professional email address too – or any service which will direct messages to their work email (ask them if they registered with the service using their professional or personal email).

Reporting is a 'people skill': it is much more important to grasp a story and be able to speak to people about it than it is to be a good writer. Your sources must, of course, trust you and your staff, which is why we go to great lengths to keep their identities secret when they ask us to. You will, of course, have your own contacts in important areas of the industry you cover so that you can get a feel for the accuracy and general appropriateness of the stories coming out of your news operation.

If you are working with inexperienced reporters, encourage them to keep their contact books up to date and safe. If they store them on a phone, make sure they are backed up (there are a number of services that do this for free).

Be wary of asking them to contact their valued sources for frivolous purposes. But there must be a general office contact book or spreadsheet listing the normal straightforward sources of information. Most magazines should acquire the so-called 'White Book', the Central Office of Information's comprehensive listing of government press officers. You will also need professional directories for the industry you are covering.

Internet skills are essential for reporters. At the very least, they need to learn:

- how to do an accurate web search, including looking for phrases and searching individual domains and sites;
- how to use news sites and news search tools;
- how to use and search newsgroups and email mailing lists;
- how to track down the creators and owners of web pages;
- how to verify online information;
- how to subscribe to podcasts and find other online audio;
- how to monitor changes in web pages automatically (such as through RSS feeds and email alerts);
- how to use online mapping tools such as Google Maps and Open Street Map – and mashup visualisation tools such as BatchGeo;
- how to use social networking tools such as Twitter and Facebook to find sources, spot leads, and exchange useful information (not just your own).

These are not terribly difficult, but depressingly few British journalists have taken the trouble to learn them. Courses are available, and there are a number of useful books and websites on the subject.

Facebook groups and mailing lists can be a useful place to find contacts and story ideas, and blogs and Twitter can be useful places to find sources too. It is possible for reporters to involve themselves in these online communities for news-gathering purposes, but they should be aware that if they attempt to hide their identities they will invariably be caught out. A British specialist publication once fell victim to a newsgroup hoax perpetrated by group members who objected to its presence. Only after it ran a prominent story based on newsgroup gossip did it discover that it had been conned. All reporters must remember that 'private' emails take on a life of their own, being passed around. Everyone who uses email should be prepared to stand by its contents should it become public.

The relationship between reporters and their sources is often rather intense, accompanied by a certain amount of self-conscious 'cloak and dagger'. This is all part of the excitement of news, and should be tolerated. Reporters should be given a fairly loose rein, providing that their absences from the office and lunches with mysterious contacts bring results. You may, however, come to feel that the source is using the reporter rather than vice versa. Beware of strings of self-interested stories pushing a particular line. In extreme cases, it is sometimes necessary to reassign the news 'patches' or 'beats', the areas that individual reporters cover.

Members of your news team should read their rivals closely, not just to see any stories they have missed (it will be too late to do anything about it) but to try to discover where those stories come from. Most experienced news editors learn how their contacts compare with the opposition's and set about putting things right.

Geographical coverage is sometimes a problem. Increasingly, even our national newspapers cover everything by telephone from the capital. But the problem is hearing about stories in the first place. Young reporters should be encouraged to leave the office. They must make contacts across the industry, but also across the country. Those 'ad-get' features provide an opportunity for your reporters to meet sources in the provinces, who will often be surprised and delighted to speak to someone in person. Of course, local paper reporters and newsdesks can sometimes be persuaded to offer you material that might suit your news agenda as well as theirs. You can also follow the activities of the regional press through their websites.

Inevitably much of your news material will come from sources in which the interesting items are deeply buried: press releases, reports by government, companies and industry bodies, transcripts of speeches, and so on. Emails from readers sometimes lead to stories, and even a magazine's own small ads should be monitored, particularly for information on people changing jobs, but also for more human stories.

You might also monitor activity on social networks: if someone changes their Facebook status to 'single', for example, and you work on the type of publication where this constitutes news, then you have a lead. Likewise if someone RSVPs to a particular event on Facebook, then you already have a head start in trying to get an interview. If there's a flurry of updates to someone's LinkedIn profile then that may indicate that they are preparing to leave their job. If they are suddenly bookmarking a series of web pages on one topic then it may indicate they are working on a project in that area. Remember that these are just leads at this stage – you need to chase up confirmation from them or another source.

There are various tools to monitor social networks. Most are free, but some particularly sophisticated ones (normally used by PR companies to monitor mentions of their clients) charge. HootSuite was originally designed to monitor Twitter but now monitors multiple sites including MySpace and LinkedIn. Booshaka and OpenBook are two that monitor public Facebook updates (you cannot monitor private ones, for obvious reasons). Some you have to manually check, but others offer RSS feeds – and most social network monitoring can be done via RSS feeds: Twitter's own search engine (search.twitter.com) offers them, for example, as does Boardreader for searches on forums, IceRocket for mentions of a particular term on blogs, and Kurrently for Facebook. Take an hour to subscribe to each of these RSS feeds in an RSS reader like Google Reader, then review them periodically to see if you need to add or remove names.

Often the task of a reporter in the professional press is to 're-angle' a story from other sources to make it relevant to a particular audience. An obvious case is the publication of honours lists, which should be combed to find awards that have gone to members of the profession in question. The same goes for lists of victims of major accidents and rich lists. Set up Google Alerts to notify you whenever the names of significant figures in your industry are mentioned online.

The main thing, though, is that all your journalistic staff, not just your reporters, need to keep their eyes and ears open. Good stories often originate in things people have seen from the bus, or overheard in the bus queue. They are certainly more likely to come from people than from handouts or web pages.

Leave your reporters to do their jobs, but with the inexperienced you should be prepared to offer guidance on reporting technique. Often this comes down to interviewing. Interviewing has two aspects: conducting the conversation, and recording what is said. To take the easy part first, news reporters must use proper notebooks rather than scrappy pieces of paper. Each book should carry their name and telephone number, in case it is lost, and each entry should be properly identified and dated. Notes should be clear and comprehensible, and should be transcribed immediately if shorthand is being used. (Teeline shorthand is not hard, and is definitely a sensible investment of time for any journalist who takes reporting seriously.)

For complex and contentious stories and long interviews, particularly on the telephone, reporters may prefer to use a digital recorder, making sure they have fresh batteries, enough recording space, and the right kind of telephone pickup if they are doing that kind of interview. Interviewing is conversation for a purpose, and people's abilities here are related to their personalities and conversational skills: it is about how well you listen, and how you respond to what you are told, as well as what you ask. But any story requires you to think about whom you need to interview, and when. Often the order in which you speak to those involved is critical. If you speak to A, will she tip off B and give him time to get his story straight?

Tell your reporters to go to the top and work down, unless they can get straight to the person who actually witnessed the events in question. Many organisations now have specific people charged with speaking to the press, which is not an unmixed blessing. These people should be told you need to speak directly to the relevant person: you don't want to waste their time running backwards and forwards with messages, since you will certainly have lots of follow-up questions. With luck they will get the hint. Otherwise, people at the top of an organisation generally have the clout to speak freely without asking anyone's permission, as well as having the appropriate information.

Encourage your reporters to establish whether people are able to talk freely. If you are ringing the office, it can be better to try to get a home number and talk to them later. Face-to-face interviews are better still, but you need to be polite, especially if you go to see people at home. Calling absurdly early in the morning or behaving in a threatening manner is not acceptable.

Encourage interviewers to work from a list of questions. This will ensure that they don't miss anything, but also, if carefully constructed, it should help them put their story together later: the quotes should follow the natural order of the story. And encourage them to shut up occasionally: a patch of silence sometimes persuades people to digress revealingly.

Your reporters will sometimes lack experience in covering court cases and tribunals, a specialist area that needs both experience and careful study of a good textbook on press law. Meetings, conferences and press conferences, however, are more of a free-for-all. In these cases, encourage them to arrive early and speak to the participants. They should establish whether there will be time for a few private questions later, or collect a telephone number. Or go along and show them how it's done: ask questions if you like, but nothing that will give your opposition an inkling of what you are up to. Competition is an essential part of news journalism – as well as being good fun and a tremendous motivator of your team.

News writing

News style is one of the dialects of journalism, a type of writing that every trained and experienced magazine journalist should know. News is a style that can be taught. It uses the facts of a story to attract readers and carry them along. It is much less reliant on literary flair than feature writing, which makes it the ideal place for inexperienced journalists to start.

News should offer both great economy and narrative drive. It should be understandable in the time it takes to read it. In other words, the reader should never have to stop and puzzle out construction or vocabulary. At its worst, though, news writing can degenerate into a series of clichés.

Like the design of news pages, news writing evolved for functional reasons. The object is to grab people's attention, give them the key points as quickly as possible and then supply the rest of the information they need in order of importance. Some versions of news history trace this back to the American Civil War, when the telegram lines were often cut while the correspondents were still sending their battle reports. They might only have sent the moving introductory preamble, leaving the editors in New York unaware of the really important thing: who won. From then on, they were encouraged to start with the important facts first (the story is largely apocryphal, but illustrative). Writing news in this way helps copy editors to 'cut from the bottom' without losing anything vital. More importantly, though, it reflects a fact of life, which is that few readers make it all the way through a story. Give them the gist of the thing first, then make sure what follows is fair and accurate.

If you are employing people without journalistic training, this is a concept they will find difficult to grasp, especially if they have been in the habit of writing college essays that demand an introduction, several discrete points and a conclusion. News writing is not like that.

The key to a news story is the introduction, or 'intro' as it is invariably known. It must grab the attention, but it must do so by conveying the essential point of the story. Even experienced reporters sometimes find themselves taking as long over the intro as they do over the rest of the story, only for it to be rewritten by the sub-editors. If your news writers are struggling, suggest they write the story first, using a working intro, and then come back to it at the end. Quite often they will find the first par can be chopped entirely.

The problem is always the same: you have to get the 'gist' of the story into the first paragraph. But if it is a complex story, you are in danger of running out of words: no news intro should go much beyond about 25 words. Various techniques have been devised to achieve the necessary compression. They include 'the inverted pyramid'; 'five Ws and an H'; 'the telegram'; and 'the key word'.

Journalism textbooks, particularly American ones, are particularly keen on the inverted pyramid. But all it tells us is that the weight of a story, the important elements, should be at the top, followed by less important material. This is helpful advice about the shape of a news story, but does not assist in the creation of an intro.

The 'five Ws and an H' will be familiar to literary types as Kipling's 'six honest serving men' from the *Just So Stories*. They are, obviously, 'Who? What? When? Where? Why? and How?' All those questions must be answered in the story. Some say they should all be answered in the intro, but that is wrong. Such an intro would be terribly confused, as well as making the subsequent news story virtually redundant. But it does work when you are writing 'briefs' or 'nibs' (from 'news in brief') where you must sum up the whole story in compressed form.

A more useful way of looking at the five Ws is that they offer five ways to angle an intro. Say you have a story about building workers blockading a site in the City of London. Who? 'Angry builders ...'. What? 'Work on the new Barcloyds Bank ...'. Where? 'The City of London came to a standstill ...'. When? 'At first light this morning, angry ...'. Why? 'The accidental death of a colleague drove ...'. How? 'Using their excavators as barricades ...'. Some of these work better than others, but they are all possible. If you get stuck, run through them and see if you can't find something that works.

Harold Evans, in *Essential English for Journalists, Writers and Editors*, has a good suggestion to help find the key points for your intro. He suggests writing it first as a kind of telegram, then fleshing that out to produce something literate. So our builders story could be reduced to 'Builders paralyse City in site death protest'. Fill in the missing words with real grammar and detail and you are getting somewhere near a real intro: 'Building workers paralysed the City of London on Tuesday morning this week in protests over the death of a scaffolder.'

Evans also suggests finding a key word or phrase and making that the core of the intro. Is there a word that sums it up? Here it might be 'paralysed'.

This approach forces you to make a decision about what is important. An intro really needs one idea, and one idea only. Often stories lead in several directions at once. If you discover that a company is opening a new factory in a depressed area which will create 2,000 jobs to build a product that safety experts say should be withdrawn from sale following worries about its safety, you can only write a sensible intro by deciding which of those things is more important to your readers.

Usually your intro should explain to your readers why it is relevant to them. For local paper readers, the fact that the story takes place in their town is enough. For the editor of a professional journal or specialist consumer magazine, the relevant detail may be the fact that the story concerns an architect or a company that produces replacement exhaust systems. Test your intro by writing a heading from it. If you can't do it, something essential has been omitted.

Not all intros give everything away at the start. One of the characteristics of a good story is the element of surprise, often signalled by the use of a dash. 'Computer manufacturer Smallbits is to cut 3,000 jobs – despite having its best year ever.' There is also an old journalistic tradition called the 'delayed drop', or the 'slow burn', in which the point of the story is held back as long as you dare. It can make a change from the routine, but its use should be sparing.

If you like this sort of thing, look at the *Daily Mail*, where an inordinate number of stories tell us that 'It was a day like any other for Mildred Jones', only to reveal seven paragraphs later that she has been elected president of MENSA or found garrotted by her own dog-lead.

This story-telling approach works better in features, even news features, than it does in news. But the straightforward news intro can become terribly repetitive. In supervising news pages, you need to ensure that there is variety, otherwise you are going to lose your readers. In particular, most news sections ought to have one or more lighter stories, signalled by a more imaginative type of intro.

Once you have your intro, the rest of the story should follow, filling in who did what, when, where, why and how. Most of your stories are likely to be accounts of things people have said or written. Reporters need to evaluate the importance of the speech or report's content to your readers. The most important point becomes the intro, and depending upon its strength it may need to be developed immediately and anchored in direct quotation. Any other relevant points follow on.

The eventual shape of this kind of story might be something like this:

- (Para 1) INTRO (the gist, but not the whole story)
- (Paras 2–3) EXPAND AND EXPLAIN (filling in the bits that the intro omits)
- (Paras 4–6) POINT ONE of speech/report + direct quote
- (Paras 7–9) POINT TWO + direct quote
- (Paras 10–12) POINT THREE + direct quote
- (Remaining paras) REACTION + quote from opponent + BACKGROUND (other information of interest). The Reaction paragraph or paragraphs represent the 'balance' in the story.

Sometimes the reaction will be so strong, and so important, that you will want to place it nearer the start of the story. Like this: INTRO EXPAND + EXPLAIN REACTION (in summary) POINT ONE + quote POINT TWO + quote REACTION (in more detail) + quote and so on. Background that is essential to understand the story really needs to be higher up, probably in the Expand and Explain area:

> Troubled hardware giant Smallbits has recalled the entire production run of its latest server, following reports of overheating. This is the third serious hardware problem the company has experienced.

Stories about events are different. You need to get the most dramatic or important points across first, concentrating on their human impact, and you need to explain why they are relevant to your readers. But after that you may turn to a chronological treatment. Human beings like narrative, and a passage that tells them 'the story began when …' is one of the few occasions when chronological writing appears in news. After that comes reaction and background as usual, perhaps relating this incident to similar events in the past or elsewhere: INTRO EXPAND + EXPLAIN, INCLUDING RELEVANCE/CONTEXT THE DRAMA BEGAN WHEN … WITNESS ONE + quote and so on.

Quotes are important in news stories but should be used for a purpose. They are too often incomprehensible, flabby or dull. Straight exposition or reported speech ('The director of Smallbits denied that there was a problem …') often does a better job of getting the story across quickly and plainly. But you do need quotes to show that you have spoken to someone about the story, preferably someone who has seen the events or knows the issue and thus gives the story authority.

This is why quotes should be attributed to named individuals. But it helps if they are also vivid or controversial. You should also use them when you want to indicate precisely what someone said, for instance when the story concerns a particular insult or promise. Too many stories these days use 'quotes' that were never actually spoken. These are taken from press releases or written statements.

They look like quotes, typographically, but they have often been composed by groups of people and designed to be self-interested and bland. Make your writers quote people they have actually spoken to. Email quoting, unless unavoidable, is a bad idea for the same reason.

It is also easier for interviewees to put off responding to an email, whereas a phonecall is more likely to be taken, and an appointment kept. These also help build closer relationships with contacts. Email should be a last resort, and should still be chased with phonecalls.

If your writers are speaking to people and still coming up with dull quotes, the problem is in their interviewing. They have to chat to people, in a relaxed way, and if those people are dull or monosyllabic they must coax or needle them into saying something more interesting.

Remember, too, that you are under a general obligation to get all sides of the story. If someone is mentioned, they ought to be asked to give their side, and their response to an accusation should not necessarily be left to the final paragraph, where it is in danger of being chopped in the sub-editing process.

The most comprehensive accounts of news writing come in Evans's book and Winford Hicks's *Writing for Journalists*. You might also enjoy Richard Keeble's *The Newspapers Handbook*, which has a useful discussion of the whole subject.

Features

When we think of magazine writing, we are not usually thinking of news but features. In magazines, the word features covers a vast range of material, from interviews with celebrities or the leaders of giant industrial concerns, to advice and instruction.

News provides chunks of useful information to your readership, but features appeal to their wider interests and aspirations. There must be a balance. You must cater for the range of your readership with different approaches: straight information, inspiration, education, amusement, provocation, and so on. It is a mistake to fill your magazine with identical interviews or instructional features, and then to rely on design to differentiate between them. A classic magazine feature is a single entity, a words/design/pictures package that has to be planned as such from the outset.

One obvious starting point is the 'news feature'. This can't simply be a news story that has overrun. It needs to be considered from the beginning as a feature based on a topical incident or issue. News features explore their subject matter at greater length than simple stories, and they include more analysis, explanation, colour and background. They do not need the punchy intro of a news story, starting instead with scene setting, a key detail or an argumentative statement. Even so, their news point needs to be established early on. News features allow writers to explore a wider tonal range than simple news stories. Subjectivity, for instance, may be permissible. But because they involve detailed knowledge and topicality, they are really part of the reporter's job.

More elaborate features may take more skill. There is, unfortunately, no simple pattern to follow. Most people learn to write features by trial and error or by emulation. The starting point is an idea, which may be yours, or the writer's, or may arise in a meeting. Opinions vary about the value of ideas, as such, as opposed to their expression: often the best features come from no very promising start. But nothing should be wasted. Your writers should be encouraged to keep lists of ideas, along with the relevant bits of cutting that sometimes give rise to them.

When an idea presents itself, it is important to work it up into some kind of brief or proposal, if only for the writer's own benefit. Narrow ideas, which crystallise themselves in a single encounter or incident or place, are often better than those which try to cover some huge and amorphous subject and fall short. 'I want to write about global warming' excites nobody. 'I want to write about a small community which is having to move 200 miles because of global warming' is specific, new, and much richer for it.It is good to discuss a proposed feature before the planning and research goes very far, if only to weed out the obvious and the over-familiar.

You need to brief writers, and it is good practice to do this on paper if only to concentrate your own thoughts. Briefs presented to writers range from the airy 'give us one of your usuals, about 1,500 words, by Friday week' to detailed specifications laying down precisely who should be spoken to and what questions they should be asked.

Too many commissioning editors work on the basis that they already have the perfect feature in their minds. Then they send someone else out to flesh out the idea. The commissioning letter becomes a series of questions to which the writer supplies the answers. This may make sense with inexperienced writers, but it makes for predictable and clumsy features. Writers need to find their own story, their own narrative and argument. Responding to such a brief leads to features without logic or drama.

There is, however, more of an argument for this kind of commissioning in the case of informational articles for the specialist consumer and business press. Here the brief needs to be precise to ensure the important questions are addressed. All briefs must include such details as the delivery date, length and fee. It even makes sense for in-house features, though you might save a bit of your time by getting writers to give you a couple of sentences explaining how they plan to cover each feature. They won't thank you for this chore, but if they are honest they will admit that it can help them to focus on what exactly they are doing with the piece.

Feature planning

The starting point for planning a magazine's features is the editorial diary. A high proportion will be 'date-tied' or 'pegged' to some external event, either as specific as a company's annual results or the release of a film, or as general as Christmas. The key to running a features desk is time: there is a right time for any feature, and if you wait until an event has happened and then try to respond you will usually be too late.

In the case of a company profile intended to tie in with someone's annual results, you have to have approached the company, made any necessary visits and conducted interviews well in advance. You will very often need to carry out any photography at the same time. Your profile can then run at the same time as the results are released: as long as the general tenor of your piece is appropriate they need not be mentioned in it, taking their rightful place on a news page instead.

Editors always want to be first. But this is not something that much concerns the readers, many of whom will buy your title out of general enthusiasm rather than an interest in any particular subject matter. (You can, in fact, increase your readership slightly by carrying unexpected features from time to time, attracting new readers without dissuading the regulars.) But you must not become complacent. Don't put a tired old subject on your cover: as you get further away from being first, so the size and prominence of your coverage should shrink.

This causes difficulties in the case of celebrity and arts material, where everything you do, including your timing, is not a matter of journalistic flair but of negotiation. Securing most film or music interviews will mean revealing when you propose to publish, which is extremely unwelcome. The PR companies involved have their own agenda. They will be manipulating the coverage to ensure that it appears at the most suitable time for them, and they will also have struck deals with other publications about timing. You can mislead them and publish when it suits you, but you should expect repercussions. This kind of bluff and double-bluff, coupled with hurt phone calls from the PR people concerned, becomes exhausting. In any case, it is not uncommon for editors to be expected to sign 'binding' undertakings. These may not be legally enforceable, but they have a certain moral force.

The celebrity interview area is increasingly problematic. Even the highest profile newspaper supplements are faced with extraordinary demands by studios, record companies, PR companies and their clients. Often they will attempt to specify the writer, the photographer, the size of the eventual piece and its prominence. You should resist this, but if celebrities constitute the cornerstone of your feature coverage, you will usually have to live with it.

Unfortunately, this creeping disease is spreading to other areas which have fallen in thrall to professional PR people. The word 'no' often comes in useful, and steering a more unique course that serves your readers rather than the PR agencies can be both more satisfying and more successful – depending on your market.

Few interviews or product previews are so essential that they are worth surrendering your right to make editorial decisions. Obviously freelance writers are at liberty to make individual arrangements, but you should ensure that nothing has been agreed that will bind you. Celebrity writers – if they are allowed – may also expect to sell their material to several customers. You should ensure that you get the first instalment. If you fix the interview and then choose a writer, you can set the rules. Some interviewees are sensitive about where they want interview material to appear, and you must be able to assure them that your writers are working for you alone: that may give you a little bargaining power.

The most irksome aspect is probably 'copy-approval', whereby celebrities and their agents demand the right to edit what is written about them before it appears in your magazine. This is a serious intrusion into your affairs. It turns every magazine into vanity publishing. And yet it is on the rise, and not only in cases involving the giants of the entertainment industry. In March 2002, the

Press Gazette reported that show-business freelance Garth Pearce had been asked to sign a pre-interview contract with 'former All Saints singer Shaznay Lewis', whom he was interviewing for the *Sunday Times Culture* magazine. She wanted to restrict his reuse of the material and demanded copy-approval. He refused, and the interview went ahead. He subsequently found that both the *Observer* and the *Sunday Telegraph* had signed the agreement, although the *Sunday Telegraph* magazine had crossed out the copy-approval clause. The *Observer* magazine signed it, but said it planned to disregard it. It would have been better not to have signed in the first place.

In some areas it is widespread. Simon Caney, editor of free magazine *Sport*, told *Press Gazette* in 2008:[5] 'With footballers [copy approval] is almost unanimous, everybody wants to have copy approval. A lot of them want to see the questions beforehand. But what we say is, you can approve the copy but if you change it and it detracts from the feature, we just won't run it.'

While Caney appears to be happy for editorial interference the line is, interestingly, drawn at commercial interference. The interview notes that: 'One England football star failed to grace the pages of *Sport* after the player's agent tried to dictate what advertising could run in the issue.'

Luckily, much of your feature material will come about through your own ingenuity and that of your writers. All your staff should keep ideas files, and you should constantly be aware of the possibilities for turning simple news items, even one-paragraph briefs, into features. You should also feel no shame about borrowing other people's ideas and adapting them: they will do it to you. Of course, this does not mean copying your rivals, although it is worth studying their features to see how they came about and how well they have been put together. It is better to take inspiration from different fields and markets and adapt them to your own purposes – whenever you're at a train station pick up a few magazines and look at their ideas. In your routine meetings, allow room for free-ranging features discussions. Sometimes a hackneyed idea picked up from another magazine can be transformed into something quite original.

This is particularly important when it comes to the great annual landmarks in the world your magazine covers. Some of these will be specific to your particular topic – the start of the season, the beginning of term – but many will be more general. The obvious example is Christmas, which most magazines will feel some obligation to celebrate. There is a terrible tendency to look at what was done last year and reproduce it, but each time you do this some of the original inspiration has ebbed away. Better to start early and come up with new ideas.

Scheduled features

There is another aspect to features work, and that is the creation of a features schedule designed to be publicised as a lure to advertisers. The schedule should be drawn up in conjunction with the advertising department, since there is no point in programming a series of 'ad-get' features for which there will be no advertising support.

But this is not an area in which you can abdicate editorial responsibility. These features must be planned, commissioned, edited and presented to the best of your ability and must meet the standards of the rest of your magazine. Within the broad headings listed in the features schedule, there is room for considerable ingenuity and editorial flair. They can also serve as a useful area in which to try out inexperienced staff and new freelances before you give them some more prominent commission. But they must remain true editorial products. You should not, for instance, allow the advertising department to commission and edit them.

Instructional features

Instructional features, whether knitting patterns, recipes, advice on chord structures or notes on dealing with tax, present a problem. Despite their unglamorous image, they demand high standards of commissioning and editing. The task must be 'do-able' and within a time-scale that is meaningful for the magazine: a weekly is ill-advised to carry constructional projects that take a month to put together. Projects that demand deep pre-existing knowledge and skill should be avoided, as should those with hidden costs and dangers. It is essential that writers giving the instructions have done the task and can show that it has worked.

The instructions themselves need to be perfectly clear, and all quantities, temperatures and other numbers need to be checked back against original copy and with the author. Common sense should provide a further line of defence against absurdities, especially in cookery. If you are producing large numbers of magazines, and you are trying to establish an atmosphere of genuine communication with your readers, you cannot afford to ruin their dinner parties or Sunday tea.

These sorts of features tend to prove particularly appealing on the web, where people often go to ask 'How …?' questions. They also suit the platform editorially: think about how the following might add to the piece or to your instructional feature offering generally:

- multimedia (e.g. video, audio, animation, maps, galleries);
- databases (e.g. of similar recipes, patterns, etc.);
- tools (e.g. converters that change pounds to ounces and vice versa).

Make sure to provide space for reader communication around the online feature, too, via comments, forums or chats – as this is where users can exchange corrections, tips and improvements to the original.

Other features

The classic magazine feature consists of a single continuous narrative illustrated by photographs. Increasingly, however, even a straightforward narrative feature will now be accompanied by boxes and panels.

Then there are other types of feature altogether. Picture features are common. A picture essay by a single photographer can be an appealing way of dealing with a hackneyed subject. If an appropriate fee is agreed it need not be more expensive than filling the equivalent space with words.

Graphic-based features are worth trying, but they need careful research and design. Anything that involves grading or testing a large number of subjects is often better dealt with by some kind of graphical grid or chart than it is in words. With the increasingly visual nature of communication, it is worth asking yourself if an idea can be conveyed visually, either as an accompaniment to a traditional feature or as a replacement for it. These treatments – including infographics – obviously need a skilled designer.

Interviews and profiles

Interviews of various kinds will provide a great deal of the feature material for many magazines. Most features involve interviews, often to provide evidence on either side of an argument. But here we are discussing features that are entirely based on a single personality.

An interview needs as much preparation as any other feature. If you have specific points you want raised, or issues covered, tell the interviewer. Interviewers must do enough research to ensure that their questions are intelligent and to the point. Reference books and directories should allow them to establish the basic facts of people's lives and careers so that they don't have to waste precious interview time on uncontroversial matters. Your writers must also look at cuttings, but they should not incorporate unchecked quotes and anecdotes into their features. If there is any incident that they find particularly revealing, it should be brought up in the interview and the interviewee given the chance to confirm or deny it.

Most interviewers will use an audio recorder, although the inexperienced should be reminded of the necessity to use new batteries and to find a quiet place to conduct the conversation: this can make all the difference when it comes to transcribing. Recording an interview allows journalists to have a natural conversation with their interviewees, listening to the answers and responding to them rather than simply writing them down, although it is worth making notes as you go – not just of what the interviewee says (and when – look at the time elapsed on the recorder), and their expression when they say it (which cannot be recorded on audio) but what questions you might want to follow up with when they finish. It also allows them to bring back plenty of material beyond the words: the interviewee's appearance, dress, manner, body language, and so on, and the setting for the meeting.

Often these are what brings the interview alive, giving it a sense of immediacy. If you don't want that sort of interview, you should make that clear to the writer at the outset. You may only have a telephone interview, of course, but you don't have to announce that in your piece. The tone of voice should still come across. Some telephone interviewers invent the details of the setting and the interviewee's clothes and mannerisms. Ingenious, but an abuse of the reader's trust.

Experienced interviewees, particularly 'celebrities', often become predictable in their responses. It is not uncommon to see the same phrases in several interviews done in the same period. More interesting questions might help, although people with something to promote will tend to use any question as an opportunity to repeat their prepared answers.

If your interviewee is likely to be jaded and workmanlike though being repeatedly interviewed, think of ways to take them off the 'factory line' – interview them in an unusual location or situation, 'eavesdrop' on the person at work, or attend some event. Get a sense of how the person reacts to other people, and different situations. This will make for more interesting material and a more memorable relationship.

A profile can mean several different things. It can be a simple interview, even of the 'Q&A' or questionnaire variety. More often it means a more elaborate interview, supported by comments from colleagues, family and friends of the interviewee, including extensive details on his or her family or professional background, domestic circumstances, and so on. This is a major undertaking that should only be done by a skilled journalist who will be given appropriate time and support.

It can also mean an analytical article, or character sketch, of a person written without the benefit of an interview. Such pieces are often disparaged as a 'cuttings job', thanks to the source of much of the material, but this is too negative. A good profile is often more revealing than an interview. It can have more attitude, more of an argument, which means it is not necessarily either quicker or easier than an interview. It should be seen as a different approach, not an inferior one, part of the palette of colours available to the editor. Nonetheless, readers tend to prefer a new and exclusive interview to even the most erudite of profiles. An interview is also valuable as a 'property', something you can sell on your cover and in your cover-lines.

It has become common for magazines, particularly in the women's weekly sector, to pay people to be interviewed if they have startling stories to tell. This is understandable, given the intensity of competition in that market, where magazines are also competing with tabloid newspapers and daytime television. But it is a nuisance for everyone else.

If you are paying for stories, however, such payments must be covered by an appropriate contract to secure their exclusivity. A person must agree both to provide you with appropriate interview and photographic opportunities (also, in some cases, filming for the website) and to refrain from being interviewed or photographed by anyone else until after the appearance of your magazine's article. You may also want to ask them to write a few blog posts for the website to coincide with publication, or to take part in a live chat.

Part of the payment should be withheld until publication to encourage compliance. Unfortunately, once you are dealing with people who will sell their stories, you can always be outbid. The fact that you have signed a contract with someone simply means that their price increases: the rival publisher must build in a sum to pay your compensation for breach of contract.

Achieving that, however, can only be done by the threat of legal action, which is unlikely to prove cost effective and may prove damaging to your image, especially if you are having to contemplate action against people whose story involves some tragedy. The act of 'buying up' someone's story should not be seen as the end of the negotiation: you must continue to convince them of the non-financial merits of telling the story to you and no one else.

Feature writing

Unlike news writing, where there is effectively a standard approach, feature writing offers great scope for creativity and ingenuity. It is not always necessary to be distant and objective. The word 'I' is even permitted, and the writer is allowed to be a participant in the story, although this should not be overdone. There is no agreed form for an intro.

All this can make feature writing rather bewildering for the inexperienced and difficult to direct. It is certainly important for editors not to impose any kind of uniformity. You need people to try different approaches so that you have a range of styles and treatments to choose from when you are creating the editorial mix.

Research will often help feature writers through their material: they will have discovered the key points, the crucial incidents, the most relevant quotes. Now they need to be persuaded to put those things in some kind of order before they start writing. They will always need to think hard about construction. Many experienced and skilful feature writers still draw up some kind of point-by-point 'essay plan' before they begin. At its crudest, this can turn a piece into a series of points, each matched with a quote to illustrate it. But it helps the writer to keep to the argument, and to decide on the correct order for the material.

Any feature needs a shape, whether that is telling a story chronologically, starting with general principles and moving down to a specific example, or starting with an individual case and drawing a broader lesson from it. Most people find the last version is the most effective: an opening section dealing in detail with a particular incident or individual will always have more appeal than generalities. By the time the feature is finished and polished, this scaffolding should be invisible. But it will have given the feature great underlying strength.

An arresting opening is as important for a feature as it is for a news story. The difference is that a feature will usually be presented on the page with a separate introductory paragraph (a 'standfirst' or 'sell') written by the sub-editors. This will usually explain who is being interviewed and why, or why a particular issue is topical, or what the story is actually about. That leaves the writer free to start with something bold that sets the tone.

One useful idea, particularly in narrative features, is to start in the middle, at a point of great drama: when you, the writer, fall off the raft and into the churning waters of the Colorado River rather than when you get a call from the travel company asking you if you'd like the trip. The same kind of thing can work in interviews: you start with the question that made your interviewee lose his or her temper, rather than with the one that happens to come first on your tape.

For those who are interested, this approach is called *in media res*, meaning 'in the middle of things', and was first identified by the Roman poet Horace, who detected it in the works of Homer.

In both these cases, you may need to double-back on yourself to tell the story from the beginning. You only want to do that once, returning immediately to a straightforward chronological sequence. But you will have grabbed your readers' attention, and you should have a greater chance of taking your readers with you than if you creep up on the subject by telling them about your difficulties in fixing up the interview or your adventures at Heathrow while you were waiting for your plane.

Some people habitually put their best quote at the beginning, but that is not always a good practice. Starting with a quote creates a number of problems. It is an irritant to readers to hear someone's voice before they know who is speaking. And if your design calls for features to start with a 'drop cap', starting with an open quotation mark (or omitting it, which is often done for design purposes) is never satisfactory. Besides, it is not advisable to make the rest of your piece an anticlimax.

Consider whether anything in the piece would work better as a graphic or diagram – or online animation – than as a piece of prose. And individual elements in a story that can be separated out – long digressions, interviews, explanatory passages, definitions of key terms, passages of historical background – should often be presented as separate panels. These must be discussed with your designers, preferably at an early stage in the feature-planning process.

If you do break away from continuous narrative, you must ensure that the reader can still navigate through your feature. There is a particular problem with tenses. You may wish to make use of the 'historic present', for its immediacy: 'It is 3am in Cheltenham, and the narrow Georgian streets are throbbing with the sound of powerful car exhausts.' But you may then have to switch to a straightforward narrative. 'Cheltenham's problem with the cruising fraternity began ...'. This needs careful handling. You can't keep switching backwards and forwards.

Features, unlike news stories, are not designed to be cut from the bottom. Writers need to spread their insights throughout the piece, to keep the reader intrigued, rather than throwing them all at the reader in the opening. And features need a satisfying ending: a conclusion, a powerful quote or a reference back to the introduction (sometimes your ending can help you construct an intro, or vice versa). The sub-editors must leave this alone, which makes cutting features tricky.

Stylish writing deserves to be indulged, but features must still comply with the basics. Feature writers must understand the need for their stories to make sense, to be fair and accurate, for names to be spelt correctly and facts to be checked.

Learning to write features is often just a case of doing it and reading the efforts of masters in the field. You can help inexperienced feature writers by the quality of your briefing and by talking the brief through with them. Writers get better with practice, and there is nothing more rewarding for an editor than to recognise and nurture a new talent.

Writing for the web

While news articles and features are regularly published on the web in the same format as they were written for print, this is no more ideal than printing radio scripts. The web is a different medium, consumed in different ways and with different qualities.

One of its core features, for example, is the link: an online article without links is poor online journalism. You should ensure that all material published online links to places where the user can find further information on any key concepts, people, organisations, or documents. If this information is on your site, all the better, but do not hold back from linking because it is on someone else's site: links are part of the quality of your journalism; users will come back for more if they are good.

More broadly, a good mnemonic to remember in writing for the web is BASIC: Brevity, Adaptability, Scannability, Interactivity and Community and Conversation.

Put simply:

- Keep paragraphs and multimedia short (the BBC's news website is an exemplar of how to do this).
- Be adaptable in the medium that you use to tell the story – video, audio, maps or photos might work better than traditional text.
- Use subheadings, bullet lists and other features to break text up into scannable 'chunks'.
- Think of ways to allow the user to do things with your content too, for example exploring it in their own way.
- And think of ways to allow users to communicate with each other around your content.

The regulars

A large proportion of your magazine's content is intended to be reassuringly similar from week to week or month to month. These elements, called the 'regular features' or the 'departments', are extremely important to the magazine's appeal. New editors tend to neglect them, concentrating on the more noticeable elements first. But research shows that the regulars are often as well read as the features, with columnists and readers' letters getting a particularly high score. You must find the time to look at each of these elements and ask if it is performing well.

The editor's letter

Many editors find the 'editor's letter' (or 'leader' or 'editorial') a chore. This is a shame. It provides you with an opportunity to communicate directly with your readers. One obvious use is to draw attention to parts of the issue which might otherwise go unnoticed. Some editors go beyond that, using it to draw their readers into a relationship with themselves and their staff. Certainly it is a good place to announce awards that have been won, major redesigns, new sections on the way, and so on. It is worth switching between all the above from month to month to maintain interest in the editorial (both that of readers and your own).

Press Gazette columnist Janice Turner lists six functions of the editor's letter: The Meet and Greet (which rounds up that week's contents); The Friend of the Stars (name-dropping celebrities they have met that week); The People's Editor (the just-like-you diary of their personal life); The Product Placement (this is what you ought to be buying this month, at least according to our advertising department); The Spokes-editor (launchpad for a campaign); and The Attack Dog (picking fights with editors of other magazines). You could of course alternate between them depending on your mood.

In the business press, particularly, the 'letter' becomes a true 'leader column' and plays a different role, allowing you to comment on the state of the industry, and specifically to point out and uphold the interests of your readers. All your coverage should demonstrate that you are 'on the same side' as your readers. But the leader column is where you say that, explicitly, and where you offer your considered thoughts on the development of the profession and the world it inhabits. This is vital to establish common cause between the magazine and those who read it, although on occasion you may need to play the part of the 'candid friend' and offer well-grounded criticism.

At the very least, the editor's letter should stimulate correspondence for your letters page. Increasingly, editors are expected to maintain blogs along the same lines – doing so also makes the editor's letter easier to write.

Readers' letters

It is a common belief among journalists that only lunatics and the very stupid write to letters pages. The great American editor H.L. Mencken put it like this:

> The volume of mail that comes in to a magazine or a newspaper or a radio station is no index of anything, except that you happen to attract a lot of idiots, because most people who write letters to newspapers are fools. Intelligent people seldom do it – they do it sometimes, but not often.[6]

It's not true, of course, but your own letters page may perhaps have too much correspondence from readers with axes to grind, complaints, and nothing to say but a burning desire to appear in print.

If this is the case, it is your own fault. Readers' letters are copy like any other, and need to be edited. It is not enough to stand aside and let material dribble in. Contributions need to be edited so that they make sense, cut to enhance their impact and placed in order of interest. And give each letter an appealing headline. Letters which demand a direct answer from you or your staff should be answered on the page, but this can go too far. You should not allow letters to be used as a starting point for the exercise of sarcasm.

But it is worth asking people to write letters on occasions. If you are a professional journal, you need the leaders of the profession to use your letters page as a forum for debate. If they are criticised (make sure such criticism does not slip over into defamation) they should be told about it and invited to respond. A letters page which boasts contributions from important names in your field will become a fashionable place to appear. You'll get plenty of letters and enhance the authority of your journal. And if the supply of letters increases, the quality will rise. To this end, remove merely informational letters, requests for assistance, form letters, and so on, and find somewhere else for them.

'Letters' of course now rarely come on paper – they arrive via email and through comments on your website and blogs. You should also monitor blog posts written by other people that comment on what you have written (most blog systems will alert you to this via a 'pingback' email, while you should also be using an 'analytics' package which will list other web pages from which visitors arrive). Sometimes these 'letters' are quoted separately in an 'On the Blogs' section. Likewise you might present a sample of Twitter opinion in a 'Twitter Talk' column, and so on. You should have a strategy for attracting comments and pay attention to the issues which generate the most debate on your site and others that link to it.

Columns

Columnists are part of the same communication process as a lively letters page. Find columnists who will enhance your magazine's reputation. They may be authoritative figures from your industry, or good writers with strong views and a good turn of phrase. Ideally, they would be both. Blogs are a good place to find potential columnists – but remember that blogs are not columns and a blogger may need help adapting their style for print, and meeting the deadlines and word limits that columns require (the same, of course, applies to columnists who you might ask to write a blog).

They must be reliable and self-sustaining. There is nothing more dispiriting than a columnist who has to be told what to write every week. But you must not let columnists feel they are working in a vacuum. A courtesy call to ask what they are writing about, to praise a previous effort, or to suggest a thought, will usually be appreciated.

Columnists hired to be funny need only do that: it's hard enough. Humour is very subjective, of course, and what amuses you may not have the same effect on your colleagues. But this is a case where rank has its privileges, and if you find something funny you should stick with it. Your columnist should be answerable only to you: it is impossible to be funny for a committee. Nor does a humour column benefit from subbing. If a piece doesn't fit, it can be cut, but only by removing whole chunks and not by delicate trimming. Clipping a word here and a phrase there is liable to destroy the delicate rhythm on which jokes depend. Humourists should also be exempt from house style. Some things are best left alone.

Columnists are not obliged to be objective, but their material must be read carefully for legal reasons. The law defends strong opinions honestly held, but only if they are based on the accurate statement of facts. Libel juries are perfectly capable of detecting that something is a joke, but they may also feel someone should be compensated for having such a thing said about them.

Diary columns

All publications need a little humour, and many, especially in the business press, do it through the diary column. Sometimes this is little more than a notice board of events and causes, mentioning a retirement here and a charity ball there. More often, however, it attempts to become a kind of gossip column. But there are a number of problems with that idea. Suitable gossip is rarely available. When it does become available, it is not usable, principally because your readers do not expect to see their peers written about in that way.

If you do run genuine gossip, you can expect outrage from those written about, leading to all manner of threats from withdrawn advertising to a libel writ. In the end, your hapless diarist will be reduced to looking for amusing misprints. In any case, readers sometimes enjoy these columns less than those writing them.

Nonetheless, a good diary column does serve a purpose. If it is filled with events it gives a strong sense of the magazine being active within the world it covers. It also makes a good place to store reports of good works, promotions, awards and the kind of positive, semi-promotional information that doesn't make it into the news section. Local newspapers have a policy of photographing as many people as possible, especially groups of children, on the grounds that their doting relatives will buy copies. Something similar can be achieved with magazine diary columns.

The gossip element can still be there, if you have someone capable of researching it thoroughly and writing it up with a light and inoffensive touch, respecting both taste and the law. Such writers are hard to find. You should certainly not expect to challenge *Private Eye*.

The contents page

A magazine's contents page is as much about design as writing. It should be considered as a selling device for the content, an extension of the billboard or the cover-lines. The object is to present the material in the most appealing light, while at the same time providing basic information for those who use the page to find things. Research suggests that they are a small proportion of the total readership, but you should not frustrate them.

Most magazines give most of their pages over to regular features of one sort or another, but to use the bulk of the space on the contents page (or pages) simply to list them is a waste of a valuable selling pitch. So your design needs to accommodate some way of dividing off those 'regulars' from everything else, and listing them simply by page title and number. If there is something extraordinary in those pages, there is no reason why it shouldn't be listed twice, in the 'regulars' section and in the main listing of features contents. It may suit you to break your long list of contents into many different sections, but you should be wary of simply using those divisions if they have no meaning for the reader. A heading saying 'Features', for instance, is meaningless to most people who will read your magazine, whereas 'Road Tests' or 'Health' over a group of features will make sense. Increasingly magazines are also explicitly highlighting those stories that are on the front cover.

The emphasis should be on the straightforward 'sell'. Where strong pictures are available, they should do most of the talking. Alongside, above or beneath the relevant picture should be the heading from the piece (providing it is not too obscure) and a brief, positive outline of its contents. Using different headings on the contents page and on the actual feature is to be avoided, simply because readers have to know they've arrived at the right place. But if you must, you must: it is essential for the casual reader of the contents page to know exactly who is being interviewed. Above all, keep contents page blurbs to one short sentence and keep the type size high.

People pages

Most magazines will have some sort of 'people' page or section, either a list of professional moves, as in most business-to-business magazines, or the short interviews that are common in consumer publications. For the latter it is important to try new approaches. There are many ways of writing and illustrating interview material and they should all be used to avoid making the material too 'samey'. 'Q&A' format interviews, 'as told to' first-person interviews and questionnaires can alternate with normal feature-type interviews. The same section might usefully accommodate quotes of the week, gossip, and so on. It is a useful place to introduce new faces, stories and personalities into your magazine. It can also be a good place to allow new feature writers and editors to practise their skills.

Products

Most magazines will have some sort of 'products page'; some, often known as 'product books', consist of little else. The degree of editorial input required will vary. Some product pages will amount to no more than press releases sub-edited to fit, with the more outrageous claims removed. Others will involve detailed tests and ratings for the objects described: this has been a successful formula for *Which?* magazine.

The common denominator is accuracy. Any information must be accurate, and this is particularly the case with telephone numbers and prices, which must be checked as near to publication as is feasible.

Comparative testing of equipment is an expensive and complex process, but it may be right for your market. Computer and hi-fi magazines are constructed around such tests, both objective and subjective, and go to considerable lengths to ensure their credibility. In particular, you should be aware of all the commercial relationships of your testers. It is not unheard of for the reviewers of hi-fi equipment to be involved with manufacturers as design consultants, publicity advisers or simply brochure writers. Those who take this kind of work must declare it to you and, if appropriate, to the readers. Unexpected exposure of such links can be very damaging.

More informal comparisons, without pretensions to true objectivity, are appropriate for less technical products, from household appliances to foods, but they still require fairness from the writer and skilled editing. Like must always be compared with like: a simple printed form may be the best way of ensuring that the same points are addressed when each object is examined, and if more than one tester is involved this becomes essential. The results need not be presented as a table, but the use of a printed form ensures that the underlying structure is solid. An online alternative such as a Google Form generated from a spreadsheet can allow you to store the results in a format that allows you to easily find top and bottom values, calculate averages, and so on.

If you are simply reporting the availability of a range of new products, then there are two common approaches. The first is pictorial, but this depends upon photographic material of suitable quality being available. For high-quality consumer magazines, the free publicity shots will be unsuitable, so you must expect to do a shoot. In business-to-business magazines this may not apply, and standard publicity shots can be used in a tight grid.

The other approach is to apply news values to the material. Which of these objects is the most interesting and why? This then leads you to a hierarchical approach to writing them up, with the most important products given the most space and prominence and the others reduced to fillers.

Video reviews are increasingly being used for products on magazine websites. This gives the viewer a chance to look at (and possibly listen to) the product from a range of angles and in different contexts, while a reporter talks through the key features. An expensive studio is not necessary – clean sound and good light are more important. Stuff.tv reviews some gadgets at the journalist's desk, for example, but most shots are close-ups on the gadget itself.

It is becoming increasingly standard for product review information to be stored in some sort of database that can be used internally by the editorial team and externally by users of the website. This has obvious advantages not only in allowing users to make direct comparisons on features that are of interest to them, but also in providing commercial opportunities in selling access to those databases or advertising against them. Motoring magazine *Auto Trader*, for example, generates 90 per cent of its profits from its database-driven website.

Diary/listings

Most magazines will include some sort of weekly diary of events: this is not to be confused with a 'diary column' as discussed above. The object here is simply to list, accurately, a selection of useful and interesting events for your readers. Some magazines, of course, are composed of little else. It is essential that a smooth and fairly foolproof method exists for ensuring that the information comes in in the first place and makes its way into print. Your copy deadlines need to be published prominently, and whoever deals with the post needs to ensure that the material is moved swiftly to the person or persons compiling the section.

Outside organisations whose events you are publicising must understand exactly what you require and when. Your diary or listings editors should be able to 'train' them to keep the right information coming. If something has not arrived, they must be aware of that and seek it out. In the writing, a balance needs to be struck between the simple listing of facts and something more elaborate: the difference here is between listings and critical previews. Where that balance is struck will depend entirely upon the nature of the magazine.

Again, the nature of this content is well suited to the web and many magazines maintain a more comprehensive diary online. You should direct readers to this and, if possible, allow them to contribute to it. You will need to strike a balance between the value of the information provided and the income from it. Some publishers operate a 'Yellow Pages' approach, letting people add basic information for free but charging for higher prominence or advanced features.

Campaigns

One useful tool in the struggle to develop and maintain a close identification between the magazine and the reader is the campaign. But it needs careful planning if it is not to be either a long anticlimax or, worse, a positive embarrassment.

The cynical would say that there is no point in pursuing a campaign which you cannot win. One London newspaper, for example, launched a campaign for 'A Seat for Every Commuter' and claimed its first victory when more carriages were announced. Of course conditions for commuters never did get any better – and within a few years train passenger numbers had reached post-war record levels. In the same year the newspaper campaigned to 'Save Our Small Shops' – only to do anything but help small newsagents with its transformation into a freesheet.

On entering a campaign, it is important to know how you are going to withdraw, with honour, at the end. The impetus from the magazine must also be met by equal or greater enthusiasm from the readers and the outside world. It helps if the campaign is not entirely self-interested: publishers' efforts against VAT on reading material have suffered from that accusation. The Internet has transformed the way that campaigns are conducted – and is often a good source of inspiration. If a particular issue generates a lot of passion on your website, or one of your users has started a fast-growing campaigning Facebook group, this is just as likely to form the basis as a news story or feature article about something that 'needs to change'.

Tapping into that sort of groundswell of opinion is a good way to ensure that your campaign doesn't flop at the outset. But it is just the start. You will need to be careful not to appear to be hijacking someone else's bandwagon – if someone is already taking a lead then help them to do so. Your role will be more one of endorsement than initiation. This is not a bad thing, as it builds your relationship with your readers and reinforces the fact that you are serving them, and not vice versa.

It is good to enlist users early on in the crafting of a campaign – find out what are the most important elements of an issue, and the outcomes that people want. Identify people who want to help. There is a danger in online campaigns of 'slacktivism' – people signing up to support the cause, but doing little else. To avoid this there must be specific activities that you can enlist their help in – beyond raising awareness or funds. Some campaigns have even said 'Do not donate – act' to ensure members actually do something.

Putting an online campaign into print will be an important move, and will turn the relationship into a partnership. The first article will need to have considerable emotional impact if it is to generate enough response to carry a campaign. It also helps if there is a specific objective, such as a change in the law.

That should bring in the readers' letters, but if the intention is to make a campaign on this basis, they must be edited and projected for maximum impact. Thereafter, the campaign proper can take off.

A campaign needs a logo and a slogan or two, and someone must be given responsibility for running it – or supporting it if it was initiated by a reader. After the first article, report on the reaction – online as it comes in, while every issue after that must keep up the pressure in print. A list of objectives or demands must be drawn up and published. Look for celebrity or industry support (get a sympathetic celebrity to tweet a link on Twitter, or ask an industry body to email it to their members) and perhaps some kind of official backing.

Members of Parliament must be contacted and persuaded of your good faith, and you should ask them about the possibilities. Eventually there may be questions in the House and demands for government and opposition support. Some campaigns of this sort end in the drafting of a Private Member's Bill, but this can be frustrating, since the drafting of a bill is no guarantee that it is to receive any kind of reading.

And if the government won't support your campaign, you are heading for a defeat. You may, though, be able to create some sort of pressure group or charity that will continue the fight once you have moved on to something else. No magazine campaign will succeed unless it is driven by enthusiasm on the part of editor and journalists. Unfortunately, campaigns can very quickly become tedious if no one is passionate about them. Choose your battles with care.

6   Pictures and design

The magazine is a visual medium. True, a small number of text-only publications continue to exist, usually for official purposes. But every other editor, from the creator of a church newsletter to the editorial director of a major consumer magazine, must consider the visual aspects of the job. Publishing always involves design decisions, even if only the selection of typefaces. Magazine design also requires the intelligent use of photographs, illustrations and colour.

Sadly, there is sometimes a clash of cultures between journalists and magazine staff with a design background. Few editors have much opportunity to work with designers or photographers before they take on the role. This means that in the early part of your time as editor you must train yourself to think of ideas in visual terms, from the start. Among other things you must train yourself not to think of pictures as 'illustrating', 'accompanying' or 'supporting' the words. It is not a case of prettifying a story. The relationship should be more equal and organic than that.

At the same time, it helps if your designers understand that magazine design is an applied discipline, not a form of fine art. Magazine designers are, or should be, visual journalists. Their designs may be aesthetically appealing but more importantly they should serve to make reading pleasurable on a number of other levels too, including the readability of the content, and communicating the spirit of the magazine brand.

In other words, design should be dictated by the needs of the audience, the style of the magazine, and what is being communicated.

This is, of course, an ideal. Much of the routine work of a magazine's art department will not approach it, mainly for reasons of time. Nonetheless, it is important to keep the ideal in mind: page creation as one process, rather than the merger of two.

Editing by design

The magazine designer Jan V. White, art director of Time Inc. in the early 1960s, used this expression as the title for his classic book on the subject.[1] The book tried to place design at the heart of the editing process, complete with procedures for doing that in practice. White wanted editors to see their magazines as three-dimensional objects, in which the third dimension, depth, is created by the progress *through* the assembled sequence of pages. This dimension is easily neglected. You need to ensure that that sequence is always visible to those working on an issue, by intelligent use of page proofs or thumbnails (reduced-sized print-outs of the finished pages).

The same principles also apply – half a century later – to designing on the web, where pages should not be designed in isolation but with an awareness of how the user arrives there, where they might want to go next, and where you might want them to go too. This discipline – 'user experience' or UX – is more complex than catering for the progress of a reader through a physical magazine, however, as the user's progress online can go in any number of directions, from other pages on your site to pages you link to elsewhere on the web (or links that launch applications such as iTunes), to sharing the page on email, social networks and other platforms, or leaving to conduct a related search.

Much editing takes place on the 'micro' level, as editors fiddle with individual articles to ensure their accuracy and to get the tone right. But the other end of the scale is vital too: the way different elements are physically ordered, massed and emphasised, both on individual magazine pages and across the whole magazine. It is here that we manipulate 'pace', the rate at which a magazine presents its material to its readers. The usual pattern is to use short elements at the front and back, where they will appeal to the casual reader or the person flicking through in adverse conditions, leaving the centre of the magazine for longer, more time-consuming reads.

These decisions are made in flat-planning an individual issue, but they take place in the context of the magazine's original publication design (the website, likewise, is originally planned using a site map, and most subsequent content is placed into that site using a content management system which formats it accordingly). That must provide visual landmarks for the reader, starting with the cover format, typeface and cover-line style, which provide a high degree of consistency from issue to issue. Nowadays we are inclined to call this aspect the magazine's 'branding'. Branding elements normally include the overall grid, typefaces, bleeding or non-bleeding of pictures, use of illustrations, and the positioning of the contents page or pages, which will always start on, say, the first or second right-hand page, and section openings, which might also open on right-handers. There might also be particular shapes, colours or icons that are repeatedly used, such as a coloured square to indicate the end of an article, or the thickness of a line under each article author's name.

Decisions must also be made about how to handle longer features. You can specify a number of page permutations, designed to accommodate different volumes of words and different levels of prominence. These might include single pages, simple spreads, spreads followed by several singles, a single right-hand start followed by a spread, and so on. The designers then provide suitable typographical and visual styling for each option, some of which will become regular 'slots' dedicated to a specific purpose. For instance, your opening interview might always be allocated to a single spread, which is then commissioned, edited and designed to make a particular impact. It becomes a regular 'event' for the reader.

American magazines favour starting each new feature on a spread, and then continuing it at the back of the 'book'. The idea is to create a fast-moving feature 'well', in which browser and casual reader are given lots of potential starting points to hook their interest. Unfortunately, those who want to read the pieces in full are led on a paper-chase through numerous follow-on pages scattered through the back of the magazine.

This approach has rarely been favoured in the UK, where the tendency is to start with an eye-catching opening spread and assume that the reader will follow. The density of the page (the ratio between words and pictures) can increase rapidly beyond that first page, because the assumption is that the reader is captivated. This might mean an opening spread which is largely composed of picture, headline and standfirst, then a left-hand page with a reasonable selection of pictures, then another with a single picture, then a final page with almost no decoration, except perhaps a pull quote. This soaks up large numbers of words, bringing the feature to an end and allowing the next one to start. The American method, in contrast, writes off the back half of a magazine as a sort of filing cabinet.

There is already a danger that the back of a magazine becomes a place to put things that no one on the staff is very interested in: competitions, readers' letters, regular items. But good magazine designers work backwards as well as forwards, aiming to accommodate those readers who flick from the back. You must always anchor the final editorial page, usually the left-hander opposite the inside back cover. Save it for a strong column or something equally striking, and then you can build backwards from there.

Altering the running order can have a dramatic effect on a magazine's usefulness and readability, and this is particularly true for magazines with a high information content, for instance listings titles. It is essential to finding a logical structure for this type of material.

White also recommends bringing design into the initial story-planning process. He proposes a 'story conference' for each significant feature, to include writer, commissioning editor, designer and picture editor (nowadays you would also add the web editor). This is an excellent idea that is rarely practised, mostly for reasons of speed and cost.

Those who have the staff and the time to do it, however, will find that it works both for individual stories (which really benefit from bringing together words and pictures before either actually exist) and for the improved understanding between writers and design people.

Even if time does not permit full-scale story conferencing, the question of how a particular story is to be expressed on the printed page should be foremost in the commissioning editor's mind. If there is one, the picture editor must be involved at this stage. Picture desks and designers rightly dislike being presented with a written feature and told to find some visual material to 'liven it up'. Commissioning new photography or finding the best agency material needs time. A good picture editor can call in material from agencies with surprising speed, especially using online facilities, but this doesn't make it the best way to operate. Better, and often more economical, results are obtained by a thoughtful personal search of agency resources. So discuss what is required first and then leave your picture researcher and designers to use their skills and experience.

The art director or art editor

The relationship between an editor and an art director (or art editor – both titles are used) is critical. A magazine's design can affect its readership and circulation more quickly than almost anything an editor can do directly, although the influence of words may be more important in the long term. An art editor should ideally be a close ally throughout, responsive to both parts of the job's title: 'art' and 'editor'. Of course, small magazines may have to manage without. The selection of a new art editor is a difficult task, especially for those whose background is in words. Like editors, art editors have a two-sided job. They set their magazine's visual style, but they also have a managerial role. Prospective art editors will present a portfolio providing evidence of their visual abilities and tastes. Study this in detail before you meet them. It should include covers, feature spreads, even whole magazines. There should be evidence of both adaptability and strong visual taste: that's a mysterious quality that makes everything, whatever its purposes and provenance, look 'right'.

Much of what you are shown may not be directly relevant, unless you are poaching from a competitor, but you want to see the way a brief has been tackled and developed. It is important to see how mundane work is handled too: look at simple news pages and product pages. It is vital that all these things express themselves, their own essence, rather than merely reflecting typographical fashions or their designer's fondness for certain typefaces.

Since they are vital to any magazine's success, you should pay particular attention to your candidate's covers. It is one thing to find or commission a high-quality portrait photograph and use it for a cover based on an interview. It is quite another to find an appealing visual analogue for a complex issue or subject. If your magazine intends to base cover stories on ideas, rather than people, then you must be confident of your art director's ability to come up with ways of expressing them.

This is not an area in which many designers will have much experience. The heyday of the 'idea' cover was in the American magazines of the 1950s and 1960s – although it has made a mild comeback in recent years. Some contemporary art director candidates will never have made a cover out of anything except a portrait photograph. If you intend to move beyond that, you must be sure your art editor is prepared and enthusiastic. Most relish the opportunity.

In the interview, you should ask searching questions about how various finished pieces of design came about and about the constraints involved, particularly of cost. You need to know how your candidate is used to working, the level of consultation expected with editorial staff, the amount and nature of direction required. Your candidate must be able to interpret a brief, and to work imaginatively within a budget. You must, naturally, ensure that the candidate is familiar with all the technology you use or intend to use in the future, as well as that used by your printers.

The job also has important managerial aspects. Few art editors can lay out every page in a big magazine on their own. Most will direct other designers or use freelance help. Your candidate must be able to run a studio, including ordering new materials and liaising with the magazine's printer. Large sums of cash flow through a magazine's studio, and you need reassurance that the candidate is entirely confident in handling both people and money. Is your candidate a leader? Is he or she disciplined and rigorous? Studios, like production departments, depend upon the rigorous tracking of incoming and outgoing material, from digital files and prints to page and picture files, and close adherence to deadlines.

Art directors will also be expected to commission photography and illustration, and to organise and run photographic shoots. Their portfolios should show ample evidence of competence in these areas. Remember that you are assessing temperament as much as ability. Searching interviewing must be followed up by the use of references.

But should aesthetic flair win out, or managerial competence? It is for you to consider how important each aspect is to you. A competent deputy in the studio and a production editor and office administrator can help with the managerial burden. But no one else can provide the necessary flair and inspiration to give your magazine a strong, confident, visual identity. You may feel that a certain managerial vagueness is a reasonable price to pay for aesthetic excellence. But this is a senior management post. Your art director or art editor must accept full responsibility for the art domain within the magazine, in terms of both aesthetic quality and management. Not all creative people find such responsibility easy.

Here is one art director's thoughts on editors:

> The art director and editor must have a good working relationship based on mutual respect; their two disciplines, when combined in a magazine, are mutually dependent.
>
> Publish fantastic content that is illegible or beautifully designed content that is poorly conceived/written and you'll lose the reader rapidly.
>
> The best magazines combine the images, words and designs to create something greater than the sum of its parts. Magazines are the only medium that demand that word and image combine so closely.
>
> The best editors understand design and the best art directors understand editorial. The editor and art director need to have an agreed agenda and work closely from the beginning of a project in order for a magazine to be seen by the reader as successful, confident and desirable.
>
> Too many art directors today are seen merely as designer-decorators; a good editor expects more from their art director than mere decoration; an art director should be able to tell the editor 'no' just as often as the opposite occurs.
>
> (Jeremy Leslie, magculture.com)

Working with designers

When briefing for a new publication design or redesign, give the designer the same information you have used to understand your readers and plan their magazine. But some factors are more important in this context than the normal stuff about the readers' social status, sex, professional status, and so on. The designer must know how the magazine is going to be used. Is it to be a leisure publication to be read at home after being brought home or delivered? Is it intended to be read by commuters? Is it to be delivered to people at work and kept there for reference? Each makes different demands on the design.

Home-use publications are built for continuous reading in relaxed conditions, permitting longer articles, longer line lengths and elegant, timeless design and photography. That is not the case in magazines intended to be read on a crowded bus or at the hairdresser's, where short articles, big type and attention-grabbing design would seem to be essential. Professional publications, intended to be shelved and referred back to, on the other hand, will have a deeply sober look. The age of readers is another critical factor, not just in the specifying of type, which must not fall below a certain minimum size, but in assessing the degree of design excitement that is advisable.

These are extremely complex decisions. The range of available typefaces, for instance, is vast. But you should not try to design the magazine: you don't have either the aptitude or the expertise. Instead, you must be the perfect client. You should set out the problems in as clear a way as possible and let the designer work the process through. There can then be further discussions. This is one task you must delegate, specifying the job you want done but not the means used to achieve it.

On the other hand, your requirements should be honoured. And any decisions must be tested before they are put into practice. It is not enough to make decisions on the basis of proofs. You should see pages after they have emerged from the printing process. If the budget does not run to having your new design elements printed on short-run presses, find ways round it. If you are planning to use a new body typeface, for instance, you must find a corner in your existing magazine, a small house advertisement or an announcement, put it into the new face and have it printed.

Magazine history is littered with fatal decisions made by designers and editors intoxicated by a vision of elegance that proved unreproducible, or unreadable, in practice. *Event*, a 1970s rival to London's *Time Out* produced by Richard Branson and designed by Pearce Marchbank, failed in part because many people thought the typeface was too small.

You must think through the logic of particular design solutions to see how they will affect every aspect of the working process. Increasing the leading between lines of type, or introducing more generous gutters, may bring much needed light into your pages but at what cost in terms of loss of space? Do you really want to lose that amount of material? Or is it a worthwhile price to pay for greater elegance and ease of reading? Your readers must be your guide: are they paying for information or for elegance?

Consider the effect of adjusting the hierarchy of headings and standfirsts. It may seem a good idea to give each news story a two- or three-word 'kicker' label above its headline. But how much time will writing it require, and how are you going to ensure that it simply doesn't repeat what's in the headline itself? Those centred standfirsts might look elegant when they are properly filled out to fit, but do you really want your sub-editors tinkering with that when they could be doing something more constructive?

And there may also be cost implications. The most notorious of these is paper format. The reason most magazines are produced in standard formats is that they come off the print web with no wastage. More innovative shapes, which designers tend to favour, can involve horrendous levels of paper wastage as standard paper widths are trimmed to fit.

Less radical design tasks, for instance the creation of new sections in existing magazines, should be much simpler to accomplish. It is important that you say precisely what you want the new page or section to achieve and what elements you want it to include. A 'people' spread, for instance, might be expected to accommodate between three and five small interviews of 300–500 words each with a headline, standfirst, photograph and caption, plus a slot for snippets of gossip and quotes of the week. A columnist's page might require 1,000 words of copy, a prominent by-line, a pull quote, a headline and standfirst, and a photo or caricature. It is perfectly acceptable to give your designer sheets torn from other magazines, but only to show the kind of elements or feel you require rather than any typographical specifics. Most designers would rightly feel rather insulted at being invited to imitate someone else's design.

Working with web designers

This is not the place to explore the various technicalities of web design but an understanding of some of the basics of the medium will serve you well as editor. With any new technology it is easy for those who know a little about it to 'blind you with science' and pretend to know more than they actually do, leading to inflated spending where simple solutions may be best.

Technically, websites should separate content from design. The content should be contained within the HTML; the way that the content is presented should be determined by Cascading Style Sheets (CSS). The advantage of this separation is that the same content can be presented in different ways depending on whether it is being viewed on a computer screen, mobile device, or by someone with visual impairment. You can also have a style sheet that changes the appearance when something is printed.

Another advantage is that you can change the look of every single page on a website by simply changing one stylesheet (assuming that all those pages link to that in their HTML).

There is obviously much more to web design than this, and a variety of languages from Javascript to PHP, ASP, Ruby on Rails, Python and others. All have their strengths and weaknesses – and quite often web designers and developers will have strong preferences for one or the other. Do not be persuaded too much by these prejudices: a good designer or developer should be able to learn a new language if they have to; and they should also be prepared to continue to learn new skills as technologies develop and change. Designers who previously worked in Flash, for example, may have to switch to HTML5.

As editor you should be wary of hiring web designers who can create stunning mockups but do not think about the broader issues of information architecture (IA) – that is, the structure of a site – and user experience (UX) – that is, how people act when they use your site. Their role is likely to involve problem solving as much as – if not more than – making things look good. Ask them what they would do in certain situations, or with certain editorial ideas. And ask them what they would change about the current site, if you have one. If they treat the site as something to be used as well as looked at, then they have the right idea.

When it comes to designing for tablets, designer Craig Mod sums up the differences well, pointing out that whereas magazines and books have an 'axis of symmetry' – i.e. the spine – devices such as the iPad lack similar simple sources of orientation: 'On one hand, designers can approach tablets as if they were a single sheet of "paper," letting the physicality of the object define the central axis of symmetry – straight down the middle. On the other hand, the physicality of these devices doesn't represent the full potential of content space. The screen becomes a small portal to an infinite content plane, or "infinite canvas."'[2] Bear in mind these differences when dealing with designers.

Routine design tasks

As far as day-to-day involvement with design goes, there should generally be a discussion about a significant feature before it is written. This is certainly the case with features that depend on tabular and graphical material. These should be discussed early and material commissioned as appropriate. Illustrations can sometimes be commissioned before anything is written, but only after considerable discussion and at the risk of a mismatch that will have to be corrected by adjustments, most likely to the written material.

There is always a danger of Chinese whispers. The commissioning editor may explain the concept to the designer responsible for commissioning the illustrator or photographer. The designer then discusses it with the illustrator, while the editor talks to the writer. At no stage do the writer and illustrator speak, and the distortions introduced in the discussion and briefing process mean that they may be working at cross-purposes. It is not entirely practical for the writer and illustrator to be brought in for a discussion with the editor and art director, although that is probably the ideal. If such a discussion takes place, it is a good idea to put something on paper at the end of it. If no such meeting takes place, both designer and editor should make an effort to read one another's briefs before they are sent out to ensure that they, at least, are clear about what is required.

Certainly designers must read the written material and raise any queries with the writers or editors concerned. Most editors will have come across designers who considered it no part of their function to read the copy around which they were creating pages. The view was sometimes expressed that reading the material would in some sense 'distract' from the task of creating pages. This is nonsense, of course, and no editor, indeed no art editor, should stand for it.

It is for the art editor to supervise individual page and spread designs for visual elegance, adherence to the established style, appropriate use of type, appropriate colour palette, and so on. But the editor should not be excluded from the process, and either the editor or a trusted member of the team should be responsible for passing finished pages. So that this is not a traumatic process, it is advisable for an editor to keep an eye on work in progress, both informally by wandering around and watching what goes on, and formally by receiving proofs of pages under construction.

When you look at a page or spread or whole feature you must ensure that it works. It must lead the eye logically through the material. The page itself must tell the reader what is the most important thing. News pages, which are made up of numerous different stories, are designed specifically for that purpose: to embody a whole hierarchy of suggested importance. The lead story should stand out from the rest, something that can be achieved in any number of ways: size of story, position of story, shape of story, size of headline, shape of headline, typography of story, typography of headline, size, shape and impact of any accompanying photograph, and so on. Thereafter, immediate visual impact should be reduced, on a sliding scale down to simple one-paragraph 'briefs', which should have almost no impact individually, but should have an appealing and obvious presence as a group.

In feature material, the hierarchy of emphasis is applied not to different stories but to different elements within a single overall story: headline, standfirst, body text, panels and boxes, pull quotes, by-lines, and so on. A magazine needs a clear hierarchy for this kind of material, which should be laid down in some kind of design manual, indicating acceptable typefaces, sizes and styles for each job (it is likely these will be expressed technically in style sheets and page templates). When you look at an individual piece of layout, you should ensure that the theoretical ordering of elements has been carried through in practice.

The editor must not be deterred by the mystique of design from applying standards to the whole editorial domain, which certainly includes the look of the magazine. Any failings in the magazine's visual appeal will result in poor bookstall and circulation performance, and responsibility for that will certainly be laid at the editor's door. At the same time, wise editors recognise their deficiencies in visual matters and let well-chosen and well-trained design staff get on with the job.

The picture editor

Some journalists think that handling pictures is all about housekeeping: ordering photographs, negotiating fees, and paying bills. Those things do form part of the job, but a picture editor has a passionate interest in visual material. You need someone who can bring that interest to bear on the very specific problems of producing magazines, which are not so much about aesthetics as about uniting images and words in a single act of communication. If you have no picture editor, it becomes your job.

Aesthetic questions are a matter of taste and experience. You may wish to produce a beautiful magazine, but beauty has a rather static quality. *Impact* may be a better criterion for picture selection. Again, this ideally requires a discussion between yourself, your picture editor and your art director, but it is your responsibility to have the last word.

Pictures can draw in readers or repel them. They can say as much as the accompanying piece, or they can simply sit alongside it: a bad picture, which is to say a dull image or a technically incompetent bit of photography, can destroy an otherwise acceptable page. There are many ways of assessing photographs, but start with the content: is this the right person, the right place, the right object to accompany the copy? Then you need to ask about the timing of the photograph: is this what the person looks like now? Is this the right moment in the story, or could we get closer to it?

Finally, and most elusively, you have to consider the quality of the photograph. Remind yourself that the resolution of a computer screen is much lower than that of glossy printed pages. An image that looks fine on screen can still look pixelated in print. Your designer and picture editor should have enough experience to help you make intelligent judgements about this. They should also make sure that there are no obvious compositional howlers that only appear on a second or third glance: lamp-standards emerging from people's heads, for instance.

But technical quality is not the only important aspect of a photograph. You are also looking for its inherent qualities as a piece of observation of, usually, human beings. There must be a sense of life about it: this can come from something as simple as a facial expression or an unusual posture. For feature photography, you need something that tells a story, that reveals something about the people or situation pictured. And it helps if there is an element of drama in either the material or its composition. Again, the word is impact. Does the person in the picture communicate with the reader? Does it invite an emotional response? It probably should.

As an editor, your immersion in the world of visual images may have been limited but you should take the time to develop it now by looking at photography and the visual arts whenever you have the opportunity. Picture desks and designers spend hours poring over Continental and American magazines in search of visual inspiration: it would not hurt you to take the occasional look, nor to attend photography exhibitions and graphic and fine art degree shows.

Your picture editor, if you have one, must be invited to rise above the routine aspects of the job (while continuing to handle them efficiently) and become a vital part of the creative process. A picture editor must be part of the editorial team, which is both a privilege and a responsibility needing effort and understanding on both sides.

Editors do not need to involve themselves in the practical side of the picture editor's job, but they do need to be aware of what is possible and what is not. There is a tendency for editors to imagine that because they have seen a picture, or think they have seen a picture, it is available for inclusion in their magazine. But that image may have been something they saw on television or in a film that does not exist in still form. It may be something they have imagined. Or it may simply be outside the practical and financial range of the magazine's resources. Of course, it may be possible to create the image, by commissioning photography, but that is a separate issue.

If you are using existing photography, it pays not to approach a feature or cover idea with an image in mind that is too specific. On the other hand, it does not help your picture editor if you say that you have no idea what you want, but you'd like to see everything.

Agencies and libraries

Picture editors need time to seek out new or forgotten images to give features their fullest visual impact. Unfortunately, much of their time is devoted to telephone discussions and negotiations. More than anyone else in the editorial team, the picture editor has to deal constantly with people and money. This is where experience is invaluable, in making deals with agencies, libraries and photographers. Your magazine's circulation and distribution pattern and the size and prominence with which the picture is to be used form the basis of the discussion. You should also make sure that rights include the ability to publish the image online, worldwide.

But the eventual price struck has as much to do with your picture editor's knowledge of the market and negotiating skills. You can also negotiate to stop anyone else using the same picture during the circulation period of your issue.

There is an exception to this pattern of payment. It is possible to buy 'royalty free' pictures. These are stock shots using models and timeless scenes that are sold without reference to how a magazine intends to use them. So there is no premium for large circulation or prominence, and they can be used several times. You can buy them on CD, and they can be a good investment for people who simply want decorative material rather than specific shots of individuals.

The disadvantages are inherent in that. Royalty-free pictures are necessarily anonymous reusable pieces of visual material. They may capture a mood, but they do not express anything specific or refer to individuals. Because they use models, they tend towards the kind of blandness you see in newspaper advertisements for financial services. And because you aren't paying for a special use, you do not get the right to control whether anyone else is allowed to use them. All of this means they are fine for eking out the budget, but are no use in high-profile jobs like your cover and your lead interview, where you want to give people images they have not seen before.

Royalty-free pictures are one way of saving money if you have to, but they should still be of high technical quality and from a good source. Nothing betrays a magazine on a shoestring budget so much as inadequate photography. You can also reuse a single photograph at various points in an issue. A section of your cover photograph, for instance, makes a good eye-catching device when used on the pages of the accompanying feature. The price for these subsidiary uses will be much lower.

If you really have to use bad pictures, get the designers to give them a thorough treatment. Radical cropping, different screens, and treatments such as posterising and solarising can all transform a dull free picture into an original artwork, and at very little cost. The best comment on this came from Alexey Brodovitch, art director with *Harper's Bazaar* during the 1930s: 'A layout man should be simple with good photographs. He should perform acrobatics when the pictures are bad.'[3]

Good picture editors affect not only your costs but the quality of the photography in your magazine: they know where to go for particular pictures, which photographers are bringing new material into the market, what other magazines are looking for at any time, and so on. This makes them invaluable, although that is not always reflected in what they are paid. An experienced picture editor will cost more than a beginner, but the difference is likely to be made up in what they will save the magazine. You will also get better quality material and use more interesting photographers.

Celebrity pictures are a constant problem. The famous do everything they can to control the way they are photographed. That means that the agency pictures may be extremely familiar and uninteresting. Your picture editor must know how to look further afield. But most agencies now charge a fee for 'research', even if your picture editors or researchers go and look through the material themselves, so the more trawling you do the more expensive it becomes. Even if the research is free, conducted by your picture editor online, it will still be time consuming.

Photographers and shoots

Original photography should be as much a part of magazines as original writing. An original picture to your specifications can be precisely matched to the mood of a story. It can express the values of your magazine as a brand. And it is yours and yours alone, at least for the period you agree. It can, however, be horribly expensive. Those who are used to dealing only with writers are sometimes surprised by the fees commanded by freelance photographers, not to mention the cost of hiring studios, models, stylists and hair and make-up artists when these are required.

The reason advanced by the photographers is that they have to carry high overheads, although often you will receive a bill for studio hire, film and processing on top of the fee. But unlike writers, photographers operate with one foot in the world of advertising, where extraordinary fees are commonplace. Editorial photography doesn't pay as well, but most photographers need editorial work for their credibility. Having established that credibility, they get more money for their advertising work, which means that their editorial rate will increase again.

A skilled picture editor selects a photographer for a job not merely on technical quality and artistic merit but also on temperament. The best photographers combine a high degree of competence with amenable personalities. The photographer must match the job. If the picture is a portrait, two personalities have to be matched. They won't necessarily form a lifelong friendship, but they should be able to establish a working relationship that will last the length of the picture session.

In the case of celebrity photography, this can be problematical. Show business public relations is about the control of imagery. If you want to photograph a star for your cover you must enter lengthy negotiations about access, timing and exclusivity. But it may go further. Some 'stars' now insist on specifying their own favourite photographers. Even then, the star's 'people' may expect to choose which images are used. You may end up asking them to choose a possible three from perhaps 40 or 50 originals.

Photo shoots take a lot of planning. Aside from matching the photographer to the job, it is often a good idea to present the photographer with a mock-up of the layout the picture is supposed to suit, especially if it is a cover. If special props are required, or a backdrop, this should all be done and approved far in advance. Then the art editor or the picture editor should go to the shoot and take responsibility for it. This means ensuring not only that any necessary studio hire, equipment hire, catering and all the rest are competently and economically controlled, but that the actual photographs that emerge are what is required. Some photographers do not need to be told what to do, and don't appreciate any such guidance. Others welcome a clear explanation of what is required. The picture editor or art director must take responsibility for managing the photographer to get the desired result.

The practical requirements should be clear. A cover photograph has to be a particular shape. The composition must allow room for the fixed elements of the cover (the logo, price, barcode, and so on) and also for cover-lines. Be more precise if the cover is more than a mere portrait and has to express a particular idea or represent a particular activity. The photographer's ideas on this may be welcome, but get the picture you really need first.

Photo sessions involve paperwork. If you are photographing models rather than identifiable people, your picture editor must be provided with appropriate 'model release' forms for models to sign. These make it clear to the model, who may sometimes be an ordinary member of the public, how few rights she or he actually retains over the way the finished work is used. They can be rather alarming documents: no one likes to lose 'rights', even those they have never previously thought about. Such forms generally require models to acknowledge that they have no claim to copyright and that the magazine can use the photographs in any way it sees fit. They also state that the photographs and any accompanying copy are deemed to be of an 'imaginary person', rather than of the model her- or himself. This is to permit their use in contexts which would otherwise permit an action for libel.

For instance, you might take a picture of someone looking glamorous in a bar and at some subsequent date use it to illustrate a story about prostitution. This is one of the hazards of professional modelling, particularly at the lower levels, where reputation is preserved by the simple line 'posed by models' accompanying the photographer's by-line. Ordinary members of the public should not be treated in this way. If they have signed the release form, however, you have some protection against disastrous mistakes, when a photograph taken for one purpose inadvertently ends up being used for something else. A famous case concerned a photograph of a group of sinister-looking motor-cyclists in black leather, accompanying a piece about gangs. Unfortunately the group in question was a Christian motor-cycling club, run by a clergyman.

The presence of a name on a caption attached to an image, without any indication that the person in question is a model, should be a warning. People who give their names to photographers do not consent to the photographs being used in any unspecified context: they think the picture is for a specific purpose. They retain the right to protect their reputation in a libel action based on the photograph's appearance in a defamatory context. Those who are photographed but whose names are not known or recorded also retain their rights to take action in the same circumstances. A typical example is to show a picture of some peaceful football supporters walking home after a match with a caption stating that they are members of a notorious hooligan gang feared throughout Europe. If they are identifiable, they can sue.

Pictures of models may well come with no names attached. If models' real names are, however, published alongside their pictures, or attached to any statement about them or by them, they regain their right to have their reputation protected, and your model form should make that clear.

The real problem with commissioned photography is one of perceived value. No one begrudges paying for a sparkling portrait for a cover or a feature. But high fees are often asked for mundane 'mug-shots' destined to end up on the people page or the news pages, where they will be used small and will do little to enhance the layout beyond simply identifying the person being written about. A simple mug-shot can easily cost you as much as a short feature, and you can expect to pay for it again each time you use it unless you acquire the copyright.

It is no wonder that most small magazines are keen to acquire and store free photographs of the sort dished out as publicity material: technically there is usually an implied obligation that the photograph is used only for the purpose for which it was originally supplied, but that is rarely enforced. Another option, frowned upon by some, including the trade unions, is the use of an office camera for basic news mug-shots. The results are likely to be poor, but using cheap or free photographs in non-critical places releases money to pay for proper commissioned photography elsewhere. Every so often, you should have a blitz on your photo files to ensure you have reasonably up-to-date pictures of anyone you are likely to need in your news section. If you have omissions, hire a photographer for a couple of days on a daily rate to take as many as possible. Make sure you buy the rights to use them as often as you like.

Illustration

Illustration is subject to fashions in magazines, but it can provide a welcome change of pace and mood. Illustration is not neutral: however hard or combative the artist might try to make them, illustrations invariably have a more 'subjective' air than photographs. They label a piece as a feature, as something driven more by opinion and analysis than by hard reportage. They create a distancing effect, giving things an unreal, storybook quality. But they have their uses.

They are helpful where the use of photographs is impossible for practical or legal reasons:

- no photographer is available;
- the situation is too dangerous or impractical;
- there is nothing to photograph, because the piece is about an abstraction;
- a court case is pending;
- you have other reasons not to identify any individual;
- or for legal reasons.

But they are also good for emotional and abstract subjects, where the illustrator finds an image that goes to the heart of the matter in a way no photograph could. And line drawings are ideal in instructional material, where photography simply isn't clear enough.

One type of illustration that is still used is caricature, which is a good way to make a 'character' out of an interviewee or profile subject who may otherwise be rather bland. Here the effect can range from the flattering to the grotesque and insulting, so your artist should be chosen with care.

Sourcing video

An increasing number of magazines now offer video online – either as part of a website, as a standalone TV channel, or on an app for phone or tablet. There are a number of sources you might obtain video from. The first is broadcast footage – this is most likely if your publication is an offshoot from a broadcast production. You will want footage to be optimised (its file size reduced) for the web, and probably edited to a manageable length as well: anything longer than three minutes or so is going to test most users' patience.

The second option is syndication – buying video that has been produced for something else. This presents similar issues, along with those of relevance and value. A third option – using video from PR agencies – presents all sorts of ethical issues and will probably undermine your reputation.

User-generated video may not have the same quality as a slick PR production, but it will at least have integrity, and will reinforce the relationship you have with readers. The question to ask here is not whether it fits your own production values, but whether other users will want to interact with the content and its author. They will not see it as your content, but rather content that you are allowing readers to share. Do not be too precious about this.

The final option is to create your own content. The temptation here is to spend lots of money on a television studio simply because you believe that that is what broadcasters do, but you are not a broadcaster, and there is no reason to do this: broadcasters build studios because they need to produce large amounts of content to fill schedules. As a publisher you do not have the same pressure – or, indeed, the same finances. Simple video filmed with good sound in your office or a place that represents the subject matter will be fine for most examples. If you are filming yourself reading the latest headlines you have to ask 'Why?' The only reason that broadcasters do it is because they do not have a choice. You do: and if text suits your story best, don't use video for the sake of it.

Information graphics

The term information graphics (also called infographics) refers to visuals used to explain. They range from simple tables and grids, used to compare a number of different objects or services, through various types of maps, flowcharts and graphs to elaborate exploded diagrams.

In each case there are two essential tasks: assembling the information and finding an appropriate way to express it. Sometimes this is obvious: if you are writing about a network of long-distance footpaths, you will need a map. At other times things are more difficult. Ask yourself how many variables can safely be incorporated in a single graphic, and, indeed, how many the reader requires.

Take a simple line graph showing the rising cost of living (on the vertical axis) over time (on the horizontal one). You might complicate this with an extra line showing falling house prices, which would require a different scale, but could be done. But if you attempted to include salary rates for different jobs you would be in danger of overcomplicating things.

Presenting information as a table or graph is, unfortunately, more complex than it seems. Computer software has made it easy to conjure up these things, but it has not made it any easier to use them intelligently as devices for explanation. You should turn to a specialist in the field, or perhaps encourage one of your design team to become one. It is never a shortcut. Collecting the material for a detailed graphic, perhaps showing some piece of technology or the scene of some incident, can easily take as long as producing a feature on the subject. But a graphic should be used when words and photographs don't do the job.

Online infographics have huge appeal in terms of distribution: compelling and clear infographics can be shared thousands of times so it is essential that a credit and a link is included in the image itself. They can also be particularly 'sticky' (that is, people spend a longer time looking at them) if given a life of their own. Unlike the static nature of print, you can make graphics respond dynamically to user manipulation – from allowing users to sort a table by a particular column, to hovering over positions on a line graph to see individual details, or selecting from drop-down menus or clicking on parts of a chart to re-draw the graph.

Commissioning visuals

Commissioning a photographer, illustrator or graphic artist must be approached with the same seriousness as commissioning a writer. There must be a brief, a fee, a delivery date and some statement of the rights to be acquired. Illustrators and graphic artists will also require information on the size at which their material is eventually to be used, although they may work much larger. A photographer will need to know exactly how many photographs are to be delivered, whether they are to be colour or black and white, and in what digital format. Everything must be recorded on paper for the benefit of both parties.

The briefing will be handled by your picture editor and art director. But if your feature or cover concept depends entirely upon a particular visual image, it is essential that this is clearly discussed in-house before the commissioning process begins. This is where the mock-up or rough layout comes in. The illustrator should also produce roughs before proceeding too far, so that you can be sure the message has been passed on accurately.

Copyright

Photographers and illustrators were the major beneficiaries of the 1988 Copyright Act. Copyright is the right to exploit your own work and, more importantly, to prevent other people exploiting it. For the first time, photographers and artists were considered to be 'authors' for copyright purposes. But there was a more crucial change. Previously copyright in visual material had belonged to the person or organisation commissioning the work. Since the passing of the 1988 Act it has belonged to the photographer, just as it does to writers and artists. This is a logical change and a beneficial one for photographers.

It makes it necessary, though, that magazines reach explicit agreement about the material they buy from freelance photographers and illustrators. Precisely the same disputes have raged over visual material as over writing, with publishers attempting to buy out copyright so that they can reproduce the material in other media without further payment. In practice, however, successful photographers tend to be represented by agents, who are canny about their clients' interests, and photographers tend to know the value of the rights they are signing away.

It is worth noting that the 'moral rights' aspect of the 1988 Copyright Act applies no more to photographers and illustrators than it does to writers, assuming all parties have voluntarily made their works available for publication in a magazine. That includes the right to prevent 'derogatory treatment' of copyright works. This means that in theory photographs can continue to be cropped, reversed out and subjected to various types of digital or darkroom distortion without fear of legal consequences.

Such techniques should not, however, be employed in a cavalier fashion. Photographers, especially those with artistic ambitions, are increasingly demanding the respect traditionally accorded to illustrators, whose work is rarely cropped or amended. The more successful exponents of the art will have agents who will expect you to sign contracts agreeing to do nothing of the sort. So although you have nothing to fear from statute law you could face a breach of contract action if you do not comply. Even if no such contract has been signed, it is good manners to discover how sensitively your photographer wishes to be handled.

A particular aspect of copyright to be aware of is the Creative Commons licence, which is used by many photographers and writers online (look for an icon or link).

This allows authors of creative works to assert how they wish any individual piece of work to be used online. This includes whether it can be used for commercial work, or only non-commercial work, and whether it can be modified. They can also specify that if you do modify their work you can only do so on the basis that you share the results under the same Creative Commons licence ('share alike'). All Creative Commons licences require that you attribute authorship.

A similar issue comes into play when sourcing images posted to Twitter. As with any images online, the photographer retains copyright. Services such as Twitpic which allow users to post images easily to Twitter make this explicit in their terms. Others, however – such as Plixi – include clauses in their terms and conditions that allow them to sell any images that are uploaded using the service. If you are approached by a company like this, beware: the person who took the image may not be aware that they agreed to such terms, and may not be pleased if the first time they hear about it is when it is published.

Photographic ethics

Ethics are the unwritten rules regulating the conduct of a particular professional group. They run alongside personal morality as a guide to behaviour. As an editor, you will have your own sense of values, and you must ensure that those working for you understand your standards and are prepared to comply with them. This is particularly important when you are dealing with photographers, whose potential for causing offence and distress is huge.

The professional ethics of photography are especially important when matters of privacy are concerned. There is no explicit privacy law in the UK, but there is an increasing body of case law in the country based on EU legislation – specifically the Human Rights Act – that affect the photographer's job.

The Human Rights Act itself recognises both a right to privacy and the right to freedom of expression, including press freedom. It has been left to the courts to balance the two. When Michael Douglas and Catherine Zeta Jones tried to use it to prevent *Hello!* publishing snatched pictures of their wedding (they had sold the real thing to *OK!*) they obtained an emergency injunction on privacy grounds. However, the Court of Appeal took the view that what had happened was a commercial matter and not a matter of personal privacy, and publication was allowed to proceed. On the other side, Princess Caroline of Monaco won her case arguing that her right to privacy was breached when she was photographed in a public place. It is worth following the latest legal judgements involving privacy as these establish 'case law' on the issue.

Within the confines of the law of trespass, photographers can go anywhere and take pictures of anything – although the Terrorism Act 2000 has been used on more than one occasion to prevent photographers taking images in a public place (the key part of the act – Section 44 – no longer applies, but there are other parts that can still be misused). There is also the issue of members of the public putting themselves in danger in order to take newsworthy images with their mobile phones. Of course, you as an editor do not have to publish them, nor indeed to encourage this sort of photography in the first instance. The question of publication is regulated, for the time being, not by law but by the Press Complaints Commission's Code of Practice and the Code of Conduct produced by the National Union of Journalists, to which many news photographers, particularly, belong.

The NUJ Code of Conduct (see Appendix 1) begins by stating that journalists have a duty to 'maintain the highest professional and ethical standards', although these are undefined. It states also that information, photographs and illustrations shall be obtained 'only by straightforward means. The use of other means can be justified only by over-riding considerations of the public interest.'

This clause implies that photographers should identify themselves if asked to and specifically rules out the tabloid tradition of sweeping the mantelpiece of family pictures of those in the news. But it does not deal specifically with invasions of privacy. The only mention of the concept comes in Clause 6: 'Does nothing to intrude into anybody's private life, grief or distress unless justified by overriding consideration of the public interest'. Nothing there, however, about moments of private happiness, the depiction of which has so often been the cause of public outrage.

The Press Complaints Commission's approach is rather different. Rather than the sweeping statements favoured by the NUJ, it deals with specifics, leading to some suggestions that it is designed to allow unscrupulous editors and proprietors to hide behind the letter of the 'law'. The text of the Code of Practice (see Appendix 2) needs to be interpreted in the light of a growing body of precedent. In broad terms, the Press Complaints Commission (PCC) outlaws invasions of privacy, misrepresentation and subterfuge, intrusions into grief, the photography of children in many cases, and the photography of individuals on their own property without their consent.

This idea was expanded to include people in what had previously been considered public places, for instance restaurants and hotels. The *Dorking Advertiser* carried a picture of the interior of a café as part of a review. Unfortunately, some of the diners were identifiable. One man complained that his privacy had been infringed, and the PCC upheld the complaint. It said that he had a 'reasonable' expectation of privacy in such a venue, and instructed publications to ask diners' permission before taking any such photographs. This would seem to make all sorts of photographs rather hazardous.

Most of these prohibitions, however, are overruled by what is called 'public interest', defined by the PCC as the detection of 'crime or a serious misdemeanour', the protection of 'public health and safety' and 'preventing the public from being misled by some statement or action of an individual or organisation'. Nothing here is straightforward: each of these exceptions is a knot of semantics and interpretation, apparently designed to provide hours of quasi-legalistic debate rather than to make it clear what is and is not permissible.

The PCC Code of Practice was designed to discourage Parliament from legislating to shackle the press, and as such is to be supported. But it is terribly time consuming for editors. Better to steer well clear by telling your staff and contributors, including photographers, that they must do nothing that you would have any reason to apologise for or feel ashamed about. If your own conscience does not guide you, consider the feelings of your readers.

One area in which ethical standards have yet to be established is the manipulation of photographic images to make them show things that have never actually existed. Crude photomontages, in which one person's head is placed on another person's body, or two people at opposite sides of the frame are moved closer together, have been with us since the photographic process was invented. They have usually been sufficiently inept to make detection simple, even by non-expert readers. They were not meant to mislead, but to amuse or make a satirical point. They did not profess to be something they were not.

Digital picture manipulation has changed all that. Once the image is digitised (the point at which the shutter is pressed, with digital cameras) it can be distorted, adjusted and merged with other images in a way that is often undetectable by the naked eye. Indeed, there are already cameras on sale that will automatically produce flattering images, for example, through manipulation without the user having to do anything.

This manipulation need not be extreme. Many magazine editors, particularly those whose covers feature photographic models rather than known public figures, routinely retouch their cover photographs. In some cases this is simply a matter of removing blemishes caused in the photographic/scanning/reproduction process. In others it is done to correct human blemishes caused by Mother Nature. Teen magazines are particularly keen to zap spots. Sometimes the hapless model becomes merely the raw material for an exercise in creating a perfect man or woman, using Photoshop rather than a scalpel. Some editors and art directors stop just short of the point at which their model ceases to look human, perhaps recognising that their readers have to identify with a person rather than a Stepford Wife or an Action Man.

On occasion these 'Photoshop jobs' have backfired. When the German GQ magazine, for example, did a photoshoot with Lindsay Lohan, the Dead Butterflies blog pointed out:

> This is crazy. Lindsay Lohan's navel is missing from the cover shot, and then ridiculously high for the bow and arrow shot, and then probably the least photoshopped in the last one where her waist has a normal soft appearance. Come on people, if you are going to turn photography into a 'painting-like' art form, at least be consistent.

The NUJ campaigned for some time, with no obvious effect, for such photomontages to be labelled, probably with a symbol. In 1998, the PCC changed its Code of Practice so that its very first clause, on accuracy, applied to pictures as well as text. It was a decade later before the first high-profile judgement on the issue, when the PCC ruled against the *London Lite* newspaper after it combined images of a celebrity and a model to suggest that they were dating. Each image had been taken at a different time. The PCC commented that the case was 'A useful reminder to editors that photo montages should be labelled as such so that readers are not misled – even if the image itself seems relatively innocuous.'

It is a simple matter for editors to take a stand on this. Any montage, or digitally manipulated photograph (where the intention is to alter, rather than to correct losses of quality in the process), should carry two by-lines: 'Photograph by …'; 'Digital montage (or enhancement, or treatment) by …'. This both gives credit where it is due and tells the reader the truth, which is that the picture is a fiction. Of course, it may be a fiction designed to reveal a 'greater' or 'deeper' truth, but readers are perfectly capable of working that out for themselves.

Those who are using a montage to provide the momentary frisson of excitement that comes when the readers wonder whether something is real have nothing to worry about: that will still work. Only those who want to leave their readers in doubt or confusion, or positively to mislead them, will have anything to fear from such a scheme. The only real opposition is likely to be in-house: art editors and picture editors will not enjoy making it explicit to photographers and models that they have 'improved' on their original work.

The cover

The cover has more impact on an editor's life than any other design issue. A magazine's cover is its most prominent and useful selling tool. Many otherwise excellent publications are damaged by their editors' apparent inability to arrive at a suitable cover style. On the other hand good covers alone will not, in the long term, save a bad magazine. The cover must be true to its subject, but also have an unchanging quality from issue to issue: it is the principal carrier of the magazine's 'brand' values. But finding a style and sticking with it is made no easier by the undoubted fact that everyone has an opinion on the cover, from the managing director to the person who comes in to mend the photocopier. Many of these opinions will have little to do with reality.

There has been research on the importance of the cover to buyers, but it is of strictly limited use. The most famous report was commissioned by Comag, the magazine distributors, in 1990. Thanks perhaps to its great age, it has achieved a status it barely merits. Only 200 people were surveyed, 15 of them in depth, and most of what they had to say was obvious.

The survey discovered, for instance, that readers prefer an attractive, eye-catching cover to an unattractive one and that they don't care about the relevance of the picture to the subject matter. They want to know what is in the magazine, using the cover-lines for this purpose. But most people buy regular magazines irrespective of their covers: spontaneous buyers of unfamiliar magazines do so because they are going on holiday or, in the case of specialist titles, because they want them for reference.

On the basis of these findings, Comag's report produced a set of recommendations on the ideal cover treatment which mesmerised publishers (and bemused editors) for years. It suggested that there should be five cover-lines, which should not be meaningless and should not obscure the cover picture. The cover picture must

Figure 6.1   Components of a standard cover

be clear and not crowded. Men expect the cover picture to have something to do with the content, but women don't. The cover subject should fill the frame and preferably be in the middle. Models must 'reflect the right image for the title', and 'their body language is vital'. Bright colours are preferable to dingy ones, but really there should only be three, preferably black, white and red. And people don't like free gifts obscuring the cover, but they will buy magazines that do this because they want the gifts.

What this research seems to be saying is that readers prefer a competent cover to an incompetent one. A competent cover will not look crowded. It will look bright and not dingy. It will have the right number of cover-lines, and all of them will make sense. In short, it will look 'right'. It will have a certain inherent quality. But how that quality is achieved is largely irrelevant. The cover must have a sense of confidence and strength. But as to the means used to achieve that effect, it is almost the case that, as William Goldman famously said about the movie industry, 'no one knows anything'. Certainly, any slavish attempt to follow a formula is wrong-headed.

Effective cover creation depends upon your being clear about what you are trying to achieve. The point of a cover is to sell the issue, both to your regular readers, whom you want to buy this particular example, and to other people's readers, who might be looking for a change. Obviously those two objectives may not be entirely compatible. Then again, you may not have to sell your magazine. It may have a controlled circulation; it may be distributed solely (or overwhelmingly) by subscription, or as part of a membership deal for an organisation; it may even be distributed without a cover price as part of some other package, with a newspaper for instance. Not being on the news-stand will give you some freedom to assume how the reader will encounter the magazine – but you still have to 'sell' the issue. You may not have to persuade people to take the magazine off the shelf and up to the till, but you still have to produce a cover appealing enough for people to want to pick it up when it falls on their mat.

You also have to make sure that you are 'selling' it to the right people – generally, those that your advertisers want to reach. Sex may sell copies, for example, but that is not your only objective. A good exercise is to have keywords that represent your brand and ask yourself whether the proposed cover represents the same words. Is it 'authoritative', for example (if that is a word you feel describes your magazine's image)? 'Cutting edge'? And so on.

Likewise, the story that is chosen for the cover might not be the best one – but should be the article with the most appeal, and which represents the values of the publication. Explain this to journalists whose egos may be bruised by missing out.

Finally, remember that the cover is your territory, and is not to be given to celebrity agents who demand that their client occupy that space in exchange for providing an interview. You set the terms when it comes to editorial coverage and any short-term gains to be had by making those sorts of deals will be outweighed by the long-term loss of authority as your negotiating power is inevitably further weakened.

None of these things should divert you from your main task, which is to create covers that sell, thereby keeping your staff in work. Sometimes it is necessary to explain this harsh reality to those who think that covers are about 'supporting' various initiatives and organisations or about 'encouraging' various writers.

Subject matter

Subject matter is the fundamental decision. Some covers, of course, especially in the women's general interest market, are no more than attractive visual billboards upon which cover-lines are hung. Sometimes the connection between cover and content runs no deeper than the outfit the model is wearing: winter, summer, Christmas, summer holidays, and so on. In those cases there is no cover subject as such: the cover's success depends upon style rather than content.

Many magazines, however, will have a cover subject (or, less straightforwardly, several subjects). Naturally, each publication has its own interests. This makes generalising difficult, but there are a few thoughts which may be useful. The first, once again, is the appeal to self-interest. Ask yourself what you can produce that will convince your readers that they have a positive, identifiable advantage over those who do not read the magazine.

You know your readers by now. What are the things they are really concerned about? And what ideas, stories and features have you generated that will really get them 'where they live', as the Americans say? You don't have to be a professor of psychology to know that in the general population this means money, family, sex, career, health, home – and not necessarily in that order.

These things rarely form the subject matter of either professional press magazines or specialist consumer publications. But stories about subjects apparently remote from those visceral concerns may well tap into them. A piece about new banking technology, in a magazine for people who work in banks, is really about job security. It does not do to become too rarefied in your thinking about cover subjects: professional people and hobbyists are human beings too.

What you must do is offer something new, or unexpected, or surprising. The guidelines for what constitutes a news story can be helpful here: your cover stories should all be 'news' in their own way, even if they are only offering new recipes by a well-known cook or the first review of some piece of hi-fi equipment. You must be absolutely clear about what people want to know, and what they know already. Miscalculating here can kill a cover story stone dead, which makes it essential that you know not only what is happening in your subject area but also, in general terms, what your rivals are up to.

You should not be overly distracted by your rivals, however: choose subjects on their own merits, and if other people do them at the same time, so be it. A successful magazine is an ocean liner: you set your course, you try not to collide with other craft (or icebergs), but ultimately other people have to get out of your way. You must obviously react to events in the real world but you should let rival publishers look after themselves.

These things come into particular focus with 'people' covers. The use of an appealing person, one your readers are already interested in, is an obvious, easy, straightforward and endlessly seductive cover formula. With the reservations about celebrity work mentioned above, there is no reason not to pursue it. In an industry or specialist publication you will have to make your own stars, building up their editorial visibility over a period before you give them the cover treatment. If you need more than their name, and possibly a simple memory-jogging phrase, to sell them as a cover subject then you are too early. If your readers already feel they know exactly what they think, you are too late.

In the case of cover 'stars', timing is everything. It is better to catch people on the way up, when the readers are still interested in them, and that applies whether they are running ICI or presenting the National Lottery. Of course, you can catch them again on their way down, but that's a different kind of story and a less immediately appealing one. Even magazines for hard-nosed professionals should not scorn 'aspirational' (or 'directional', as the fashion fraternity say) features and cover subjects. Yes, you cater for the realities of their lives at the lower end of the professional ladder, but at the same time you show them what the big names are doing, and how they have achieved their present status.

NME's Conor McNicholas says the cover is 'the thing that affects sales more than anything else and it's also an incredibly fun part of the job. The cover of *NME* is an iconic thing, it's shrouded in myth and legend. We try and have a lot of fun with the cover – if we're not enjoying it, how can we expect our readers to?'

Achievers always make a cover subject. Those who might well achieve in the future are more tricky, and here one idea is to group them: 'The 10 best new bands', 'Tomorrow's award winners', 'High flyers'. Old chestnuts all, and potentially disastrous for the future careers of those you tip, but a great way of making readers feel you share their concerns.

Abstract subjects ('The future of accountancy', 'Be a better lover') do not lend themselves to simple photographic treatment. They need a more thoughtful approach, involving the creation of a genuinely expressive image. That should not rule them out, but their success depends upon coming up with good images and persuading your readers to use their mental faculties. This makes them tricky: allow plenty of time and have a fall-back position if the essential image fails to come.

What makes a bad cover? Every editor has a store of horror stories, of covers sweated over and polished that died a horrible death on the bookstalls. It is important to get a sense of perspective. You should examine your monthly or weekly figures in as much detail as is available to you, but you must take all factors into account. What was the weather like? What else was going on? Were there any distribution problems? You are not responsible for those things.

Everything else is likely to be your fault, however. There are few impossible cover subjects, except those that are ruled out by taste. But there are dull cover concepts and inept executions. You will find it a good idea to avoid depressing things that your readers can do nothing about (as opposed to depressing things that you are helping them overcome). That rules out a lot of the world's death and destruction, except in hard news magazines whose readers define themselves by their ability to confront such material without flinching.

The worst mistake you are likely to make in the selection of cover subjects is to provide your readers with too much of what they already know. This is another example of the 'so-what?' factor at work, and it is greatly to be feared. In practice, it might mean interviews with predictable people, instructional articles that don't inspire, previews of equipment they already know all about or analyses of professional problems they have already confronted and solved.

There is a particular problem about seasonal events: it may be a good idea to do a cover to mark Valentine's Day, or Halloween, but if you are approaching it with any sense of obligation, you'd do better to give it a miss. Such forebodings on the part of editor and staff are not easily concealed from the readers. Christmas covers in particular demand early consideration if they are not to be predictable. Coming up with fresh thoughts in this context will not be easy, but that's what you are paid to do – and so is your team.

Cover treatments

At its best a cover fuses image and type. Historically, there have been magazines which used 'poster covers', images without type, but today they exist only in specialist markets appealing to the self-consciously artistic. Most magazines will settle on a picture with some kind of written label, to indicate an attitude to the material: a picture on its own, unless it is a particularly striking image, rarely expresses anything.

Several elements go into creating the average cover: the logotype or logo (sometimes erroneously known as the masthead); the image; the cover-lines; and the standing elements (price, barcode, date, etc.). The logo is really not part of the cover discussion. Almost invariably it stays the same from issue to issue. Historically, there were exceptions: American *Vogue* used different logos from issue to issue in the 1930s, a gesture of supreme confidence. Today, logos are branding and hence untouchable, although some publications permit changes of colour and positioning. They may also be partly obscured by the cover image.

The logo represents the magazine well beyond this particular context: it will usually be used in stationery, advertising and everywhere else. In some cases it will be licensed for use in clothing or other merchandise. It needs to be designed in the first instance to work in all those situations with the right 'appropriateness'. Once designed, it must be legally protected and looked after: keep it away from tacky merchandising.

On the cover, the safest approach is for it to stay in one place and be completely visible for maximum recognition and efficiency on the shelves. For some reason, art editors love to interfere with the logo: you don't have to accept this unless you can see any point in it. Some sort of slogan under the logo may be a good idea, particularly if you have something to boast about: 'Britain's biggest …', 'Europe's only …'. More tenuous claims often do more harm than good. Claiming to be the country's 'best-loved' magazine in your field, on the basis of a survey you conducted yourselves, won't enhance your authority.

The standing elements, too, need to be neatly packaged. Barcodes in particular have to conform to tight technical specifications concerning size and background colour if they are to work. If they work technically, you have to do your best to ignore them. Readers manage it.

All these elements must be seen in context, meaning their typical setting. Bookstall magazine covers should have impact at a distance of at least three metres. Logos need to be at the top to be visible when they are racked, and they should be recognisable when only half-visible. If you need to know how your magazine performs in real life, spend some time looking at the shelves in a big newsagent or supermarket.

Cover image and cover-lines must also work at the three-metre distance, which is why so many magazines opt for a big face looking straight at the reader. But there are other approaches. The temptation is to change radically from issue to issue. You might use illustrations, reportage photography, caricature or studio portrait, as the subject suggests. But it might be more effective to stick to one basic type of photograph and layout, by the same photographer if possible. A formula, in both artwork and typography, enhances recognition. But take it too far and you are in danger of destroying the sense of excitement that a new issue should create. You want people to recognise that you have a new issue without having to study the date.

Photography generally looks harder, more 'modern' and more 'classy', at least when you are using properly commissioned originals rather than agency shots or PR pictures. A cover shoot is expensive, but at least you should get what you want, even if all you want is a new, stylish portrait of a person. On the other hand, you can make striking covers out of poor photographs, but you need an ingenious art editor. Illustration can be stunning, but it is difficult to keep up the standard and establish a visual style without using just one artist, and that may be undesirable. The same goes for caricatures.

Rhoda Parry, editor of *Country Homes & Interiors*, notes a change in how covers are now used in her field: 'Today we use the cover to generate a feeling,' she told *InPublishing* magazine. 'There has to be an emotional significance to our covers. We create this by producing a strong seasonal sense ... Five to ten years ago, this wasn't happening. Magazines like ours are about creating a dream ... and today's covers have to offer readers more than a room set.'

Covers based upon images of objects rather than people are difficult to sell. Even a number of male hobby publications, which tended to use pictures of hi-fi equipment, cars, and so on, have moved on to adorning their technology with female models.

Most magazine covers now feature portrait photographs. Some subjects will be famous (at least to the magazines' readers), and here quality portraiture should repay its high price. When viewing images, look with the eye of the reader. Is this person recognisable? If not, you may be in trouble. Many magazines, particularly in the women's consumer field, prefer simple face-on head-shots of anonymous models. The model's attractive, appealing look is supposed to correspond to the way the readers see themselves. They have to like the person, or want to be the person. This means that while high-fashion magazine covers will feature more extreme looks, middle-of-the-road titles want the 'girl next door'. That should be easy enough to achieve, but these covers can be problematical as every aspect of clothes, hair, make-up, posture and expression is subjected to minute analysis.

Interestingly, women's magazines rarely feature cover pictures of the opposite sex. When fashion-based men's magazines started in the UK they took the same approach, and used pictures of male film stars and sports personalities. But men are not the same as women. As soon as some iconoclastic editor started placing attractive women on his covers, sales took off. That is now the standard ploy in that market.

Cover-lines

Ideally, there should only be one cover-line. Your readers would buy your magazine because they were confident that it would contain the kind of things they were interested in, and the cover would give wonderful projection to a single brilliant idea. But relying on that kind of reader loyalty is unwise. The old 'solus' readers, loyal to one title, have become 'repertoire' buyers, choosing every month from a range of four or five. They make that choice on the basis of what they believe the magazine contains. Many of us love the purist idea of cover design, but if we are honest we will admit that there is no alternative to telling people what they are getting. In the past, people would open the magazine and scan the contents page. Increasingly, with plastic wrapping and unfriendly newsagents, that information has to be on the front.

There is no special magic about cover-lines, but you need to be clear about the point of them. They are there to tempt the reader, to intrigue and invite closer scrutiny. They should be positive and enthusiastic. It is very difficult to 'sell' a negative idea: 'How to avoid …'; 'Things not to buy …'. Above all they need to be short, colloquial and absolutely straightforward. Sub-editors and editors love puns, clever wordplay and allusions of all sorts. There are plenty of places for such things, but the cover is not one of them. Readers should be able to glance at the line and understand what it means. They shouldn't have to puzzle it out.

In the last few years the number of cover lines has crept up to around six or seven. *Glamour* magazine has played a large role in this, compensating for its handbag size by cramming in cover lines, and proving hugely successful.

The main line needs to be visible at the usual three-metre distance or so. Its usual position, since the mid-1960s, has been in the bottom third of the cover: that leaves the area just above halfway as the visual centre of the page, for your picture to do its work. Subsequent lines can be smaller, but they shouldn't become illegible. Any number of styles of line are available. Some magazines use a sort of 'heading-and-standfirst' style: 'GOING TOPLESS: New convertibles for the summer'. This may satisfy the need to be both clever and informative, but it requires complicated typography and should be accompanied by a general reduction in the number of cover-lines.

Here are some examples of folk wisdom about covers and cover-lines, collected by David Hepworth, editorial director of *Development Hell*.[4]

> Quality of picture is the best guarantee. Women sell better than men. People buy the one they pick up first. Leading left edge works. Use active not passive grammar. Quotes imply access. Numbers bolster the impression of quantity. 'See page 76' works. Best cover-line refers to shortest piece. Sex sells – as do hair and chocolate. Beware green and black and white. Never put 'part 2'. You've got to be up! Magazines are here to celebrate and validate.

You should avoid adding more and more cover-lines simply to satisfy various parties in the office: promotions departments, disgruntled feature writers, even, in some cases, advertising departments. Remind yourself once again: only the readers count. Select your most appealing material for promotion on the cover and sell it as hard as you can.

Coping with cover-mounts

Your cover can be as artistic and full of impact as you like, but if your rivals have thicker paper, lamination, a fifth or sixth colour of ink and a cover-mounted free gift, you are fighting an uphill battle. Once rarities, these things have increased significantly over the past decade. If you are competing in such a market, ask your publisher to look again at the production budget. You might have to shave some of your own costs, but you will need to find the money to compete properly.

There are all sorts of issues to consider with a cover-mount: if it means polybagging the entire magazine, this will mean that readers cannot browse through it. There are also increasing legal issues to consider around free gifts, such as health and safety considerations: see Chapter 4, p. 111 for more on this.

Multiplatform design

Most magazines now have a presence across a variety of online and mobile platforms. In addition to a website they will probably have a Facebook page and/ or group, Twitter feeds, YouTube or Last.fm channels, Flickr account, and perhaps an app for iPhone or iPad.

The branding of these presences should be consistent – but you should also recognise that these are different platforms with different qualities, and often different audiences and commercial objectives. You will probably use smaller, fewer, and more tightly cropped images on your website, for example, than in your photo pool or Facebook pages, where there is less competition for space and the emphasis is more photographic and you can include all the images that didn't make it into print.

Some magazines have websites built for them; some publishers launch magazines online first and then design a print version if there is sufficient demand; and some design the website and the print product simultaneously. All approaches have their own challenges. The key thing is to remember that design is about functionality as well as aesthetics: a well-designed website will not only look good but it should be *usable*.

7   Managing production

Magazine editing is not just about content, nor even about content and design, but about producing an experience for the reader in which the physical object plays an important role. Magazines are, typically, luxury items, and high standards are expected. The gloss of a fashion magazine, the flourescent colours of a gossip magazine, and the smell and weight of an independent music publication – or even a specialist business newsletter – are key parts of the reader's experience. Creating this reader experience can be just as creative an endeavour as maintaining editorial or design standards.

You may not be responsible for the physical quality of the manufactured product, but you do want it done well, and on time. That means the editorial part of the process has to be efficient. Editorial pages must be handed over at the right time, they must occupy the right spaces and they must match the physical requirements of the printing process. This is a matter of copy-flow, scheduling and the flat-plan.

Before that, however, words have to be edited and cut, brought into house style and placed on pages. Headlines, standfirsts and captions have to be written. These are all jobs for the sub-editors or copy editors.

Sub-editing

Sub-editing has three strands:

- quality control – ensuring that everything is accurate, well written and legally safe;
- production – ensuring that everything fits and that deadlines are kept;
- projection – presenting everything to maximum effect, through headlines, standfirsts and captions.

Depending on your staffing and structure, some of these tasks may not be done by sub-editors. Many editors like to write headlines and standfirsts themselves, but it is good to give your sub-editors their fair share. These are among the more enjoyable aspects of their job.

Dealing with copy

Writers and sub-editors should approach a piece of work from different directions. Writers' loyalties will tend to be to their sources, their interviewees and the facts of the story itself. This can mean a lack of detachment, the inclusion of too much confusing detail and, on occasions, deliberate obscurity. Sub-editors represent the readers' interest. That means making everything as clear and as accurate as possible. Sometimes this leads to the loss of nuance and subtlety, but that is the price that is paid for clarity. Writers and sub-editors will sometimes disagree, but editors must adjudicate between the two sides, bearing in mind their separate loyalties. Since the editor's loyalty, too, is to the readers, if the sub-editors are making the right decisions they should generally be able to count on the editor's support.

Pieces must be constructed for clarity. Everything in a story must follow logically, and there should be no internal contradictions. Having established that, the sub-editor can look at individual sentences and paragraphs to ensure that they are as well expressed as they might be. The writer's language must be shorn of padding, clichés and jargon. Every sub-editor will have a favourite library of authorities on the language. No sub-editor's desk should be without the *Oxford Dictionary for Writers & Editors*, the Fowlers' *The Kings English* and *Modern English Usage*, the excellent *Chambers Guide to Grammar and Usage*, *Essential English for Journalists, Editors and Writers* by Harold Evans and *Writing for Journalists* and *English for Journalists* by Wynford Hicks. Even in the business press, subs should encourage language that makes sense to the mass of the public rather than acronyms and technical buzzwords. Jargon is only justified when the jargon word is the right word. Trendy buzzwords irritate even those who understand them.

The sub-editor must also look out for inaccuracies. While the main thrust of a story will necessarily be taken on trust, subs must check those things which can be verified from printed sources or by a simple, uncontroversial telephone call: names, telephone numbers, dates, registered trademarks, and so on. Using online sources such as Wikipedia for verification is obviously problematic – although the site is a good source of information on material that a traditional encyclopedia may not cover (such as popular culture), it is also targeted by users who add hoax information to catch lazy journalists out. If you have to use Wikipedia for any element of fact checking then follow up its references and check those too. If there are no references, then you should be suspicious. And if you find inaccurate information, correct it. Also useful to check is the 'Discussion' page that accompanies every entry on Wikipedia, where users debate changes and where you can also find subject experts.

Subs will usually have at least as much general knowledge and topical awareness as the writer, and should always apply their common sense. It is their job to be sceptical. Spelling should be checked too. Computer spellcheckers will only detect misspellings that do not form words. If the writer types 'there' rather than 'their' or 'the rapist' rather than 'therapist', the spell-checker will not raise the alarm.

Subs must also spot defamatory and potentially actionable statements. Libel cases often come about by accident. Any critical statement about any living person, company, product or organisation is potentially troublesome. Stress that you need to be informed of such statements. Subs should get into the habit of asking 'Would I like this said about me?' If not, there is likely to be a problem.

Subs will often make substantial cuts in submitted articles or carry out major rewrites. If the changes are more than minor, inform the author. Cutting a feature for length can mean removing whole themes, episodes or characters rather than mere verbal tinkering. You should guide the subs so that they know which parts you want to come through the process. It should be standard practice for subs to work on copies of computer files rather than on the originals, since the option of returning to the original form of words must always be available.

Rewriting should only take place when necessary. It is usually preferable to leave well alone. A competently commissioned article should be publishable on arrival, or at least once the author has provided a second draft. Feature writers, especially, are prized for their style, which may be more adventurous than would be acceptable on a news page. Subs should concentrate on re-angling and re-ordering. Sometimes this can take the form of pulling passages out and turning them into sidebars, panels and captions, although it is better if such things are discussed at the commissioning stage.

Rewriting does not usually mean recasting a piece's whole approach. Sometimes changes will be necessary to reflect new developments in a story or to match the tastes of your readership, which you may understand better than a freelance. Don't let the necessary discussions become personal or founder on the minutiae of taste. Subs will sometimes have to salvage otherwise unpublishable pieces, without the help of the author, and you must be ready to defend their work.

Sub-editing and production

A magazine's schedule allocates time for all the editorial tasks, from initial commissioning, through picture research to sub-editing, online production and layout. The subs have to enforce that schedule, ensuring that copy arrives and pages leave on time. Lateness costs money. The subs should have your support in their struggle to enforce deadlines. They are also responsible for keeping control of copy-flow, ensuring that the correct files come in and go out. A logical structure of filenames is important here, as is a system to log traffic between editorial office and outside facilities. Subs must know your editorial computer programs and system inside out.

As well as sending material through on its first pass, subs should read paper proofs. A much higher proportion of errors is detected on paper than on even the best screen. As well as checking for typographical errors and missing lines and words, subs must watch out for wrong fonts, type sizes and weights, all of which are easy to do, and hard to spot, in layout programs.

Sub-editing and projection

On some magazines, particularly those professional publications which use newspaper-style layouts, it is common for subs to handle page layout as well as copy editing. They have a key role in the projection of editorial material, and it helps for them to have received proper training to do the job, probably among newspaper subs rather than magazine designers.

But even subs who aren't involved in the visual aspects of the magazine will have some responsibility for writing the words that project the editorial matter. They have to persuade people to read. That means writing strong cover-lines, headlines, standfirsts and captions. There are as many approaches to these as there are magazines, or, indeed, as there are subs. The editor should set the pattern and keep an eye on quality, but that does not mean stamping out individual inspiration.

Your magazine's cover is its most important selling tool, and you may like to use your subs' expertise in this department. The picture makes a direct appeal and the main cover-line supports it. The remaining lines represent the five or six most appealing articles inside, rather than the longest, most prominent or most costly. Once again, offer the readers an advantage. Phrase that offer in a straightforward and appealing way. Clever puns and allusions are rarely required in cover-lines. If you can intrigue the readers, do so.

Headlines inside the magazine can be less commercially minded. They should have respect for their function, however. News headlines are the most straightforward: they tell readers the gist of the story. They should also have some relation to a story's standfirst, if your design includes one. But they must not use the same phrasing: that's a waste of space.

Outside the news area, headline style will depend on what the design requires the headline to do and the space it provides. A reader looking at a page or spread needs to know exactly what it is about. If your design allows you to incorporate basic information in a strapline or sub-heading, you don't need it in your main head, which can therefore be more allusive and clever. For instance, if you have an interview with someone whose name is well known to your readers your strapline can say 'Interview: Joe Smith'.

Your standfirst can then say what Joe Smith is all about, as well as introduce the interviewer (if your design does not demand a separate by-line): 'The head of Amalgamated Rivets foresees a hard time ahead for industry' etc. Meanwhile your headline attempts to tell readers more about what Joe Smith is like: 'Man of iron' or 'Hammering out a grim message'. The trick is to use the various elements to ensure that between them they provide all the necessary information, without necessarily providing it more than once.

Headlines must be legally sound. It is disastrous to amend copy to remove its defamatory undertones only to reinstate them by sloppy choice of a headline. Some consumer magazine subs tend to think that writing a heading is about writing puns. It is not. Readers don't like puns half as much as subs do, and if they are allowed it must only be when they are appropriate as well as funny. A play on words based on someone's name must be meaningful as well as humorous. If the pun is particularly appealing then it must be integrated with the standfirst so that it makes sense, but don't use the standfirst to explain a heading that is otherwise meaningless. Other types of wit are often more appropriate, including topical or artistic allusion.

Editors should be aware that there are fashions in headline writing, even within a single sub-editing department. Occasionally you must issue an order: no more first names to appear in headlines, no references to the names of songs the readers won't have heard, and so on. This is not to cramp anyone's style, it's to try and make inspiration run on less familiar lines.

Standfirsts are another essential element of the feature package. They are useful for writers because they free them from the chore of identifying precisely what the feature is about in the first 50 words. They can also indicate the tone of what is to follow, or set the scene. Brevity, though, is of the essence. Most contemporary standfirsts consist of no more than a single punchy sentence, two if the writer's by-line is to be incorporated.

Crossheads are short headings between paragraphs in the body of a feature or story. They are rarely more than two or three words long and are placed for design purposes, usually, rather than for editorial reasons. They should have some relation to what is immediately beneath them. Sometimes they are fixed on the page rather than embedded in the text, and the copy runs round them. If you cut earlier in the story, the copy moves up and the crosshead (or sidehead, which is a left-aligned variant) now appears after the text it refers to. This irritates some readers.

Captions are there to label the elements in a picture, but not to describe them. Those who are writing captions should ensure that they know exactly what the cropped picture will show, and be careful not to state the obvious. The caption should, where possible, add something to the picture that the visuals alone cannot convey, whether that is actual information – 'Minutes before the fatal crash ...' – or simply atmosphere. There is no need to say 'This picture shows ...'. You can safely omit the obvious. Readers do expect to know the identities of the people in any picture. If you don't have their names, or you don't think they're relevant, you need to find a way of explaining them away. Subs must also check that the correct photographs are being used. Confusing two people with similar names can be a costly error if one is a known criminal and the other is a blameless Sunday-school teacher.

All these things are the product of solid basic skills, a high level of education and awareness, and sharp verbal intelligence. Editors should value their subs at least as much as the more vocal and visible members of the team.

Search engine optimisation (SEO)

Some sub-editors will also have to edit copy for online publication. In other cases this will be the web editor's job. In either case they will probably need to rewrite headlines and other elements for the web to ensure that they use plain language and include key names and phrases that the content relates to. A headline that may read 'Selling the family silver?' in print might be rewritten as 'Janet Jones on selling Smithco' online on the basis that users will be searching or scanning for those names rather than a colloquial phrase that is meaningless out of context.

Just as in print content, the first paragraph of an article is particularly important online as users and search engines scan for key terms. Likewise, crossheads – more plainly known as subheadings – are useful in helping users find the relevant part of the article that they are scanning for. Both – like headlines – should include key names and phrases where relevant to ensure that search engines correctly categorise your content. The sub or web editor may also need to tag and categorise content effectively for similar reasons.

There is much more to search engine optimisation than this but other parts are likely be the responsibility of other people. For example, the person who decides which content management system (CMS) to use (this is the software you use to add content to the website, most often web-based) will need to make sure that the system embeds all of this information into the code of the page: its title and web address (URL), for example www.engineeringmagazine.com/janet-jones-smithco is more search engine-friendly than www.inspiredmag.com/32427648376.asp. Your publication may also have someone responsible for trying to generate 'inbound' links to your content from other sites, too, such as a community editor or social media manager.

Copy-flow

Copy-flow is a complex matter. It determines the sequence of events from initial ideas to the moment the magazine leaves the editorial floor. It is not one single sequence. At various points, things happen simultaneously. There will be numerous 'feedback loops' where work, once done, is assessed and if necessary done again. And, to add to the complication, schedules for several issues will overlap.

Given these difficulties, it is no surprise that most editors stick with the schedule they inherit, rather than taking a clean sheet of paper – or perhaps a stack of paper – and working out the most logical system. But systems that 'just about' work, without being planned, have a way of failing when one key person goes missing. They also bear more heavily on some people than on others. That's not good management.

You might start tidying up by drawing up a flowchart, a working drawing that will let you take account of your resources: people, materials and time. Don't expect to get it all on one neat diagram. Isolate various aspects of the problem and deal with them one at a time. Separate sheets of paper might show you what all your people are doing at various times, where editorial copy is going in both paper and digital form, what proofing materials are being generated and the paths they take, and so on.

In the end you might be able to reconcile some of these elements into a single chart, festooned with different coloured inks, but it's fairly unlikely. Still, the point is to try to work out how it works, not to make a nice picture. With luck, you'll be able to reconstruct things in a more efficient and transparent form. Every magazine is different, of course, both in its staffing and in its actual technical procedures. The system described here is typical of that used on small to medium-sized consumer monthlies.

Drawing up a copy-flow diagram

Forget for a moment that you are working on several issues of your magazine at the same time and concentrate on the steps in the creation of a single issue, see Figure 7.1. These stages overlap in time, and they may be repeated as material comes back round the system for re-evaluation and as circumstances change. What follows is an idealised and simplified picture of what happens.

Start with planning. There will probably be some kind of initial meeting. Your section editors, if your magazine is that big, or your writers will bring their ideas, but also the information you need to help you organise the issue: the dates of significant events for both you and your readers, and so on. You should have any publishing information that is available at this stage: issue size ('pagination'), the likely advertising volume and editorial allocation, and anything else that will take up editorial space, such as in-house adverts, offer pages and competitions. You discuss how to fill that space, and by the end you should be well on the way to working out an approximate running order. You already know where your regulars are going to be placed.

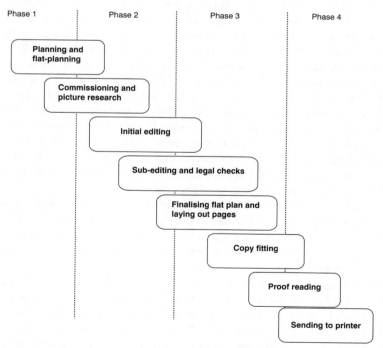

Figure 7.1 Overlapping tasks in one cycle of magazine production

The next stage is commissioning and briefing. You find suitable writers, photographers, illustrators and picture libraries and brief them, preferably in writing. In-house contributors have to be organised too. It is possible to commission photography, and start library research, before you have the words. Illustrators, though, often need the writing, because they respond to specific phrases and verbal images. All parties must be well aware of 'copy in' dates which will have been set by your chief sub/production editor.

The next stage, which you might call initial editing or rough editing, starts as soon as the first commissioned material begins to arrive. At this stage, good 'housekeeping' is essential. Most copy now arrives via email, and needs to be logged in and safely stored. There are now various online project management services that provide this sort of service. Incoming material should be copied to the correct computer folder or queue and allocated to the appropriate editor. The copied files should be renamed according to a meaningful convention devised by your chief sub/production editor to ensure that the right versions make their way into the right issues. The whole naming system should be the sole responsibility of one person, probably the chief sub/production editor, but there should be a written explanation of how it works for use in emergencies. Preferably the file name should indicate the issue of the magazine it is intended for and the status of the copy, but beware that the lengths of filenames are limited in some computer systems. You might start with a one-word title, then add the date, then the initials of the first copy editor: CatstoryOct03-JM.doc. When someone else passes it, let them add their name: CatstoryOctO3-JM-PS.doc. And so on, remembering to bear in mind your system manager's rules about file naming. For safe use of your files on a range of computers, stick to letters, numbers, single hyphens (-) and underscores (_).

A sophisticated editorial management system, built around a database, will ensure that once a file is brought into the system it cannot be lost or overwritten. It should always be possible to revert to the last saved version. Systems such as InDesign allow locking and unlocking, and checking in and checking out of files. Those who have to manage with simple networks of individual computers have to devise their own systems for ensuring that originals are kept safe and that files are opened and edited sequentially. It is foolish to spend time polishing a feature that someone else has already edited and passed. It is also essential that your designers lay out stories using the correct versions of the text.

It is a good idea to read the original story on paper – printed text is higher resolution than on-screen, and therefore easier and quicker to read, as well as allowing space for you to write notes on that you can pass on to the writer or designer. Some, however, prefer the trackability of digital file management, where you can see its progress.

Whatever system you come across or put in place, make sure that you can easily identify the latest version of a story, that others can easily put changes into effect, and you can tell where the work sits in the production line – from editor to subs and on to layout. You should also be able to find author contact details and information about the original commission, for instance how long it is supposed to be and what it is intended for.

Depending on the time available to you, and your confidence in your commissioning and editing staff, you may choose not to read original copy. But you will certainly want to read early edits of the story, and the original should always be available.

At the initial edit, editors and senior staff should be making sure the copy fits the brief, and then cutting and shaping stories, sending them back for rewrites, adding any panels and boxes, and thinking about headlines, standfirsts and other display matter. Some magazines have a single meeting at which all headlines are written in a batch. There is a danger here of allowing these important elements to become 'samey', stereotyped and tired. Better, probably, to allow individual stories and individual editors to suggest their own headlines.

The first broad copy-editing stage must be followed by a sub-editing stage, in which subs check facts, construction, legality, grammar, spelling, house style and the rest. The copy will probably go to the chief sub first, who will allocate it appropriately. Traditionally, subs have done most of the rewriting and the writing of headlines, standfirsts and captions. Increasingly those tasks have moved up the hierarchy, leaving subs to become more involved in copy-fitting.

By this stage, the art process will be under way. Editorial design should start as a visual statement into which editorial matter is brought, rather than as a mass of editorial matter which the design struggles to accommodate and prettify.

The art editor will allocate work according to the production schedule. Once designers set to work, they have to select pictures in conjunction with the picture editor and relevant editors and then combine them with real copy. Obviously, fixed elements of page design, including the basic grid or grids, folios (page numbers) and other standing elements, can be built into the master pages on which individual layouts are based.

There will also be a full set of type style sheets, set up by the magazine's original designer or the person responsible for the last redesign. There may also be more detailed templates for various parts of the magazine. This is an area where technology has obvious economic benefits, although it is a long way from the 'editing by design' ideal, in which each spread is individually designed to reflect its content. But it does mean casual freelance designers, for instance, can quickly put together a magazine with the right brand identity. Creativity can be employed where it really counts: on the major features spreads and the cover.

Art proofs are generated at this stage. The proof, with any overmatter (placed in a type box on the same sheet, outside the type area), is then passed back to the art director, section editor and editor, who will be looking at the shape of the spread as much as at details. The proof will then be returned for the artwork to be adjusted.

Next comes the copy-fitting stage. On receipt of a 'first proof' generated by the art department, the editors and chief sub will examine it before handing to a sub to fit, rewrite where necessary and add any finishing touches such as captions, standfirsts, pull quotes and credits which have not been completed at an earlier stage. This will then be run out again, and a second or 'final' proof examined in minute detail. It will then go back to the chief sub, who will give it a final check and then pass it around to all the appropriate editors. When they have added their final details and 'signed off' the page, any last-minute changes can be added on-screen by the sub. The page will then be given a final OK by the chief sub and art director before being sent on its way.

The currently favoured system of delivery is PDFs. These files work with any current computer system and most typesetting bureaux. Text, layout, fonts, photographs and computer drawings are all incorporated into a single highly compressed file that can then be sent to the pre-press house or printer.

Others continue to send more elaborate bundles to their 'repro' (for 'reproduction') houses. That might mean InDesign pages with text and images in place. InDesign and other layout programs will list the pictures, fonts and other resources they need if the pages are to be reproduced properly. All this material (not always the fonts) must also go to your colour house or printer, depending on your arrangements for pre-press work. Everything that leaves you should be logged, even if it is being sent online. Usually, physical objects have to be sent as well. You should always send hard copies of your layouts to the repro house and printers, for reference purposes. All these things make proofing critical.

The colour proofs will be returned to the magazine for examination. This should allow enough time for changes to be made, but these should be avoided for reasons of cost. In general, changes at this stage should be reserved for dire emergencies. Serious legal problems are the first example. Gross embarrassment, perhaps when someone dies or you have made a terrible mistake, is the second.

From this point, the print issue is out of your hands, but you may be dealing with stories that have already been published online or which are scheduled to (see below). You may, out of interest, attend the occasional print run yourself and your publisher may be able to spare someone to observe what happens, but there is nothing much you can do about it. But if you are operating on a tight print schedule, your office must be staffed while printing is under way so emergency decisions can be made.

Things can go wrong at any stage. Pages or files go astray or corrupt, and you receive a call asking what you want to do. It helps to have a made-up 'house ad' at the printers for such eventualities. If there is time, you should be able to find the page in the computer system and resend it. It is at times like this, when you are the only person left in the office, that you realise how important it is to know your layout program and your file-naming system.

The mysteries of printing, pre-print, repro and finishing may be new to you. Try to meet the people who do this work and get them to explain it. Few of us want to appear ignorant, but that is preferable to getting things wrong. Ask about the right software, the right file labelling system and the best way of bundling your material. See what they can do to help your workflow. If you make the effort with your printers, they may take more care with your magazine.

Figure 7.1 showed the magazine being gradually assembled in a sequence of tasks handled one at a time like a production line. In practice, the raw material of the magazine travels in a series of loops, getting closer to completion each time. The same people handle the same material at several stages in its development. A

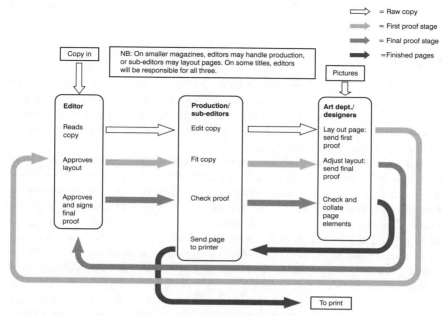

Figure 7.2 Typical editorial copy-flow around a magazine

diagram of copy-flow, showing how the different sections of the staff work on the same piece of editorial material, is necessarily more complicated, see Figure 7.2.

Imagine all those processes happening at once. How long does each task take? Which jobs can be done simultaneously? Who is under pressure at each stage? If you think about the timing of these activities, you should be able to see where production bottlenecks are likely to occur. You may need to find ways of dividing responsibilities differently.

The other factor is your computer system. Your company might have a content management system that makes it easy to manage files across the publication. If it is a small independent publisher, however, you may need to convert your theoretical copy-flow into a logical system of files and folders. A story might appear first in a folder called 'copy in' on the main file server. Editors might then work on that on their own computer, then rename it accordingly, before placing it back in another file on the server, perhaps labelled 'copy to subs'. Subs can then pull the file out to work on it before putting it back, renamed again, into 'copy to art'.

The art department is then free to pick up the file and drop it into InDesign, applying style sheets, bringing in pictures and building a layout. The finished page goes into a file called 'first proofs' and a hard copy is printed. The editor approves the layout and the subs copy-fit, moving it to a folder called 'final proofs', printing another hard copy.

The layout is now approved, proof-read and the page file placed in a folder called 'to print' or 'dispatch'. Sub-editors or designers must ensure the page elements are collated and the basic file accompanied by any photos, illustrations or special fonts.

Scheduling

As soon as you start to incorporate realistic time constraints in your copy flowchart or diagram, you are on the way to scheduling. Your publisher or print-buyer should be able to tell you the exact timings once your magazine leaves the editorial offices. These deadlines are fixed in accordance with advertising requirements as well, and cannot be changed at will.

A serious discussion with both printers and repro facilities should allow you to get a feel for how things work at their end. This will translate into a series of dates and times for you to deliver your pages. Things are much more complicated if your magazine is only partly in colour, or if it is printed on several machines before being reunited at the binding and finishing stage, or if you have an add-on supplement to be printed and bound on at the same time. You may also want an extra colour on your cover (such as a fluorescent tone, or metallic shades), or laminated effects. All of these may require extra time and your schedule will have to be brought forward to accommodate the printers.

Working backwards from these print deadlines, and referring to the sequence of events laid down in your flowchart, you should be able to schedule for a single issue. Work backwards through 'pages to repro house', 'final proof', 'first proof', 'finished layouts', 'copy editing', 'all copy in' and 'commissioning of copy' right back to your original planning meeting. It is not surprising to find that many glossy magazines are working on their Christmas issues at the end of the summer holidays.

Once you have worked out realistic timings for a single issue, it is just a question of superimposing several schedules onto a single calendar, see Figure 7.3. Use a real calendar, which includes public holidays. Now stop and take stock. Are you really going to be able simultaneously to 'pass' one issue, write headlines in a second and hold a planning meeting about a third? It may be possible to do different tasks in the course of a day, but it is not ideal to make several critical decisions simultaneously. Try not to schedule anything at the same time as events whose timing is determined by other people. For instance, you must study the colour proofs when they arrive, otherwise you will have no time to act.

A schedule needs to work smoothly almost all of the time. That way everyone involved in production will be sufficiently relaxed when a genuine crisis or opportunity arises. If you do not habitually dither about your cover, you will be better placed when you have to change it because your cover star has died or your rivals have the same picture.

Once you have the printing dates, and the schedule begins to take form, your own dates need to be worked out in detail. This will usually be the job of the chief sub/production editor, who will work back allocating a number of working days for each department – art editor, sub-editors and section editors – to handle the copy. These dates will then be recorded on a written schedule which must be distributed to each member of staff.

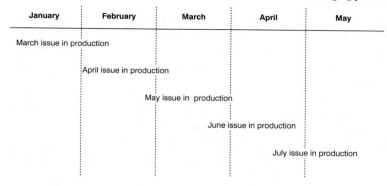

Figure 7.3 Overlapping schedules for a monthly magazine

Often the feature content of a magazine will be divided into three or four sections. The priority of sections and their configuration may be laid down by the printer or may be just a device of the chief sub/production editor to even out copy-flow. Each section will have its own schedule, and the schedules will overlap. 'Section one' copy arrives with the editors on one date, followed by 'section two' copy days or weeks later. The editors have time to work on one section and pass it down the line before more feature material arrives on their desks to be edited. This is to discourage people from leaving commissioning and editing until late in the production cycle. Chasing late copy or layouts is usually the job of the chief sub/production editor.

Schedules are built from the back, meaning the moment your pages reach the printer. The process of print-buying invariably involves some compromise about the scheduling of printing. By fitting your magazine around some bigger printing contract, your printer may save you money. But if your magazine misses its print 'slot', your incompetence will affect not only your own printing, finishing and distribution but those of other magazines around you. So print contracts include punitive clauses about late arrival of material. In return, the printers should pay you compensation when they let you down. All this becomes more complex as you go beyond simple four-colour printing to include external cover printing, finishing, binding, and so on. As editor, you need to know exactly when your issue must arrive at the printer, and what it will cost you if you don't make it.

Every editorial person must stick to the schedule or a backlog will be created. When this happens, the sub-editing department has to make up time. Always support your chief sub/production editor in enforcing deadlines. Failures in this area can have expensive consequences.

Scheduling online production

Magazine websites have introduced different rhythms into production schedules – to what extent depends on the way your publication has integrated web production processes, and the software that they use to publish content – most of which now allow you to publish not only to print, but also web, mobile and tablet formats (some are cruder than others in the way that they do this). Some magazines impose print production cycles on their websites, meaning they are only updated every month, but most have recognised that the web works to a very different rhythm.

At the earliest stages of commissioning stories you will have to consider how they might work online – indeed, you might have to decide whether they go online at all, or only partly, or if they only go online and not in the magazine.

News is a good example of a type of content which suits the web well, and many magazines publish news on their website which never appears in the print edition (because it would by then be out of date).

Multimedia content is another. Your magazine may run an online radio station (as NME.com does) or expert podcasts. It may run an online TV channel (like *Stuff* magazine's) or provide a data service. This means that journalists have to consider visuals, audio or data as they go about covering a story.

You may have to decide whether to keep web production separate from print production, or integrate the two. Separation has its own benefits, including focus on the web product and innovation; but it also has its drawbacks, including lack of efficiency and communication (both production teams may be working on the same stories) and cultural conflict (teams may look down on each other). An integrated team is able to look at a story or issue from a number of angles, cross-promoting different coverage across their respective platforms. Most new journalists are expected to be skilled across a number of platforms now anyway, and it is increasingly the case that any editorial team is able to produce great coverage on whichever platform suits it best.

You will also have to schedule when you are going to publish material online. Here you have no printers to worry about – but you do have the print product. Some key factors to consider are

- timeliness;
- exclusivity;
- whether the content supports a print feature;
- whether the content feeds into a print feature (for instance, are you hoping to use any material from the website, such as comments or images, in the printed publication);
- whether the material particularly suits the web in being 'social' or 'viral'.

As stated above, timely material such as news should go online first. Exclusive material can be held back for print publication – but you should also plan how to lead up to that with teasers and web-friendly material such as multimedia. A video for a review could be held back to support the print product – but if it's a new piece of kit that people are going to be Googling then you will gain a lot of traffic by publishing the video early.

'Social' or potentially 'viral' material can be hugely effective if used right. If you have a real-life interview with someone who resigned in a spectacular manner, then a copy of their resignation letter (with any personal details redacted) might catch a lot of attention online.

Online distribution

This idea of viral content is a small part of the broader issue of distribution online. Whereas your print product will be distributed to news-stands or subscribers, there is no distribution infrastructure online – at least, not one that you can control.

The primary means of distribution online are search (that is, people finding your content) and social (people sharing your content). Search engine optimisation – mentioned above – is a key way to ensure that people find your content; that it is well distributed on search engine rankings for particular terms. Social distribution is much more difficult, and increasingly important: Facebook, Twitter and other channels can often be the number one sources of traffic to a site.

Publishers tend to take three broad approaches to online distribution. The first is to focus on marketing the website by advertising on relevant websites, promoting the site in the printed magazine, and various other channels. This can be expensive and not always effective.

A second approach is to hire a social media manager to ensure that the magazine has a high visibility across various social media platforms. Their role may involve managing a number of accounts for the magazine, or parts of it, responding to other users and trying to stimulate conversations around issues the publication is covering.

The third approach is to ask journalists to get stuck into social media themselves, talking about the stories that they are covering and the places they are travelling to, and having conversations with readers. The advantage of this approach is that it often leads to the journalist having a closer relationship with readers, and a better understanding of what they want. It can also generate useful story leads and contacts.

Clearly, as in any situation where a journalist is representing your magazine in a public place, they should be expected to behave professionally at all times. This does not mean that they should not talk about personal experiences or opinions (which can be very effective in forming relationships), but that they should avoid being unnecessarily offensive or unprofessional. They may want to have separate social media accounts for personal use.

Online production

There is no single way of producing a magazine for the web, for mobile or for tablets, and there are a range of competing systems that allow publishers to publish across media, from adapted (and expensive) print production systems to free, simple online tools such as Issuu, which will convert an uploaded PDF into a 'page-turning' online magazine.

Production, then, can range from being exactly the same cycle as for print (with the only difference being that nothing is printed at the end, but the PDF is merely put online) to a one-off production term that ends in the release of a mobile application. It might involve managing an online community and creating content in response to what they're talking about, or asking. It might involve adding 'metadata' about your content (such as the people, organisations and locations it refers to) so that it can then be published according to a pre-defined system, or according to the requirements of users.

There are dozens of online tools that are worth familiarising yourself with. Issuu, already mentioned, takes your PDFs and allows you to embed them on any web page with the ability for users to turn pages. This is sometimes called 'brochureware' – taking a physical product and putting it online with little thought paid to using the qualities of the medium, like putting a radio programme on TV. That said, it is a cheap and simple way for those with print production skills to publish their work online.

Mygazines offer a more powerful service, which they charge for. This includes magazines that are better optimised for search, which link to social networking, and have in-page links as well (such as coverlines that link directly to a story). They also build apps for mobile phones and tablets – as do services such as Pieceable, ComboApp, and Application Craft. Those wanting to build an app for Android can also play with Google's free App Inventor for Android. Ultimately, it's worth remembering that the most popular app on mobile phones is the web browser – and building a mobile-friendly website may be the cheapest and most successful mobile strategy.

Flexible blogging services such as Wordpress can also be used effectively for building professional-looking and powerful websites. CNN, the *New York Times* and the *Telegraph* are just three organisations that use Wordpress in their publishing operations. The key is customisation: you can set up these services so that you have control over the top stories, and over layout. There are also a number of web design services such as IssueManager that will do that customisation for you.

The market in this area is in its early stages, so some of these services will fold, and new ones will launch – take some time to find the new ones.

Your own production processes will be influenced in large part by the system that you choose – and you should of course choose a production system based on the needs of your publication. These change so frequently, however, that flexibility may be the most important feature. In the case of Reed Business Information, for example, they have restructured magazine teams to separate content production from delivery channels: individual journalists working on a particular field are expected to think of the best way to cover a particular story across multiple platforms; 'product editors' are expected to ensure that there is a balance of coverage in their particular channel (for example, online, or print); and a 'Head of Content' coordinates the tension between the two.

Flat-planning

Editors must understand flat-planning, although some may find this a task that can be delegated. The flat-plan is a map of the magazine, indicating what goes where, from the cover to the back page advertisement. Its purpose, in commercial publications, is to allocate space for advertising and editorial matter, in accordance with the advertising/editorial ratio and overall pagination. In large publishing houses these matters are broadly established when the annual publication budget is drawn up. But a skilled editor uses flat-planning as an editorial tool, clarifying the order, prominence, size and shape of competing pieces of editorial material within the editorial space. That in turn determines the balance and 'pace' of the issue.

To flat-plan you need the advertising department to tell you what advertising has been sold and where. Obviously, position is one factor in determining the price of advertising. Restricting the available positions improves rates and makes it feasible to produce an editorially appealing magazine. The precise restrictions will be laid down either as written rules or by tradition.

Long before flat-planning begins, you can sketch out running orders and likely feature lengths. Indeed, you should get into the habit of visualising the final layouts of features even before you commission them. Designers, too, will sketch likely 'shapes' of your big features even before they have the copy and photographs. Draw up a simple running order, indicating the main features and their approximate lengths and the shapes you'd like, for example:

- Cover story; driving the new Focus: 6 pages = 2 × spreads + 2 × singles
- Second feature; selling a one-year-old car: 4 pages = 1 × spread + 2 × singles

and so on. These exist only in your mind at this stage, although you will be thinking about the photographs needed to make those spreads a possibility. Some shapes on the page are better than others. Features really need to start with impact. You can get that with a double-page spread, or, perhaps, by opening on a right-hand page (which is where the reader's eye naturally falls) and then going to a spread. You would not, ideally, start anything on a left-hand page. But you can finish or continue features and sections there.

It is not surprising to discover that advertisers want the same spaces as you: right-hand pages. They don't want them opposite other people's advertisements. They don't mind half-pages, vertically or horizontally, providing that you put editorial above or beside them. They won't accept a place next to someone else's half-page advertisement, or above or below it, unless the price is right.

Editorial needs a clear presence on the right-hand pages near the start of the magazine, so that browsers can tell that the magazine has something in it. But advertisers want that space most of all, and are prepared to pay for it. This is an obvious conflict, which needs to be determined at the outset by the publisher. The advertising department should have a list of acceptable positions and sizes, with prices that increase with their prominence. But there must be an upper limit: it is absurd to sell every single right-hand page in the front half of a magazine. At the same time, you want to negotiate a notional flat-plan with certain areas permanently reserved for editorial, so that you have a fixed place for certain essentials, for instance the contents page and the back page columnist.

In the UK, advertisements are generally placed between features – which actually helps punctuate the magazine – and inside features. This is less desirable, but inevitable, in a competitive climate. Designers need to be told what advertising will appear alongside their pages and react appropriately. It is almost never right to shout down an advertisement. Better to place your plain type against it and hope your readers are sufficiently engrossed to avoid being blown off track, which they should be. Worse problems come for a designer when the flat-plan somehow leaves two one-page editorial items opposite one another: it is then that wise editors will hope for another advertisement to appear.

Flat-planning is not a once-and-for-all event, although many magazines have a session where problems are thrashed out. This is one of the few occasions when advertising and editorial sides meet, which can be either helpful or the excuse for a lot of bickering. Have your notional running order in mind, as well as a full schedule of other editorial elements. Your advertising director or manager will tell you how many advertisements have been sold (or are confidently *expected* to be sold) and where they go. Take the number of ads sold, and apply the advertising : editorial ratio to it. That will give you the number of editorial pages. Add together advertising and editorial pages and you arrive at your issue pagination. For example: 72 pages sold in a magazine with a 60 : 40 ad : ed ratio gives 48 editorial pages and 120 pages in total.

There is not always an exact fit. Issue sizes go up in fours (100 pp, 104 pp, 108 pp, etc.), or sometimes 16s (64pp, 80pp, 96pp, etc.) whereas advertising is sold in units of a single page or less. If your advertising department sells 60 pages of advertising and you are working on a 60 : 40 ratio, you produce a 100-page issue. If it sells 63 pages of advertising, you can accept a reduction in the ratio to 63 : 37. It's not good for the reader, but you hope to average things up over a period. Or you go up an issue size to 104 pages, at which point your ratio returns to approximately 60 : 40, leaving you with an extra editorial page to fill, and no budget for it.

If the advertising department sells only 56 pages, on the other hand, the ratio would move to 56 : 44, a radical shift in the editorial direction. But editorial doesn't bring in any money, so in practice you would drop down an issue size or two, ending up with a 92-page issue in which you would supply 36 pages. That would mean losing a feature, and if you've already commissioned it that's bad news. And these are only small swings. They can be much wilder than that. In practice, cost-conscious publishers will always opt for the smaller issue, reducing editorial space.

It is good practice to establish the maximum and minimum issue sizes, as well as acceptable deviations from the ratio. The publisher always decides whether to go up or down an issue size and sets the number of pages you work within. Issues will not normally be enlarged for editorial reasons, because that costs money, whereas they will be enlarged for more advertising, which is income. But extra editorial pages will be permitted when advertising volumes are low but a solid presence on the shelves is required, or when particular events call for them. At that point you need to ask for some extra money for editorial material. Within these broad guidelines, it is for you and your advertising counterparts to agree the placing of advertising in and around editorial material.

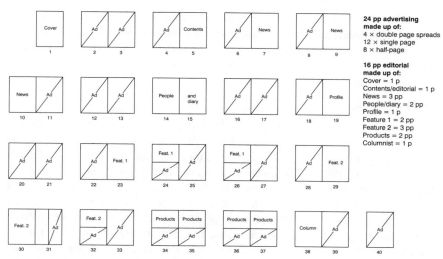

Figure 7.4 Flat-plan for a 40-page issue on a 60:40 ad:ed ratio

Flat-planning, in complex cases, demands a clear head, good mental arithmetic, an eraser and a supply of sharp pencils. A blank plan of the whole magazine is used, and agreed fixed editorial sites and guaranteed advertising sites are filled in first. These will include your contents page, the back page ad and the 'first available right-hand' advertisement. Then you carry on adding more advertising and editorial until everything is accommodated and every blank is filled, see Figure 7.4.

It helps to start with the simple areas, notably the back, before moving towards the problematical ones. Flat-planning tends to start at the ends of the magazine and works its way in to the centre. As each advertisement is included it should be crossed off the advertising schedule, as should your editorial items. Naturally this involves a lot of counting and recounting of pages to ensure that advertisements are not omitted or included more than once.

A crude flat-plan can always be adjusted at a slightly later stage, by mutual agreement. Indeed, there will generally be adjustments as the advertising department does better or worse than it had hoped. By this stage, changes to overall issue size will no longer be possible, which can mean infuriating last-minute adjustments to your cherished editorial schemes. If it happens a lot, complain to your publisher. Creating editorial matter that is not used is extremely wasteful. Providing extra editorial because advertising falls short will wreck your budget. The ratio is an essential part of the magazine's publishing strategy and should be respected.

Once drawn up, the flat-plan should be copied and distributed to art and sub-editing departments while you hold on to the master copy. If you agree any amendments with the advertising department, you should immediately issue copies of the new version, indicating the specific changes. The previous versions should be filed away where they can do no harm. The accidental use of more than one flat-plan is a common cause of production disaster. Ensuring the finished pages adhere to the agreed flat-plan is the responsibility of your production editor or chief sub, advised by your art director and subs.

Housekeeping

A good schedule, carefully policed, and a competent, workable flat-plan are the basis of a solid production regime. Whatever the sequence of events before the final stage is reached, the finished pages should be signed off by the chief sub or equivalent, by the art director or equivalent, and by you or your deputy. All three of you are doing different jobs. Your chief sub is looking at the close verbal texture and providing a final check against typographical and factual errors. Your art director must approve both general competence and such matters as picture credits and copyright acknowledgements. You look at the whole thing for the impression it makes on the reader. Do not use this as an opportunity simply to second-guess other people's work, but if you find anything wrong, and it can be corrected in time, it is right to send it back.

Most magazines leave the office in digital form. You can sign a final laser proof, which should give an entirely accurate picture of what will emerge from the printing process. Someone needs to be designated to control precisely what is despatched, to log it out of the building and to check its safe arrival. Naturally there must be backup and archive copies of all this material.

At the end of the process, a whole range of other trades and techniques are involved, including finishing, binding and distribution. Here you are in the hands of the experts, but you are entitled to expect good quality control. Listen to complaints from readers about poor binding and printing and about late delivery. Have subscription copies sent to your home, those of your colleagues and far-flung relatives. Complaints about late delivery, faulty binding, bad printing and all the rest are really not your responsibility, but they do annoy your readers. You should not ignore them.

8　Where the buck stops

Freedom of the press is guaranteed only to those who own one.

(A.J. Liebling)

The freedom to publish is hedged around by restrictions. Some of these are petty and technical, but others benefit all citizens. We may chafe at some of the absurdities in British press law, but we must work within it if we are to carry on publishing what our readers require. We have little constitutional protection, unlike journalists in the USA and elsewhere, and we cannot rely upon the support of society in general. The British constitution's attitude to free speech is that it is an important principle but not one that should take automatic precedence over other rights.

In recent times, free speech and press freedom have been recognised in the European Convention on Human Rights, now brought into British law under the Human Rights Act 1998. Article 10 of the Convention upholds freedom of expression, but most editors are likely to hear more about Article 8, which enshrines the right to privacy.

Editors operate in a climate in which freedom of the press is seen as a sectional interest rather than a human right, and in which the activities of journalists are viewed with public scepticism and hostility. This is due at least in part to the commercial and legal pressures under which journalists operate, and has played at least some part in the motivations of those who take the opportunities presented by the Internet to practise forms of journalism which are liberated in one way or another from them.

In the meantime, realistic editors recognise the conditions under which they operate. To be an effective editor it is necessary to know and observe the legal and ethical restraints on publishing to understand what can be published in our magazines. In other words, we must not allow ourselves to be defeated before we start. This is particularly problematic in an era when online publishing presents us with new uncertainties about where we stand legally and commercially.

Publishing law

Books on first aid for children invariably start with the same advice: summon adult help. Advice on law for journalists usually adopts a similar tone: anyone with a legal query is advised to fetch a lawyer. Sound though this is, it is not always practical, nor desirable. We may indeed need professional advice, but we don't always want to be told what to do. We should always take responsibility for editorial decisions, including how to research and write editorial material, what to publish and how to deal with any problems arising from that publication. That means doing everything we can to learn about the law and to keep that knowledge up to date.

That way we can use legal advice to help us find safe, legal ways of saying what we feel needs to be said, rather than, as is so often the case, asking for guidance on what we might be allowed to say. Libel insurance can force us into the latter position, since in those circumstances the lawyer's responsibility is to advise the insurers that nothing in our magazines is likely to attract successful litigation. Inevitably, they will err on the side of caution. You would be better off with a lawyer who shares your enthusiasm for lively and controversial journalism and wants to help you achieve it.

Libel is perhaps the most worrying area for many editors, with some justification, but it is not the only legal question to consider. Editors are also likely to bump into contempt of court; copyright; the law of confidence; trespass; passing off; trades descriptions; competitions law; the rehabilitation of offenders; obscenity; blasphemy; racial hatred; harassment; data protection; court, parliamentary and local government reporting rules; official secrets; and business law. And on top of all that, the editor has responsibilities as a line manager and member of management.

A book of this type cannot hope to cover all these issues. It will not give you all the answers, but it will indicate some of the questions that are likely to arise. In addition, you should have serious legal training, and keep it refreshed. You must buy the leading textbooks on media law as each new edition appears and read them regularly.[1] It is also important to monitor the trade and national press for relevant legislation and court cases.

But theoretical knowledge really won't mean anything until it is accompanied by practical experience. When you meet your legal advisers, use the time wisely. Ask them to explain rather than simply taking instructions. Use your brushes with the law, however painful and tedious, to help you become a better editor.

The four areas that cause most problems for working editors are defamation, contempt of court, copyright and the law of confidence. None of them is exactly straightforward, a reflection of the subtle intelligence of the legal minds drawn towards the lucrative field of media law.

Defamation

The law of defamation exists so people can defend their reputations and gain compensation when those reputations are found to be illegally attacked. But a publication in which no one is ever criticised is not worth reading. Your readers want to read about people and organisations behaving badly. Your task is to provide that material – stories people don't want you to print – in a way that will not bring your magazine under legal attack.

You should have the famous 'tests' for defamation inscribed upon your heart. A statement is defamatory if it:

- exposes the plaintiff to hatred, ridicule or contempt;
- causes the plaintiff to be shunned or avoided;
- lowers the plaintiff in the estimation of reasonable people; or
- tends to make reasonable people think less of the plaintiff in his or her office, trade or profession.

You should also know the types of defamation action people can take against you – libel, slander and malicious falsehood – and how they differ from one another. And you will also need to know what else is required for a defamatory statement to become the basis of a successful libel action:

- readers of the defamatory statement have to know to whom it refers;
- the statement has to have been published, even if only to a third party.

So it is easy enough to work out when something might give grounds for a defamation action. But there are ways of defending such a statement in the courts:

- Through 'justification', which means proving the truth, or 'justification', of the 'sting', or salient point, of any factual allegation.
- By demonstrating that the item in question was 'honest comment on facts truly stated in a matter of public interest' (formerly fair comment).
- By invoking 'privilege', a legal device permitting the publication of defamatory statements in certain narrowly defined circumstances.
- By proving that you undertook 'responsible journalism' in gathering and publishing the defamatory information (the 'Reynolds defence'). This latter defence is particularly problematic and difficult to construct, subject as it is to the views of the judge and any subsequent appeal judges, which have so far proved anything but consistent. It is worth, however, watching for new judgements with regard to the defence, as this may change things.

There are differences in defamation law between England and Wales, and Scotland. In Scotland, for example, there is no distinction between libel and slander, and a greater emphasis to prove that some harm has been caused by the defamatory statement. It is also possible for the estate of a person to continue legal action even if the claimant dies. In practice, with most publications being distributed physically or digitally across the Scottish border, any version of the law around defamation is equally likely to be used (although there are fewer defamation cases in Scotland as a whole).

Once you understand defamation, you must make sure the knowledge is widely spread among your staff and contributors. They don't need the detailed understanding that harsh experience will have brought you. They just need to understand when there might be a problem. The principles of libel (and, indeed, all the legal questions considered here) should be known not only to editors, news reporters and sub-editors, but also to feature writers, columnists, web editors, community managers, in-house or syndicated bloggers, and even your art editor: it is perfectly possible to libel by mistake while cropping a picture.

The trend towards filling magazines with contributions from largely self-taught freelances has certainly been a boon to the legal profession. There are plenty of writers, some well-known, who think that placing a defamatory statement between quote marks is a defence against libel. It is not: the magazine bears full responsibility for every word it prints, whoever originally said it. Sub-editors often try to 'clean up' copy in the production process. This is not the right approach. It is too late to do anything about serious defamation at this stage. A defamatory statement cannot be made non-defamatory, usually, by 'toning down' the language in which it is made. Nor should it be. If the statement is accurate then it should be told boldly and starkly. If it is not, it should be removed. The 'toning-down' approach leads to anodyne phrasing and innuendo that may, paradoxically, be no less dangerous than plain writing.

The substance of the story needs looking at, not its style. Writing the truth, and being ready to prove it, is the only solid way of dealing with libel actions. Of course, truth is a difficult concept, but we should start with accuracy, completeness and fairness and work up from there. These principles need to be understood by both writing and production staff and systems should be created to ensure they are carried through.

As editor, you can delegate initial responsibility for these questions, but you must explain the standards and ensure that they are met. If they are not, you must take action. If you employ writers, you are entitled to check on the way they research, interview and record their findings. You must be sure their notes are kept in a disciplined way, that audio recording is used for contentious matters, and that all notebooks, memory sticks and cards, printed sources and the rest are retained and stored: a libel action can be launched anything up to a year after print publication, or longer at the discretion of the court, and at any time as long as the content remains published online (here, every access of the web page is considered a new 'publication', although the 'multiple publication rule' under which this falls is currently being reviewed).

A special mention must be made here of 'cloud storage' services which allow you to archive material using an online service such as Google Docs or Dropbox. These are very useful in allowing you to work on the move or across numerous computers, but you should recommend that journalists keep multiple backup copies to cover various scenarios.

Freelance writers are a particular problem. You have no real way of knowing about their expertise, their training and their character, except perhaps by familiarity. Few writers would take kindly to being asked to present their notebooks and audio files for your inspection. Unfortunately, if they get into trouble, worse things will happen to them. It may well be worth producing a guide for your writers, outlining your standards. This would include instructions on using notebooks and recordings and storing them properly in case of subsequent trouble. Send it out with your commissioning briefs.

Attempting to offload your libel responsibilities onto your writers, by expecting them to indemnify you against any libel costs, is fought against in magazine publishing, although it is traditional in book publishing. A commission does, however, carry an implied obligation on writers to assist in fighting any resultant legal action. In any case, most libel plaintiffs will sue the author as well as editor and publisher, so they will have every reason to. A libel action is a most unpleasant experience for everyone concerned, so stress that to your contributors.

Your writers should always check facts and approach witnesses or informants with a high degree of scepticism. But the evidence behind a story takes on extra significance if you attract a libel writ. As proceedings develop, all of this evidential material, plus interim versions, layouts and notes in your computer system, will have to be handed over. When the evidence for your big story comes down to some scribbles on the back of an envelope, you are likely to suffer more than embarrassment (although in some cases such scribbles – where there was no other way to record what was being said – have proved crucial).

Solid journalism is a much more sound foundation for avoiding legal trouble than attempting to fudge things on a verbal level. Where a story makes serious allegations, it is becoming common practice for it to be supported by written statements from sources, signed in the presence of a solicitor. Stories should always be balanced. Your writers should speak to all relevant parties, and you should ensure that they do not become emotionally involved to the extent that they could be accused of 'malice', in its peculiar legal sense. Malice here means publishing something you know to be untrue, or not caring whether it is true or not.

A reporter can even fall foul of an action for slander, the spoken version of libel, by the way he or she chooses to go about investigating a story. But in a slander action the plaintiff has to show actual monetary loss, except in five special cases: accusations of a crime for which the punishment is imprisonment; accusations of having a contagious disease; suggestions that the plaintiff is no good at his or her job; attacks on the plaintiff's creditworthiness; and attacks on the sexual conduct of a woman or girl.

Naturally you should always keep your ear open for evidence of malice in its lay sense: journalists are no more immune from self-interest and petty dishonesty than anyone else, but it is essential that they don't practise them in your pages – or websites.

Sub-editors do have an important role to play in the prevention of libel actions. They should be alert to potentially hazardous material and ready to bring it to the attention of the author or the commissioning editor responsible. But they also need to be careful about the way language is used. Stories should be clear. People who are identified should be identified unambiguously, to avoid dragging in others with similar names. Double meanings and innuendo, whereby words have a special defamatory meaning to certain groups within the readership, should be removed. Care should be taken over meanings: your writers and sub-editors should not bandy around such words as 'bankrupt' unless they know what they mean.

The sub-editing of 'opinion' columns, 'angry' columns and 'humorous' columns and the like is a much more subtle matter. Here judgements have to be made about language, but they must be based on the formula of 'honest comment on a matter of public interest', based on facts that have been truly stated or accurately alluded to. The law protects outrageous opinions, but takes a dim view of the mingling of inaccurate facts and harsh comment in the same column or phrase.

This is particularly important for those publications which review products, whether babies' pushchairs or cameras. Criticism should be robust but not abusive. You must ensure that any 'objective' methods of testing used are operated with care, and that those doing the reviewing have clean hands. Any suggestion that your reviewers might be involved with rival manufacturers, for instance, might well be interpreted as malice. Reviews have to be fair, and seen to be fair. Your subs must beware of foolish mistakes that might lead to unnecessary libel actions.

Anything tricky in new copy should be brought to your attention, although you don't necessarily want to have to sort it out personally. In the end, you must take responsibility. That doesn't mean everything you publish should be bland. A magazine that never brings anyone into 'hatred, ridicule or contempt', that never causes anyone to be 'shunned or avoided', or that never makes anyone think less of a person 'in their office, trade or profession', is a dull read indeed.

All editors know that libel is often a matter of risk assessment. It's a 'percentage game'. How likely are these words to cause offence? How likely are they to lead to a solicitor's letter? How likely are they to lead to a writ? How likely is the libel action to go to court? And what is the outcome likely to be?

Some public figures will never sue, largely because they would prefer not to have to appear in court. Others – particularly those whose careers rely on a clean-cut image – are notoriously litigious and their names should ring alarm bells with any editor or sub. Trade unions and professional organisations will sometimes pay for a member to take legal action – in some cases, regardless of the strength of the case. Do not think that because a subject lives outside of the UK that they will not sue. There are numerous examples of publishers being sued in English courts for material being accessed in another country (typically online).

In the editorial office, there should be a clear system for dealing with complaints and queries, particularly those with a hint of legal menace. Complaints should be passed straight up to the editor. Allow no one to promise any kind of correction or, crucially, any apology. Prevent writers from trying to 'sort things out' by cunningly weaving some kind of correction into a new story. If anyone is going to do that it has to be you, and it is risky.

People who have been inaccurately (but not nastily) written about will generally want a simple statement putting the story straight. Such factual errors cannot cause a libel action unless they have defamatory implications. Consequently they do not actually have to be corrected, but it is good manners. If you are confident that a complainant will be satisfied, and you are sure that your magazine got it wrong, amend any online version of the article accordingly (with a note at the top of the piece explaining the correction) and place a plain correction in the next issue. Archives are particularly problematic here and it may be worth informing any syndication partners too if the material is reproduced elsewhere with permission.

You must be careful not to suggest that anyone else, either a source or the author, got it wrong, however, unless you want to make an enemy of either of them. A correction may sometimes head off a solicitor's letter, which will save you money, but is not usually enough to appease a seriously aggrieved complainant. An apology may sometimes do the trick, but here complications start to arise. It may be safe in a case of accidental defamation, where you did not realise that the words would be understood to refer to the complainant, or where some circumstances of which you could not be aware have made the words defamatory. In these cases you have no defence, so you have nothing to lose.

The problem of apologies in general is that they mean admitting a fault, which may destroy your defence. If you do print an apology, you will only be safe in doing so if the complainant agrees in writing that the apology, and any payment you might make towards costs, settles his or her claim against you. If the complainant won't agree that, then you could easily apologise, destroy your own case in the process, and still have to go to court. Any sort of apology should only be published on legal advice.

If you choose to negotiate personally, you should head any correspondence 'without prejudice', which means that they are not binding except as part of a full and final agreement. That at least should enable your lawyers to sort things out if you get into a mess. There is a saying that may be relevant: 'A man who is his own lawyer has a fool for a client.'

If the libel action against you goes further, you will pretty soon have to assess your chances of success. Newsroom bravado (or even editor's office bravado) soon withers under the harsh light of legalistic enquiry. You and your writer will have to produce the evidence upon which the story was based, and at some point, during the process of 'discovery', it will all have to be handed over to the other side, including irreverent jottings, insulting catchlines or file names, early versions, ill-transcribed interviews, crass dummy headlines and more. Journalism does not usually emerge well from this kind of scrutiny, which is why it is essential that good practices and legal awareness are universal throughout your editorial team. Defending a libel action invariably involves re-researching the original story. Journalists generally have little enthusiasm for looking backwards, but here they have no choice. Sadly, your sources, even those quoted in the story, may be unwilling to give you the necessary assistance when lawyers and courts are involved. This is a problem which could have been forestalled by asking for written statements at the time of publication. If they refuse them, too bad. If they agree, you have effectively guaranteed their involvement if anything goes wrong. Unnamed sources are, as usual, useless. If you rely on them, the courts are likely to try to make you name them, and that is not what you want at all.

At this point, many publishers and some editors will want to settle with the plaintiff for fear of greater losses at a later point. Libel insurance complicates matters, since it often doesn't even start to apply until your costs look like reaching a certain level, and at that point the insurance company takes over your defence and decides whether or not to fight.

It is important not to crumple too easily. Publications that gain a reputation as a 'soft touch' can expect a constant string of petty complaints. They all end up costing money, if only in terms of your time.

Negative reviews have cost publishers thousands of points in the past: in the wake of one such case, IPC introduced a libel checklist for its journalists. They were told:

- to log the date and time of all telephone calls;
- to date and sign all contemporaneous notes;
- to ensure that the other party in any story was aware of their intentions and was agreeable to any product test or article;
- to double-check with their original author any facts taken from cuttings;
- to refer any worries about an article to their editor and then in turn to the company lawyer; and
- to avoid 'ambivalent catch-lines and irreverent jottings', which could turn out to be disastrous as documents connected with a story have to be disclosed.

These requirements sound excessive at first sight, but there is little in them that goes beyond the normal good practice of an efficient news team. Magazines are more likely to get into trouble in soft news and features, where writers may not be so aware of the dangers.

The real threat from losing a libel action comes from costs. A case that goes to court can easily cost the losing side a six-figure sum.

The Defamation Act 1996, which came into force in 2000, introduced a number of measures to simplify and speed up the ancient libel procedure. Of these, the most important is probably the 'offer of amends'. This allows publications which have published a defamatory statement, usually by some mistake, to resolve things quickly and cheaply. The magazine must offer to publish a correction and apology and to pay compensation and costs. All this must happen very quickly on receipt of the libel writ. If the complainant accepts the offer, the libel action is halted. If it is not accepted, the fact that the offer was made becomes a defence in the subsequent libel trial; but not, however, if the magazine knew that what it was publishing was both defamatory and false. If it is used as a defence, no other defence is permitted. The 'offer of amends' is also taken into account when damages are assessed.

Another innovation in the Act was a new 'summary disposal' procedure, allowing judges sitting without juries to deal with straightforward and less serious defamation claims. For the first time this brings all defamation actions before a judge at an early stage so that he or she can decide whether the case can be dealt with in summary fashion. If the judge decides that the claim has no 'realistic prospect of success' he or she can dismiss it.

On the other hand, if the judge decides that the magazine or newspaper will not be able to defend itself, he or she can make a summary judgement. He or she can award damages up to £10,000, can restrain the defendant from publishing or republishing the defamatory material, and can demand a declaration that the allegation was false and the publication of a suitable correction and apology. The wording and positioning of this is to be agreed between the parties, or the judge will give an order about that. None of this applies if the judge concludes that there is a defence with a reasonable chance of success or if there is some other reason for there to be a trial.

At the time of writing, libel law in both Scotland and England and Wales is about to undergo lengthy reviews. Always check the specialist press and media law blogs for new laws and key judgements.

Contempt of court

A libel action can be alarming, but it does not have the air of threat that comes with a contempt of court case. Contempt is a criminal offence, carrying a maximum penalty of two years in jail and an unlimited fine. Cases are heard by High Court judges, sitting without a jury, even though the offence in question may simply be one of publishing scandalous material about a judge. No wonder editors are, by and large, careful about contempt.

Contempt of court means interfering with the proper conduct of justice in such a way that someone will be prevented from having a fair trial. There are two types, in effect: 'strict liability' contempt, where a contempt can be committed quite accidentally; and various types of 'common law' contempt, from interviewing jurors, disclosing what goes on in private hearings and breaking court orders to 'scandalising the court'.

Editors whose publications carry any kind of crime coverage or law reporting should know the rules in detail. And every journalist should know that:

- strict liability contempt occurs when a publication 'creates a substantial risk that the course of justice in particular proceedings will be seriously impeded or prejudiced';
- the danger period starts when a case becomes 'active': as soon as an arrest is made or charges are laid against someone.

The most obvious contempt is printing details of a defendant's past convictions, or speculating on the crime, during the trial. Imagery can also be relevant: during the murder trial of Ryan Ward in 2009, both the *Daily Mail* and *The Sun* published a photograph of the defendant 'posing with a gun', taken from a social networking site. Although both the *Daily Mail* reporter and *The Sun* picture desk had warned that the handgun should not be included in any copy of the photograph due to the risk of prejudicing the trial, versions of the image containing the gun were put online. The image was not online for very long, and the judge was satisfied that no prejudice had been caused, but both websites were still found guilty of contempt.

Online archives present an obvious issue here, as they will often contain information about a defendant's previous convictions or their lifestyle. The

Attorney General has said it is unlikely he would bring a prosecution on these grounds unless the archive material was published again or attention was explicitly drawn to it.

There are many more ways of committing contempt than that, of course, and editorial staff need to be encouraged to think carefully and clearly when they are dealing with any material that makes specific reference to events in the criminal courts and legal system. This is an area in which expert advice is essential, especially in view of the penalties. And everyone on your staff should know the basics. At the very least, this may be enough to prevent such headlines as 'Rapist released on bail', sometimes composed by junior subs.

On the other hand, writers should not be intimidated by those who bandy around the words *sub judice*. Only a trial can be *sub judice*, not any kind of tribunal, hearing or in-house kangaroo court. It is not enough for people to tell you something is *sub judice* just to stop you asking questions.

Remember that the law of contempt is intended to stop people interfering with a trial. It is easy (the law argues) to prejudice a jury by something you write, but much harder with magistrates, judges sitting alone, and judges hearing civil cases or sitting in appeal. No one has been in contempt of an appeal court for half a century. And contempt of court does not apply to non-judicial proceedings.

Remember that the contempt rules no longer apply once a judgement has been made (unless there is an appeal), and it is typical for journalists to continue to gather information for pieces that can be published at that point. Also remember, however, that other laws still apply: when various accusations were made in the press surrounding Madeleine McCann's disappearance, newspapers had to settle numerous libel cases from their targets, with costs running into hundreds of thousands of pounds.

Copyright

The subject of copyright has been explored in Chapters 5 and 6 in the context of commissioning and buying rights. But it has many other implications. Copyright is the right to reproduce an original work. Normally it belongs to the person creating the work but it can be sold ('assigned') to someone else, or various 'licences' to use the work can be agreed. Copyright in a work created by an employee belongs to the employer.

An infringement of copyright occurs when a 'substantial' part of a work is reproduced. A 'substantial' part need not necessarily be a high proportion of the actual words: it can be a small but very important part. It is important to note that there is no copyright in ideas, only in their expression. And the work in question need not be artistic, it need only have been put together with some element of skill to receive copyright protection. It has long been established, for instance, that railway timetables and television schedules are protected by copyright.

The defence for magazines and newspapers wishing to reproduce 'substantial' amounts of copyright material is called 'fair dealing'. The use of reasonable extracts from the work of others is permitted when it is for research or private study, criticism or review or the reporting of current events.

In all these cases, the title of the source material and its author must be identified in the text, and it must be used 'fairly'. This is the most subjective part of the law. Motive is important. For instance, you may not 'lift' large portions of another magazine's interview with a star just because you have not been able to secure such an interview yourself. It is easy to see the application of this to what are called 'cuttings jobs', meaning features based around quotes gathered by other writers.

Such features may be considered either 'criticism or review' or part of the 'reporting of current events'. But if the borrowed materials amount to a 'substantial' part of the original work they must be properly attributed, and the new work created must not be intended to compete directly with the works it has drawn upon. This obviously applies to 'instant' features devised to 'spoil' someone else's book serialisation or cover story. You certainly can't borrow from the people you are intending to compete with.

There is also a suggested upper limit to the volume of borrowing. The Society of Authors and the Publishers Association have arrived at an agreement that reproduction of text for the purposes of criticism or review will not require permission if the amount borrowed consists of:

- a single quote of fewer than 400 words from a prose work;
- a series of quotes of fewer than 300 words each, totalling no more than 800 words.

In either case, the total must not comprise more than a quarter of the original article being quoted.

This agreement is not actually enshrined in the law, so it may be possible to use more material legally. But to do so, and to use such material outside the 'criticism or review' area, may well invite a solicitor's letter.

Satire and parody is an interesting case. It is difficult to parody something, especially a picture, without using a substantial part of it. In this case a fair dealing defence could apply, provided that suitable attribution is included. Theoretically the 1988 Copyright Act also gives copyright protection to the extempore words of any speaker once they are recorded, either on audio or as notes. The person making the record, however, provided they have not been specifically forbidden from doing so, has the right to reproduce them for the purposes of reporting a current event or making a broadcast.

Editors should be aware of the 'moral rights' created by the 1988 Act, even though most of them are specifically ruled out for employees and for anyone who gives consent for their work to be published in magazines, newspapers or other periodicals. They are: the right to be identified as the author; the right not to have the work subjected to 'derogatory treatment'; the right not to be falsely named as the author of a piece of work; and the right not to have one's own private photographs published. These don't affect journalists, but they do affect authors whose work you might have dealings with from time to time.

The moral rights may not be sold but they can be waived, and publishing organisations often try to insist upon this, even in contexts where the rights don't actually exist. It is worth noting that the rule against 'derogatory treatment' of copyright works is another difficulty for satirists and parodists, although there has yet to be a relevant court case.

Infringement of copyright is potentially serious. Compensation is usually limited to profits the copyright holder has lost as a result of the infringement, or to the fee you would have been charged if you had acquired the material legitimately. But for flagrant and deliberate abuses the court is entitled to award additional damages. It is sometimes tempting to 'lift' a photograph or line drawing that can't be found elsewhere, but you are likely to be found out and made to pay compensation. This is a matter for negotiation between the respective lawyers, which makes it an expensive way of acquiring pictures, even without compensation.

Even if a case never reaches court, a magazine can suffer enormous negative publicity if it uses material without permission. Given the loud protestations that many publishers have made about the copyright of their own material online, users are understandably quick to pounce on the perceived hypocrisy of publishers who take material from the web without regard for copyright themselves.

One particularly salutary example of this is the case of the small US food magazine *Cooks Source*. In October 2010 the magazine reproduced without permission a recipe and article by a blogger called Monica Gaudio. The editor of the magazine, Judith Griggs, appeared to believe that because Gaudio had published her work online it was 'public domain' and therefore not subject to copyright. This, of course, is not true – copyright applies to material published online just as it does to material published in other media, however 'public'.

When Gaudio emailed Griggs to request payment the request was refused, Griggs saying 'you should compensate me!' for editing the piece. This response – which Gaudio published on her blog – kicked off an Internet backlash that led to advertisers withdrawing from the magazine and hundreds of users investigating possible copyright infringement elsewhere in the magazine. The reputations of Griggs and *Cooks Source* suffered enormous damage, exacerbated in no small part by Griggs' continued mishandling of the affair as it unfolded.

More serious, potentially, is the use of injunctions to prevent the use of copyright material which is intended to form the core of a news story or feature. You may be intending to build a major piece on the basis of leaked documents, but if this is discovered by the copyright holder, various legal manoeuvres become possible.

The most serious and rare is the 'Anton Piller order', now renamed a 'search order', which gives the copyright holder the right to search your premises for his or her material. In this case you have no right to be represented at the hearing leading to the order, and may know nothing about it until the copyright owner's solicitor arrives. This is a type of 'prior restraint' and must be resisted by legal means. There is a sort of 'public interest' defence against normal copyright injunctions, but no real defence against an Anton Piller order.

Copyright is an immensely complex area of the law and is likely to become more so. Material only falls outside copyright by reason of its advanced age. It only expires 70 years after the end of the year in which its author died. Editors should take it as a general principle that every piece of publishable material is likely to belong to someone and must be legitimately acquired or licensed before it can be used. The same, of course, applies to the material which we ourselves create. Between acquiring material at one end and attempting to control the use of material at the other, we are all in for a busy time.

Confidence

The law of confidence is a growing problem for magazine editors. People in a confidential relationship with anyone else, meaning husbands and wives, doctors and patients, and many more, are obliged to keep confidential anything they learn as part of that relationship. So are those who sign a contract with an element of confidentiality to it. That generally includes employment contracts, even if there is no specific confidentiality clause.

As journalists, however, we are very interested in publishing confidential material: it goes right back to the idea of news as something someone doesn't want you to print. The law of confidence exists to prevent one party in such a contractual relationship breaking that confidentiality, for instance to give documents to a journalist.

The injured party, usually the employer, can seek an 'interim injunction' from a High Court judge, prohibiting publication of the material prior to a full court hearing. This can be a year or more later, by which time the document's value as news material will have been destroyed. In the meantime, the injunction may well play havoc with the magazine's production, printing and distribution schedules.

The magazine can defend its wish to publish on public interest grounds. But there is a great danger that the judge will also order the return of the documents, which may reveal the source.

The classic situation is that a reporter receives a document and then telephones the company to which it relates in an attempt to ascertain its authenticity. This is obviously good practice, except when it is followed by an injunction banning publication and demanding the document's return and the identification of the source.

One famous case of this came in 1990 when Bill Goodwin, a trainee reporter in his first weeks on the business-to-business magazine *The Engineer*, received a tip-off about a computer company. He duly rang the company to check and found himself faced with first an injunction prohibiting publication and then an action to make him reveal his source. He refused and was fined £5,000 for contempt of court. He subsequently sought a judicial review of the case in the European Court, backed by the NUJ and his employer.

In 1996, the court ruled that the British government had violated his human rights. Goodwin's counsel suggested that as a result of the judgement the government would have to give journalistic sources greater legal protection. But in 2002, the House of Lords ordered the *Daily Mirror* to divulge the name of its source for a story based on the confidential hospital records of the Moors Murderer, Ian Brady. Its judgement said that freedom of the press only applied if the press had proper regard for the rights of others, including the 'right of preserving confidentiality'. It said that in this case an order to reveal the source was 'sufficient and proportionate'. The *Mirror* revealed the name of its source: a freelance journalist who promptly refused to reveal his own sources. The case was pursued by the NHS at a cost of more than £150,000, but was finally dropped in 2007, having already taken eight years. Stories based on confidential documents which may have been illicitly obtained will continue to present a problem. Journalists may have to write these stories without revealing to their subjects what evidence they have. Their response must come in the next available issue. This is not an acceptable practice, usually, but here there is little alternative.

In fairness, the courts generally do give some recognition to the journalistic principle of not revealing sources of stories. The 1981 Contempt of Court Act, for instance, says that courts should not insist on the revelation of sources except where it is 'necessary in the interests of justice or national security or for the prevention of disorder or crime'. Of these, the 'interests of justice' have been given the widest interpretation, but questions of 'national security' still represent the fastest route by which an editor or reporter can be sent to prison.

Privacy

If you are obtaining and using anything that might be considered 'private' or 'personal', you will need to be wary of legal issues around privacy. Although there is no privacy law in the UK, Article 8 of the European Convention on Human Rights (ECHR) does give a right to privacy, brought into UK law through the Human Rights Act (HRA).

The tension here is between the obligation on publishers not to interfere with an individual's privacy, and their right to freedom of expression, and cases will evaluate the impact of a decision on both. Existing codes – such as those of the PCC – are important here: the Human Rights Act indicates that privacy codes should be taken into account in judges' decisions, along with the public interest of publication, and how public the individual is in their general behaviour (for example, a celebrity who courts public attention).

Data protection

Any organisation holding 'personal' information about individuals on a computer or computer system, or in an alphabetical or otherwise accessible manual filing system, is subject to the 1998 Data Protection Act. The definition of 'personal' information is extremely wide, covering just about any fact or opinion linked to an identifiable individual. It is likely to include any information you store about subscribers, employees, advertisers, and anyone who registers to use website features.

The Act gives individuals rights over that information: it has to be 'fairly and legally' collected and they have the right to examine it and have it corrected if inaccurate. It introduces into law eight 'data protection principles':

1   Indviduals ('data subjects' in the jargon of the Act) must normally consent to giving their data.
2   Data must be used for lawful purposes.
3   Data must not be excessive for the purpose.
4   Data must be accurate and up to date.
5   Data must not be kept longer than necessary.
6   Data must be processed in accordance with the rights of the subject.
7   Data must be kept secure.
8   Data must not be exported to countries outside the European Economic Area, meaning the EU plus Norway, Iceland and Liechtenstein.

The person holding such information is called the 'data controller'. They must provide details of data holdings to the Information Commissioner. Not registering is a criminal offence.

It is worth going to the Data Protection Register (accessible via www.ico.gov.uk), entering the name of a journalistic organisation and seeing the range of material covered by the Act. It includes everything to do with staff, payroll, accounts, marketing, advertising, publicity, and so on. And it certainly includes information collected by reporters and writers and held on the office computer system. A data controller with responsibility for journalistic material must reasonably believe that publication based on that information would be in the public interest and that compliance with the particular requirements of the Act would not be compatible with freedom of expression. If so, data kept for journalism, artistic and literary purposes is exempt from several aspects of the law. In particular, publications:

* are not obliged to divulge what information they hold on individuals;
* cannot be stopped from 'processing' information by those individuals;
* cannot be ordered to change inaccurate data;
* are exempt from all the 'data protection principles' except one, the requirement to keep data secure.

All this is helpful, and saves publications from dealing with endless fishing expeditions by people who think they might one day be written about. But someone in your organisation must still become the data controller and make the necessary registration.

Also covered by data protection is any unauthorised access that your journalists gain to confidential databases, such as bank records, driving licence information, etc. This is an offence under Section 55, punishable by a fine, although there is a public interest defence.

Phone hacking and the RIPA

The Regulation of Investigatory Powers Act 2000, known as RIPA, covers phone hacking activities and states that it is a criminal offence to intercept phone calls unless it is done by a member of the police or intelligence agencies with a warrant. It also makes it an offence to gain access to voicemail. There is no public interest exemption.

Competitions

One peculiar way in which you might fall foul of the law is through competitions. Any competition that people pay to enter and that they win by pure chance is a lottery. And in the UK the only substantial legal lottery is the one organised by the state. If entrants do not have to pay, it is called a 'legal free draw'. You probably won't try and extract an entry fee from readers who try to enter one of your magazine competitions. But unfortunately, if you publicise your draw on the cover of the magazine, or in issues leading up to it, the law is likely to take the view that the price of the magazine includes a hidden fee to enter the draw, making it illegal. The same goes for any attempt to require proof of purchase, by way of coupons or even asking for an entry form cut out from the magazine. Allowing people to enter for free online is one way of addressing this problem that wasn't available previously.

If you are running a community or cultural magazine you can, however, run a 'society lottery' and give any profits to a good cause. You will need to apply to the Gambling Commission – see the Lotteries Council website for more details of the criteria.

Alternatively, and much more simply, you can run a 'prize competition'. This is a competition where the allocation of prizes depends on the exercise of skill. The 2005 Gambling Act raised the bar on the amount of skill required by participants: games must now be sufficiently difficult to eliminate a substantial proportion of entrants – you cannot simply provide the answers in the accompanying text (as some magazines used to), and you cannot at any point draw the winner out of a hat, since that would turn your legal competition back into an illegal lottery.

The simple answer is to ensure entry to the competition is free online.

Website terms and conditions

You will strengthen your legal position considerably in most situations by ensuring that you have clear terms and conditions for relevant parts of your operation. If you have a forum where users can exchange opinions or upload media, you should have clear guidelines in place on what is and is not acceptable, and what the process is if users object to your decisions. If they have to register to contribute you should require them to accept these guidelines as part of their terms and conditions.

As a broad guide you should cover the following:

- copyright and permissions (both that they agree not to upload copyright-infringing material and what permissions they give, if any, to you to reproduce material);
- defamation (that they agree not to defame);
- data protection (how users can access information held about them or close their accounts);
- 'flagging': how they can bring content that infringes the terms and conditions to your attention.
- a final category to consider are the broad ethics and culture of the site – is it acceptable to swear? Are users expected to use their real identities? Where do you stand on mentions of commercial products?

Take a look at the terms and conditions on a site that you like (and where users are similar) to get an idea. They do not need to be very long. Their importance is in establishing a clear definition of what is acceptable behaviour, and providing a defence if you are accused of arbitrary behaviour in punishing misbehaving users, or indeed if you end up in a court of law (where you can point to the terms as evidence of taking reasonable steps to prevent misbehaviour). A final point to remember about terms and conditions is that users of the site can use them to hold you to account, so make sure that you adhere to them consistently.

Other laws

There are a great many more legal areas that editors may need to know about, depending on the areas in which they operate. They include:

- trespass, which affects the way reporters and photographers carry out their business;
- trades descriptions, which requires that goods are accurately described: it covers advertising features and may, theoretically, apply to cover-lines;
- the Rehabilitation of Offenders Act, which restricts your right to refer to previous convictions;
- indecency and obscenity, the distinction being that indecency offends those who see it, whereas obscenity corrupts them;
- blasphemy, an offence against specifically Christian beliefs, for which there has been only one prosecution since 1922;
- hate speech laws: the Public Order Act 1986, the Racial and Religious Hatred Act 2006 and the Criminal Justice and Immigration Act 2008 cover, respectively, stirring up hatred based on nationality, colour, and ethnic origins; stirring up religious hatred; and inciting hatred on the basis of sexual orientation;
- court reporting: a complex matter that news editors, especially, need to understand and follow;
- election and parliamentary reporting: another complex set of regulations;

- local government law: worth investigating by relevant publications for its possibilities as well as its restrictions;
- business law: particularly in respect to reporting companies in difficulty;
- harassment, which can be used to prevent journalists reporting on particular individuals. The Equality Act 2010 can also be used to take action over harassment that is sexual in nature or based on gender, sexuality, disability, age, pregnancy, race or religion. If you are providing a moderated forum where this sort of harassment takes place you may be liable if you do not take action over such behaviour;
- official secrets: limited under the 1989 Official Secrets Act to security and intelligence, defence, international relations and information that might facilitate a criminal offence.

Public complaints

Your magazine's problems with the public will not always take legal form, mainly because of the cost of legal action. But complainants can kick up quite a stink and organise effectively to damage your reputation and brand, particularly if they play a key role in the community you serve. The onus is on you to provide a fair way of dealing with complaints. Larger organisations might consider having an 'ombudsman', or 'readers' editor', of the type appointed by some of the national newspapers. Many of these people report, however, that they do not have enough to do. Many people prefer to deal directly with the editor, which seems only right and proper.

The 'right of reply'

It makes sense to publish corrections of factual errors without being asked. Far from damaging your reputation for accuracy, this should, if carefully handled, actually enhance it. Beyond that comes the so-called 'right of reply'. There is, of course, no such right, although various parliamentarians and industry bodies have tried to create one. Even so, a person who has been attacked in your pages should be given reasonable space to respond – and you should include commenting facilities on most content online anyway.

Depending upon the seriousness with which you take your letters page, this might be the ideal place for such a response. Many pundits like the idea of 'equal prominence and size' for such a response, but that is hardly appealing in practice. Wounded replies to attacks your readers may have missed do not make good reading.

There are more serious objections to the idea. What type of reply is to be offered, and to whom? Is the right of reply to be limited to a rebuttal of factual inaccuracy, or is it to be a rhetorical response to the comments, not only of the magazine or its writers but of those quoted in its stories? And if those thus contradicted are unhappy, are they too to be given the right to reply to the reply?

Good editors will do everything they can to keep relationships happy. Sensible letters in response to criticism, amended to remove libellous remarks, should always be published. Controversy should be allowed to rage for its natural life, then be quietly dampened down. 'This correspondence is now closed' is a phrase that has its uses – although you cannot stop people carrying on their argument elsewhere – and if there is an indication that their feelings attract a lot of support you may revisit your decision to close the correspondence.

Comments and discussion forums

The Internet is an inherently interactive medium and most users now expect to be able to comment on content, either through traditional blog-style comment forms, rating systems, open forums – or all the above. Preventing them from doing so only leads to a frustrating user experience; they will have their conversation anyway, so best that it takes place where you can respond and nurture the most informative discussion.

Discussion on your own websites, however, raises its own legal problems. You will need to make your own decisions whether you allow anyone to make a comment, or to require registration first; whether comments go up automatically or are pre-moderated. The right policy will depend on your audience and your objectives. You are looking for a balance between the most frictionless user experience (no registration; comment goes up instantly) and the most pleasant community experience (interesting or constructive content). Typically, operations of these sorts begin with no barriers to entry as they start with low numbers, and then raise the barriers steadily when content becomes unmanageable, or community behaviour problematic. The key thing is not to abandon comment threads once they are established but participate heavily in the early days to set an example of (and reward) good behaviour.

There are certain areas where you may want to consider restricting or preventing discussion. Many publishers, for example, will not allow comments on stories relating to ongoing court cases, for obvious contempt of court issues. Likewise, you may choose to closely monitor discussion around subjects such as immigration, which may attract comments falling foul of hate speech laws. If you do change the moderation policy for a single story, explain why you are doing so.

The Press Complaints Commission

For those complainants who reject your own peacemaking, but who don't want to go to law, there is the publishing industry's own supervisory body, the Press Complaints Commission. The PCC was set up to let the press regulate its own behaviour. Established and dominated by newspaper interests, it nonetheless has a supervisory role over the whole world of periodical publishing. Members of the public may complain against breaches of the PCC's Code of Practice. The Code makes editors responsible for ensuring that the activities of staff and 'as far as possible' of freelances conform to its guidelines, which cover various aspects of reporting and editing, including questions of taste.

An editor facing a PCC complaint will be contacted by the organisation and invited to reach a settlement with the complainant. If that fails, the PCC will carry out its investigation. The editor then must provide a written response to the complaint, which goes to the complainant, and then back for further comment, and so on. You and your staff may be interviewed by the PCC's staff, as may the complainant. But there is no hearing and no confrontation between the two parties. In the end the PCC makes a ruling and publishes it. Editors who are found to have breached the Code are required to publish the relevant adjudication with due prominence in their own publications. This includes online: the PCC released guidance in 2011 on the prominence of online corrections and apologies, stating that if an article appears in print and online 'the proposed remedy will often appear in both media'. For stand-alone corrections and apologies 'consideration' should be given to placing these in the relevant section where the original article appeared. If the original article is still online then this should link to the result of the PCC decision (this could be a correction, apology or response, for example), and vice versa. The guidance also notes that care should be taken to ensure that corrected information does not remain in the URL (for example the name of a vulnerable person in a court case involving children).

The PCC's adjudications can be searched on its website (www.ppa.co.uk). They make interesting and useful reading for any editor wondering exactly how many ways there are of falling foul of the public.

The industry also occasionally comes up with guidelines on how to deal with more specific situations. One example is the guidelines on sexual content in teenage matters, created by a body called the Teenage Magazines Arbitration Panel. The TMAP, which includes retailers as well as editors and publishers, was established as a response to public concerns about the way certain magazines were dealing with such material. It now has the job of adjudicating on whether magazines abide by its guidelines, but has not adjudicated since 2005 or released an annual report since 2007.

The guidelines remain useful, however, encouraging a responsible attitude to sex, advising readers about the age of consent and suggesting they seek parental advice. They also require magazines to produce their own guidelines for staff and ensure they are properly followed. Problem pages must use only genuine letters and qualified 'agony aunts'. At the same time, retailers agree to display magazines in ways that are appropriate for the age of the reader. If you are working in this area, you do need to know and follow these guidelines.

It is also worth pointing out that the PCC Code of Practice is a living document that is constantly being reviewed by the Editors' Code of Practice Committee (www.editorscode.org.uk), which also publishes a handbook on how to operate the code.[2]

Regulation

The PCC is just one of a number of regulatory bodies which you need to be aware of – and complaints are just one of the areas they adjudicate on. Others include accuracy; privacy, confidentiality and clandestine reporting; harassment; intrusion into grief or shock; children; and discrimination.

A quirk of convergence in the industry is that an identical piece of online media can be regulated in different ways depending on whether the publisher is a magazine, broadcaster or online-only operation. Online material produced by broadcasters is regulated by Ofcom; online material produced by publishers is regulated by the PCC (if they are a member). Online material produced by members of the public and online start-ups is regulated by the Internet Watch Foundation (IWF), and of course all the above is covered by law.

In 2009, the Audiovisual Media Services (AVMS) Directive sought to regulate video-on-demand services and established a new regulator, ATVOD. The directive explicitly stated that only 'television-like' services were subject to the regulator, excluding the sort of shorter-form content that most magazines produced. Still, if you are thinking of producing anything 'television-like' you will need to be aware of the regulatory – and financial (regulated services must pay a fee) – implications.

On the advertising side you will be subject to the Advertising Standards Authority (ASA) and the Committee of Advertising Practice (CAP) Code, ensuring adverts are legal, honest, decent and truthful. Both the ASA and CAP have recently been extended to cover promotional material that appears in online media such as magazine websites and social networking sites over which you have control, such as your magazine's Facebook page or Twitter account.

Citizen journalism, blogging and the law

Anyone who produces content online in the UK is subject to the same laws as journalists – there are no 'shield laws' in this country, for example, that give people extra legal rights based on owning a press card or being employed by a publisher (as there are in the USA).

This produces a situation where content producers who have not had any legal training sometimes find themselves having to defend themselves in court against charges of libel. This could be as a result of a negative restaurant review, or criticism of the scientific claims made by a health product manufacturer – to give just two examples.

In some cases the blogger is targeted as an individual even if what they write is also available in print, as happened with Simon Singh – who was sued by the British Chiropractic Association for an article he wrote in the *Guardian* (he eventually won the case).

A frequent criticism of libel laws is that they are expensive and time-consuming to fight even if you have a strong defence – and there is no guarantee of retrieving your costs even if you defend successfully. For this reason it can be more effective for cases to be brought against individuals – who do not have the resources to fight – than publishers.

If you are blogging as a way to build a profile in your field, then a good knowledge of all the legal issues touched on in this chapter will be just as important as if you are publishing professionally. In many ways, it is more important: some lawyers will issue threatening letters on behalf of their clients in the belief that you will not be able to distinguish between a genuine case and one that is intended to merely intimidate you. You will need to know how to respond to these letters, or how to instruct a lawyer to respond on your behalf.

If you are managing content on blogs by users, or referring to content from blogs elsewhere on the web for your own journalism, you should also be aware that this does not mean that you are immune from legal action yourself. The fact that the content is already published, and the blogger has not been sued, does not mean that you will not be sued. Just as bloggers can be vulnerable targets for legal action because they do not have the resources to defend themselves, large publishers can be targets for legal action because they do have the resources: to pay out – either to settle cases out of court, or to pay damages if any are awarded.

Ethics

One responsibility the editor has is to promote ethical journalism. You can do this in your own conduct by, for instance, ensuring that complaints are dealt with swiftly and efficiently and appropriate corrections and apologies made. But you may need to alert your journalists, especially the less experienced ones, when ethical problems are likely to arise. Young journalists, especially, love pretending to be other people for the purpose of getting stories. It's very exciting, and it can be a useful technique. Unfortunately, it is rarely considered acceptable behaviour these days. Nor is failing to reveal your identity during an interview.

Assuming a fake identity online to get stories raises the same ethical issues. It is more easily uncovered than most journalists realise, and often leads to more serious consequences for the journalist, who will have to face being named and shamed across their corner of the Internet.

The exception is when a story is 'in the public interest', a phrase capable of a number of interpretations, and there is no other way of researching it.

This remains the best way of dealing with a situation in which you hear that members of the public, or your readers, are being treated badly. Your writers have to experience that treatment for themselves. They can hardly ring and say 'I am a reporter and I hear you are treating people badly. Can I come round and see?' But subterfuge of this sort must be referred up to you. You will certainly be held to account for it. And when the story is written, the subterfuge must be mentioned and explained.

Another area in which journalists often ignore ethical problems is interviewing. Both parties must understand the basis on which any interview, however informal it might appear, is conducted. Interviewers must say who they are and name the publication they are working for. It is not necessary, however, to remind interviewees that they will be quoted: that is implicit as soon as the journalists say who they are.

Difficulties arise because of those ambiguous expressions 'on the record' and 'off the record'. All interviewees are 'on the record', unless another agreement is reached, meaning that their real names are used in any story alongside their quotes. When people ask to speak 'off the record' complications arise, and a wise editor advises his reporters not to proceed without having a conversation to ensure that all parties know exactly what is meant.

In common parlance 'off the record' can have several different nuances. Sometimes it signifies 'I will tell you something but you are not to use it', while others take it to mean 'you can use the information to ask questions of others, and if they confirm it, you can then publish'. Some want you to use the information but not the words, while others want you to use the words but not identify them as the source.

The confusion surrounding the term means it is perhaps better not used. Advise your staff to be wary of people who want to tell them things, but will also try to bind them not to use them. Why are they speaking to a journalist in the first place? Sometimes this is a crude attempt to suppress a story you have already heard.

Often people will want to tell you things without wanting you to use their words, however they are attributed. Some people will even go to the lengths of having a conversation with you on that basis before ringing you back in your official capacity to give you a statement, which may even include a denial of what they have just told you. This is 'spin'.

A better form of words is to say you will use their quotes but 'not attribute them'. Then you must agree on a form of words to describe the source without revealing his or her identity. This is a matter of negotiation and trust, to be used only with sophisticated sources or those with whom you have a long relationship.

The real answer, though, is to insist wherever possible that stories are backed up by 'on the record' quotes from named interviewees, or by written documentation. Reliance on 'unattributed' remarks kills a magazine's claims to authority. Make your writers explain to the reader why they are using unnamed sources: that will discourage the practice. Anonymous informants cannot always be trusted.

In the case of longer, feature-type interviews, it is becoming increasingly common for interviewees to demand to see the piece before it is printed. We call this 'copy-approval' and agreeing to it is unethical. It makes the publication an act of collusion between editor and interviewee: the piece itself becomes a kind of advertisement. If the interviewee objects to a phrase or a passage, and a new version is agreed, an act of censorship has taken place. And if such a privilege is extended to one interviewee, it ought, in fairness, to be extended to all.

Do not let this practice take hold. Tell your staff and freelances that it is not the publication's policy. Interviewees requesting it should be warned that by agreeing the piece before publication they lose their right to take libel action. On the other hand, it is more reasonable (though inconvenient) for interviewees to ask to check their quotes to see that you have quoted them accurately. If they find an 'error', you can either adjust it or stick to your guns: it may be better to have the row before, rather than after, publication. In general, quotes can be clipped and have their grammar 'improved' – it looks odd not to – but they should not otherwise be altered in any substantial way. Interviewees must recognise their own words and stand by them.

Another area of ethical concern, particularly to those working in the business press, is that of 'insider dealing' or profiting from information obtained for journalistic purposes before it is published. In the course of their work your journalists may receive information that could fall into this category. In the past some business journalists did profit from their enquiries. The staff of investment magazines were encouraged to trade in shares, perhaps to give them greater insight.

This is no longer considered acceptable. Indeed, they are taking a legal, as well as an ethical, risk. Journalists buying, or arranging for others to buy, shares they are about to 'tip' could be prosecuted under the Theft Act for dishonestly obtaining a pecuniary advantage. Dishonest use of inside information from companies to alter share prices by judicious leaking is likely to be a conspiracy to contravene the 1986 Financial Services Act.

Bribes and inducements are hardly the common currency of most magazine journalists, but it pays for all parties to be open about any 'freebies' they may garner in their normal routine duties. Straightforward gifts ought to be tactfully refused. Every so often it becomes fashionable for journalists to be hired to make endorsements of products in advertisements. This does little to enhance either their reputations or the reputations of the publications they work for.

There is an argument that in these cases the journalists concerned are being used because of their professional status, and that this will in some way enhance the status of their magazines. But this is not convincing, and similar proposals should, in general, be rejected. Brochure-writing and other freelance work on behalf of advertisers is also incompatible with maintaining a properly objective attitude to those advertisers, but it happens when journalistic salaries are not generous. If you agree to it, make them do it under a pseudonym. You will probably feel, however, that you do not wish to encourage such cosy relationships.

Another area of ethical concern is privacy. Intrusions into the privacy of those in public office or in positions of power are more likely to be justifiable, on public interest grounds, than those into the affairs of private individuals. But annoying the powerless is likely to be legally safer. There are also legal implications, as explored in the section on privacy above. As an editor you have a duty to protect the rights of your fellow citizens from the intrusive behaviour of your staff. It is particularly important that sensitivity is maintained in dealing with the bereaved and with children and the emotionally and mentally incompetent. In the case of children, journalistic activities that might seem justifiable in other circumstances may well come into conflict with the law.

In general, editors have a duty to uphold freedom of speech and public access to information. Ours is a secretive society, and every journalist should think hard before colluding in the closure or rationing by price of sources of public information. Personally, we consider journalists to be 'citizens with notebooks' rather than a special interest group, and we disagree with attempts to restrict access to information to journalists only, except where the alternative is chaos, as in some high-profile criminal cases.

Both the NUJ and the PCC publish extensive codes of conduct. Your staff will be held to account under the second of these even if they do not voluntarily accept the first. It is as well to make sure that their provisions are widely known and understood, which is why they are reprinted at the back of this book in the Appendices.

9 Becoming an editor

There are no clear boundaries between being a journalist and being an editor. While there are plenty of new responsibilities – representing the publication, giving it direction, managing staff, resources, and above all time – it is not always clear what you must give up to make room for this. Inevitably, however, you will have to spend less and less of your time reporting on your field or writing features.

Some editors let frustration with this interfere with their ability to do the job – or even see what job needs to be done in the first place. But remember that the ultimate objective is to produce a magazine – in whatever shape that takes. You are now responsible for the sum of its parts, rather than simply some of the parts themselves.

This can – and should – be a hugely creative process. You will need to create an environment for great journalism, and for design that is either stunningly clear or clearly stunning. You will need to spot opportunities and threats ahead, and prepare for change, creatively. You will need to motivate junior reporters, writers and subs to produce work that you could never have written alone, and use your position to make a positive difference to your readers' lives.

It sounds trite, but there genuinely are days when you feel that you are changing the world, rather than simply describing it. It is the difference between wanting to write beautifully, and wanting to make great journalism happen.

Editors must be managers and leaders in a publishing business. That's rather different from chasing stories or interviewing stars. If someone offers you the chance to become editor, do not refuse. It may be years before you get such an offer again. What's more, your position after refusing it may become tricky. Managements mistrust people who turn down promotions, suspecting them of lack of commitment, laziness or ulterior motives. New editors mistrust potential editors among their own staff, though those who refuse are less troubling than those who have been rejected. So don't say no without serious thought.

Assess your own ambitions and abilities, and when an opening presents itself, see how well the two match. If they do, you may have found a niche in which you can succeed.

Assessing yourself

In the case of a journalist considering a move into editorship, the key question is one of maturity. This is not a matter of age, nor even, ultimately, of professional experience, although both can help. It is about being ready. When you apply for your first editorship, this question will be uppermost in the minds of those assessing you.

You will need the confidence that comes from knowing the fundamentals of journalism. You will, probably, have achieved most of your ambitions as a reporter, writer, section editor or sub-editor. There may have been private triumphs, for instance producing a substantial number of news 'splashes' or cover features, editing successful supplements, web or mobile projects, or mastering the complexities of production. Or you may have achieved outside recognition in the shape of awards, appropriate compensation and interim promotions. It is not always a good idea to embark upon editorship while there are still stories you are burning to write.

But there is a more important type of maturity. Ask yourself how you will cope with leadership. You will find yourself removed from your former peers, burdened with responsibilities you can discuss with no one. You will have to give instructions and advice to older and more experienced colleagues. You will have to praise without patronising and, on occasions, to reprimand. You will have to turn down people's pet ideas, refuse them pay rises, even end their employment. You must be the person everyone turns to when there is a crisis, or when no one has any ideas. You won't be able to pass the buck.

You must take full legal and moral responsibility for what appears in your magazine, what happens in the editorial office and what happens to the magazine in its market. You may end up before a judge to explain your actions in publishing a particular report, or at an industrial tribunal to defend your decision to dismiss someone. You may have to challenge a boss whose commercial schemes threaten the editorial integrity of the magazine, or fight hard to protect your team. You will need excellent technical knowledge and skills, supportive domestic circumstances, good health and great personal resolve.

Self-reliance may be the quality most needed by new editors. It is hard to overestimate the isolation you feel when you first take charge. If most of your friends have also been your workmates, you can find the new distance between you and them difficult to bear. The fact that you now have new colleagues among your peers in management is of little consolation. You may feel you have nothing in common with them, but everything in common with those whose 'boss' you now have to be.

At the same time, everyone immediately expects you to know everything. It is no surprise that so many new editors disappear into their offices and close their doors, communicating only by memo and trusted messenger. Once there, however, it is difficult to emerge. You must get used to the new realities. Throughout your career as an editor you will have to take unpopular decisions and you will not get sympathy: most journalists are, naturally, convinced that they would be better at your job than you are.

Determination will see you through. It is no good being self-reliant if you don't have the determination to take the magazine in the direction you think right. This is a quality that comes from within. But you may be able to learn techniques for demonstrating that determination in a way that won't threaten everyone else. Assertion, rather than aggression, is the key.

You will need imagination to keep the level of inspiration high, both for yourself and for your staff. Try to release the ideas and talents of others. But at first everyone will sit back and wait to see what you can do, and throughout your career there will be times when you have to take an unambiguous leadership role.

You must also have a thorough understanding of the market your magazine is intended to serve. You don't have to know everything about the area before you begin – otherwise no one would ever change jobs – but you must know enough to get you started. It helps if you can form an emotional attachment to the magazine. There are those who insist that management tasks are complicated by the presence of emotional involvement. Some insist that a good editor is a bloodless professional who can move from publication to publication without a care. Well, perhaps, but a passionate relationship with the magazine always helps.

It also helps if you love magazines in general. You should not be able to pass a news-stand without taking a look. When you return from a foreign holiday your suitcases should be bulging with local publications, even if you don't know the language. Your magazine will have a ravenous appetite for ideas, and you never know where you might find them.

Beyond that, of course, you should have unending curiosity about the world around you, but that is central to all journalism. As an editor, you will find yourself squeezing much of what the world has to offer through a particular filter: the interest of your readers.

The life of an editor can be physically and emotionally demanding, and you will need to be on solid ground. Your physical and mental health will need to be robust. Ask yourself about your ability to deal with long hours and a sedentary lifestyle, punctuated by unhealthy working lunches and periods of high stress.

Your emotional life will need to be sturdy too. Being an editor is notoriously incompatible with the demands of family life. You should make sure you get your due time off, but you cannot expect routine hours. There will be crises. It is as well that your loved ones understand that. Many people will take the decision that other people and other interests are more important to them than work. In that case, editing may not be the best path within journalism.

Assessing the job

Few turn down the offer of their first editorship. More experienced editors turn down jobs all the time, however, not because of doubts about their own capabilities, but because of realistic doubts about the jobs they are being offered.

The process of winning your first editorship may be as simple as a chat in the pub (if you are already the deputy, perhaps) or it may involve a long series of interviews and panels. You will be primed to answer all sorts of questions, but you should also be ready to ask them. Most interviewees manage a halting enquiry about terms and conditions, but there is much more that they should know before they make up their minds.

Is it for you?

An editorship may be a perfectly acceptable proposition for someone else, without coming close to being right for you. There needs to be a match between the subject matter and approach of a publication and the person editing it. If you cannot muster enthusiasm for the material and those who read it, you must look elsewhere. Other things can be changed: the way the subject is dealt with, the kind of writers used, the design approach. But subject matter and readership are usually fixed. A professional can do a good job in almost any circumstances, but as a professional you also need to be honest about where your real inclinations lie.

Your new magazine

Consider the character of your new magazine. Start with the fundamentals, for instance its frequency and format, and then work out towards the intangibles, such as its 'tone of voice' and the way it is perceived in the market.

You may be experienced in monthlies: what changes will you experience when you move to a weekly? If you know weeklies, can you gear yourself to the different rhythm of a monthly? Now look at how the magazine presents itself. Is it authoritative or irreverent? Is it friendly or austere? Informative or entertaining? Now where does it sit in its market? Does it lead or trail? Is it growing or shrinking? These are matters of fact. But how do its readers feel about it? What do the readers of rival magazines think? If it's a professional publication, what does the industry it serves think of it? What do other editors think? What new threats is it facing – technologically, socially, politically and commercially? What new opportunities may face it? These are matters of opinion, but vital in building up a picture of the task you are taking on.

What is the magazine's history? Is it a brash newcomer, an old faithful in need of gentle tidying up, or something struggling to come to terms with a changing world? And what is the magazine's status in publishing terms: is it part of a group or 'portfolio' of magazines with a common strategy, is it simply one title in a roster of scores, or is it someone's pet project?

Magazines are not a product like any other. People have an emotional attachment to them: that's why they are so successful. The magazine may be new to you, and you may be seeing it objectively, but to both existing staff and readers it may have a long history filled with emotional resonance. If you make radical changes, you may encounter an unexpectedly forceful degree of opposition. This may be the first magazine your publisher created. The typefaces and paper format may have been devised in a pub when the owner was young and vigorous. You, an outsider, may be trampling on other people's dreams.

You may, of course, be considering taking on a new launch, in which case there will as yet be no real answers to these questions. You will be providing them. Thorough discussion will help you decide whether you can create what the prospective launch publisher seems to want.

Your new employer

Taking up a new editorship will often involve joining a new employer. Aside from general questions that any new recruit would need answered, there are specific things that editors need to know. Every publishing company has a culture, but what does that culture mean for editors? How autonomous are they, or are their activities directed and regulated by a corporate vision? Does the editor handle staffing, or is that a matter for a central personnel department? Where does the editor's budgetary responsibility end? How much power does an editor have?

You may be only one editor among many. You should ascertain whether the company's editors meet on any formal or informal basis to discuss topics of common interest and to represent the editorial point of view within the organisation. If they do, you will probably find that helpful.

Learn what you can about your new employer. Producing one magazine among dozens for a giant public company, answerable to anonymous shareholders via the balance sheet, is radically different from working for an entrepreneur with a small stable of publications, where each has the potential to determine the fate of the whole enterprise. Big companies have the disadvantage of anonymity. Editors feel less 'special', less crucial to the enterprise and more like the rest of the staff. There is also likely to be considerable support, in the form of centralised training, personnel, production and other functions.

Working for an entrepreneur or small business, on the other hand, is more of a white-knuckle ride. Psychological studies of entrepreneurs have revealed a number of characteristics which may not make them ideal employers for everyone. They find it difficult to deal dispassionately with issues of dominance and submission; they find structure stifling; they fear placing power in the hands of others; they have low tolerance of independent thinking; they have a tendency towards paranoia, seeing themselves as victims and looking for plots; they are addicted to secrecy; and they need constant reassurance and praise.

On the other hand, entrepreneurs can be exciting. They are tremendously motivated, which can be contagious. They are creative, capable of swift innovation. They often have great energy and can be more passionate, even than their editors, about their magazines. When you are in agreement, this is inspiring. When you are not, it can be a problem.

Ask about the structure above you. To whom do you report? In most cases you will work with and report to a publisher: in some magazine houses, publishers and editors are placed on an 'equal-but-different' footing, both reporting to a publishing director. This may, in practice, be a semantic distinction but it recognises the complementary interests and attitudes of the publishing and editorial functions. Anything you can discover about the personalities of those holding these positions will be valuable.

Sometimes editors, particularly inexperienced editors, find themselves reporting to an 'editorial director' or an 'editor-in-chief'. Former editors also, on occasions, become publishers. This should be helpful, but may not necessarily be. The problem with having another editor above you is that it breaks the 'contract' between editor and reader. If every decision you make can be overridden, if there is always a higher court of appeal, if your operational decisions about staff, contributors, cover treatments and so on can be overturned, you are no longer the editor. You are the deputy editor.

This is not to say that there is no place for senior editors, particularly in large publishing houses, to make strategic decisions, to look at new launches, and to make their expertise available to those editors who wish to make use of it. But this is a role which needs to be performed with subtlety if mutual respect, rather than suspicion, is to be achieved.

Editors-in-chief should be available for consultation, advice and support. All editors have times when they need the assistance of someone experienced. This relationship will not work, however, if the editor-in-chief is also supposed to be sitting in judgement on those who seek his or her help. The role of any such editor-in-chief is something that should be explored in interview. In short, the buck must stop with you, or you aren't editing your magazine.

Your new staff

Before accepting a position as editor, consider your new staff. Sloppiness about spelling, punctuation, and so on, indicates problems in the sub-editing department. Weak headlines and standfirsts and a general lack of sharpness may stem from inadequacies higher up the chain. If there is a staff box (or 'masthead', if you prefer), see how it relates to the by-lines that you see. Much of the writing will tend to have been produced by contributors, but the ideas may well have been generated in-house.

Ask yourself what you would expect such an issue to cost, in terms of freelance material: when you reach the final stages of the interviewing process, your budgetary constraints should be revealed. Taking that in conjunction with staffing levels, you can begin to make some assessment of what can realistically be achieved.

It is worth asking, too, about training. Your interview is not the most intelligent time to ask about your own career development, but you should know what is available to your staff and what their attitude to it has been. Some managements persist in using training as a punishment or ritual humiliation, to the despair of trainers, and if that has been the case you will find it difficult to promote a more constructive attitude.

It is worth thinking particularly hard about two key jobs: your art editor (or director) and your deputy editor. It is fair to say that without a happy and mutually respectful relationship with both, your attempt to bring your own personality to bear on the new magazine will face great difficulties. It will be one of your first tasks to ensure that these key colleagues are receptive to your direction or to take appropriate action.

You will make more headway and gain more respect if you make an effort to accommodate your new colleagues and give them the chance to show you what they can do. Do not prejudge things: they may have been waiting for the chance to demonstrate their skills and their enthusiasm for the magazine. You may have to hold them back, rather than pushing them on.

Either way, the attitude of your colleagues will play a large part in determining the success or failure of your editorship. At the time of your appointment, you may be more preoccupied with your own editorial skills: handling stories, headlines, pictures and money. Soon, however, you will realise that successful magazines really depend upon the creation of inspiring relationships between people. Only experience – good and bad – can help you with that: but that's when you become an editor.

No time like the present

Of course the beauty (for some, the horror) of the modern age is that you do not need someone else's permission to become an editor. If this is a role that you aspire to, then you should be gaining experience now, by publishing your own online magazine (using free blog content management software, for example, with one of the dozens of magazine 'themes'), recruiting and managing volunteer contributors, sourcing multimedia, and experimenting with online distribution. Many such entrepreneurs have gone on to sell their online 'property' to an existing publisher.

If you like the feel of print you can even use an online 'print on demand' service like MagCloud. Instead of having to pay in advance to print thousands of copies that you then have to distribute and sell, each magazine is only printed and posted when someone orders a copy online. If you are feeling even bolder you may try to raise funds to create a printed version – again, the Internet introduces new options here, with various 'crowdfunding' platforms allowing you to raise money from fans.

Ultimately you can create the 'organisation' of a magazine from the spark of a good idea – and the network to reach the right people. When editor Andrew Losowsky was stranded in Dublin following the eruption of the Icelandic volcano Eyjafjallajökull, for instance, he saw a publishing opportunity in the experience that was being shared across airports around the world. He published a blog post calling for any writers, designers, photographers, and illustrators who were also stranded to help him make a magazine about the experience. More than 50 people responded to help him create *Stranded*, a magazine he described as an '88-page souvenir of a moment in time when a non-life-threatening crisis hit the world, one for which nobody was to blame, and nobody knew how long it would last'.

In the same year a group of San Francisco-based writers and editors decided they were going to try to create a new magazine from scratch in 48 hours. Eight thousand people signed up, the team received 1,500 contributions of content and imagery, and 35 editors selected 70 pieces to fill a 60-page publication – called *48 Hours* – which broke their distributor's sales records. The only tools they needed were Twitter (to reach potential contributors), Google Docs (to collaborate online), Submishmash (a tool for managing submissions) and MagCloud (to print the end result). The team went on to repeat the process for further issues – now renamed *Longshot*.

There are many more tools to play with besides the ones mentioned above: you can use a number of online marketplaces to find and pay writers, designers, illustrators and photographers around the world. And there are even virtual news-stands for independent publishers, like No Layout (nolayout.com).

Tools, however, do not make a magazine. You do. What made both *Stranded* and *Longshot* possible were two key ingredients: a great idea that motivates people, and the project management skills to deal with the contributions that then come in.

These are the same core skills that magazine editors have always needed. With these tools at your fingertips, you can start developing them now, and the cost of failure is small (a third core skill is to be able to keep trying, and learning from each experiment).

You can start as small as you like, and go from there, without needing funding or highly placed contacts behind you (although, clearly, both things help). Employers are increasingly presented with applicants who can already demonstrate 'self starter' qualities, who are not just talking about what they would do if they ran a magazine, but have already done it, and are better editors for it. And if you love magazines like you say you do, well, what are you waiting for?

Appendix 1

National Union of Journalists
Code of Conduct

The NUJ's Code of Conduct has set out the main principles of British and Irish journalism since 1936. The code is part of the rules and all journalists joining the union must sign that they will strive to adhere to the it.

Members of the National Union of Journalists are expected to abide by the following professional principles:

A journalist:

1 At all times upholds and defends the principle of media freedom, the right of freedom of expression and the right of the public to be informed
2 Strives to ensure that information disseminated is honestly conveyed, accurate and fair
3 Does her/his utmost to correct harmful inaccuracies
4 Differentiates between fact and opinion
5 Obtains material by honest, straightforward and open means, with the exception of investigations that are both overwhelmingly in the public interest and which involve evidence that cannot be obtained by straightforward means
6 Does nothing to intrude into anybody's private life, grief or distress unless justified by overriding consideration of the public interest
7 Protects the identity of sources who supply information in confidence and material gathered in the course of her/his work
8 Resists threats or any other inducements to influence, distort or suppress information
9 Takes no unfair personal advantage of information gained in the course of her/his duties before the information is public knowledge
10 Produces no material likely to lead to hatred or discrimination on the grounds of a person's age, gender, race, colour, creed, legal status, disability, marital status, or sexual orientation
11 Does not by way of statement, voice or appearance endorse by advertisement any commercial product or service save for the promotion of her/his own work or of the medium by which she/he is employed
12 Avoids plagiarism.

The NUJ believes a journalist has the right to refuse an assignment or to be identified as the author of editorial that would break the letter or spirit of the code. The NUJ will fully support any journalist disciplined for asserting her/his right to act according to the code.

Appendix 2

Press Complaints Commission Code of Practice

The Press Complaints Commission is charged with enforcing the following Code of Practice which was framed by the newspaper and periodical industry and was ratified by the PCC in January 2011. Please check the PCC website fro the latest version of the Code.

The Editors' Code

All members of the press have a duty to maintain the highest professional standards. The Code, which includes this preamble and the public interest exceptions below, sets the benchmark for those ethical standards, protecting both the rights of the individual and the public's right to know. It is the cornerstone of the system of self-regulation to which the industry has made a binding commitment.

It is essential that an agreed code be honoured not only to the letter but in the full spirit. It should not be interpreted so narrowly as to compromise its commitment to respect the rights of the individual, nor so broadly that it constitutes an unnecessary interference with freedom of expression or prevents publication in the public interest.

It is the responsibility of editors and publishers to apply the Code to editorial material in both printed and online versions of publications. They should take care to ensure it is observed rigorously by all editorial staff and external contributors, including non-journalists, in printed and online versions of publications.

Editors should co-operate swiftly with the PCC in the resolution of complaints. Any publication judged to have breached the Code must print the adjudication in full and with due prominence, including headline reference to the PCC.

1   Accuracy

    i.   The Press must take care not to publish inaccurate, misleading or distorted information, including pictures.

ii. A significant inaccuracy, misleading statement or distortion once recognised must be corrected, promptly and with due prominence, and – where appropriate – an apology published. In cases involving the Commission, prominence should be agreed with the PCC in advance.
iii. The Press, whilst free to be partisan, must distinguish clearly between comment, conjecture and fact.
iv. A publication must report fairly and accurately the outcome of an action for defamation to which it has been a party, unless an agreed settlement states otherwise, or an agreed statement is published.

2 Opportunity to reply

A fair opportunity for reply to inaccuracies must be given when reasonably called for.

3 *Privacy

i. Everyone is entitled to respect for his or her private and family life, home, health and correspondence, including digital communications.
ii. Editors will be expected to justify intrusions into any individual's private life without consent. Account will be taken of the complainant's own public disclosures of information.
iii. It is unacceptable to photograph individuals in private places without their consent.

Note – Private places are public or private property where there is a reasonable expectation of privacy.

4 *Harassment

i. Journalists must not engage in intimidation, harassment or persistent pursuit.
ii. They must not persist in questioning, telephoning, pursuing or photographing individuals once asked to desist; nor remain on their property when asked to leave and must not follow them. If requested, they must identify themselves and whom they represent.
iii. Editors must ensure these principles are observed by those working for them and take care not to use non-compliant material from other sources.

5 Intrusion into grief or shock

i. In cases involving personal grief or shock, enquiries and approaches must be made with sympathy and discretion and publication handled sensitively. This should not restrict the right to report legal proceedings, such as inquests.

ii.   *When reporting suicide, care should be taken to avoid excessive detail about the method used.

6   *Children

i.   Young people should be free to complete their time at school without unnecessary intrusion.
ii.   A child under 16 must not be interviewed or photographed on issues involving their own or another child's welfare unless a custodial parent or similarly responsible adult consents.
iii.   Pupils must not be approached or photographed at school without the permission of the school authorities.
iv.   Minors must not be paid for material involving children's welfare, nor parents or guardians for material about their children or wards, unless it is clearly in the child's interest.
v.   Editors must not use the fame, notoriety or position of a parent or guardian as sole justification for publishing details of a child's private life.

7   *Children in sex cases

i.   The press must not, even if legally free to do so, identify children under 16 who are victims or witnesses in cases involving sex offences.
ii.   In any press report of a case involving a sexual offence against a child:
    a.   The child must not be identified.
    b.   The adult may be identified.
    c.   The word 'incest' must not be used where a child victim might be identified.
    d.   Care must be taken that nothing in the report implies the relationship between the accused and the child.

8   *Hospitals

i.   Journalists must identify themselves and obtain permission from a responsible executive before entering non-public areas of hospitals or similar institutions to pursue enquiries.
ii.   The restrictions on intruding into privacy are particularly relevant to enquiries about individuals in hospitals or similar institutions.

9   *Reporting of crime

i.   Relatives or friends of persons convicted or accused of crime should not generally be identified without their consent, unless they are genuinely relevant to the story.
ii.   Particular regard should be paid to the potentially vulnerable position of children who witness, or are victims of, crime. This should not restrict the right to report legal proceedings

10 *Clandestine devices and subterfuge

i. The press must not seek to obtain or publish material acquired by using hidden cameras or clandestine listening devices; or by intercepting private or mobile telephone calls, messages or emails; or by the unauthorised removal of documents or photographs; or by accessing digitally-held private information without consent.

ii. Engaging in misrepresentation or subterfuge, including by agents or intermediaries, can generally be justified only in the public interest and then only when the material cannot be obtained by other means.

11 Victims of sexual assault

The press must not identify victims of sexual assault or publish material likely to contribute to such identification unless there is adequate justification and they are legally free to do so.

12 Discrimination

i. The press must avoid prejudicial or pejorative reference to an individual's race, colour, religion, gender, sexual orientation or to any physical or mental illness or disability.

ii. Details of an individual's race, colour, religion, sexual orientation, physical or mental illness or disability must be avoided unless genuinely relevant to the story.

13 Financial journalism

i. Even where the law does not prohibit it, journalists must not use for their own profit financial information they receive in advance of its general publication, nor should they pass such information to others.

ii. They must not write about shares or securities in whose performance they know that they or their close families have a significant financial interest without disclosing the interest to the editor or financial editor.

iii. They must not buy or sell, either directly or through nominees or agents, shares or securities about which they have written recently or about which they intend to write in the near future.

14 Confidential sources

Journalists have a moral obligation to protect confidential sources of information.

15 Witness payments in criminal trials

i. No payment or offer of payment to a witness – or any person who may reasonably be expected to be called as a witness – should be made in any case once proceedings are active as defined by the Contempt of Court Act 1981.

This prohibition lasts until the suspect has been freed unconditionally by police without charge or bail or the proceedings are otherwise discontinued; or has entered a guilty plea to the court; or, in the event of a not guilty plea, the court has announced its verdict.

ii.   *Where proceedings are not yet active but are likely and foreseeable, editors must not make or offer payment to any person who may reasonably be expected to be called as a witness, unless the information concerned ought demonstrably to be published in the public interest and there is an over-riding need to make or promise payment for this to be done; and all reasonable steps have been taken to ensure no financial dealings influence the evidence those witnesses give. In no circumstances should such payment be conditional on the outcome of a trial.

iii.   *Any payment or offer of payment made to a person later cited to give evidence in proceedings must be disclosed to the prosecution and defence. The witness must be advised of this requirement.

16   *Payment to criminals

i.   Payment or offers of payment for stories, pictures or information, which seek to exploit a particular crime or to glorify or glamorise crime in general, must not be made directly or via agents to convicted or confessed criminals or to their associates – who may include family, friends and colleagues.

ii.   Editors invoking the public interest to justify payment or offers would need to demonstrate that there was good reason to believe the public interest would be served. If, despite payment, no public interest emerged, then the material should not be published.

The public interest

There may be exceptions to the clauses marked * where they can be demonstrated to be in the public interest.

1   The public interest includes, but is not confined to:
   i.   Detecting or exposing crime or serious impropriety.
   ii.   Protecting public health and safety
   iii.   Preventing the public from being misled by an action or statement of an individual or organisation.

2   There is a public interest in freedom of expression itself.

3   Whenever the public interest is invoked, the PCC will require editors to demonstrate fully that they reasonably believed that publication, or

journalistic activity undertaken with a view to publication, would be in the public interest.

4   The PCC will consider the extent to which material is already in the public domain, or will become so.

5   In cases involving children under 16, editors must demonstrate an exceptional public interest to over-ride the normally paramount interest of the child.

Glossary

Terms which have their own entry are printed in SMALL CAPITALS.

ABC   Audit Bureau of Circulation, the organisation which provides independent confirmation of a magazine's sales.

ad : ed ratio   the ratio of advertising to EDITORIAL in an issue of a magazine.

ad-get feature   an EDITORIAL FEATURE commissioned to encourage advertisers to take space alongside.

advertisement feature   the approved term for ADVERTORIAL.

advertorial   an advertisement written and designed to resemble EDITORIAL material.

all rights   the right to publish a piece as often as required in any medium and in any territory.

analytics   information about who is accessing your website, how and where, as well as additional information such as the websites they have come from and go on to, and the computer systems and browsers that they are using.

angle   the particular point of interest within a news story, either to the writer or to the readers.

appraisal   a formal meeting in which an employee's performance is assessed and discussed.

artwork   (a) the visual elements on a page, excluding text; (b) the physical components of a page, including HALF-TONES and typesetting, prior to being turned into FILM.

ascender   the upper strokes of LOWER CASE letters such as b, d, h, etc.

ASCII   American Standard Code for Information Interchange. Pronounced 'askey' and used to mean plain text in digital form without formatting.

assign   to sell COPYRIGHT material outright.

attribution   connecting a quote or information to its source. A note 'attrib?' in copy is a request that a quote be linked to a speaker.

back issue   an earlier copy of a magazine.

background   the context in a story or FEATURE.

backup   another copy of computer documents made in case the originals are lost or damaged. 'Backups' are the copies themselves.

bad break   where automatic HYPHENATION produces ugly or misleading results, e.g. 'therapist' becoming 'the-rapist'.

band   a wide plastic wrapper allowing an extra supplement to be attached ('bound on') to an issue.

barcode   a machine-readable serial number placed on a magazine COVER.

baseline   a notional line along the bottom of a row of type. DESCENDERS fall below the baseline.

bind   to fasten pages together to make a magazine.

bleed   to print beyond the boundary of the page after trimming. Pictures are said to 'bleed' or be used 'full-bleed'.

blob par   a paragraph starting with a black dot or BULLET. Used to emphasise extra points of interest.

blog   a content management system which allows anyone to publish online. Typically entries are written in a less formal manner than traditional publishing, and organised most-recent-top, but the increased sophistication of blog software has facilitated various professional blog-based publishing operations which are neither.

body copy or body text   the main text of a piece.

body type   the typeface in which the BODY COPY is set.

bold   heavy type.

bookmarks   a list of favourite WORLD WIDE WEB pages stored in a BROWSER program.

boost   a BOX telling readers what to expect in the next issue.

box   area of type marked out by rules.

brainstorming session   an ideas meeting in which critical comments are forbidden.

brief   (a) instructions to a writer, photographer or designer; (b) a short news item.

brochureware   websites containing content produced for another medium that has not been re-edited for the web. Also known as 'shovelware'.

bromide   photographic paper produced by a typesetting or image-setting machine.

browser   a computer program used for reading the WORLD WIDE WEB.

budget   a statement of expenditure and income allocated to a department for a given period.

budget forecast   a forecast of expenditure and income for a department in a given period.

bug   an electronic pick-up used for recording telephone calls.

bullet   a black dot used for emphasis or in lists.

business-to-business   the current term for trade magazine publishing.

bust   to be too long for the space allocated. Used of HEADLINES, STANDFIRSTS and CAPTIONS.

by-line   the author's name when used on the page.

caps   capital letters.

caption   a piece of text associated with a photograph, usually to indicate what it shows.

caret mark a mark used in PROOF-reading to indicate that something must be inserted.

cash-flow the pattern of an organisation's income and spending over a period, recorded on a cash-flow chart.

cast off to calculate the space occupied by a piece of text.

casual a freelance journalist employed temporarily in the office.

catch-line a short identifying name given to a story as it passes through the production process.

centred a form of typesetting in which space is distributed at both ends of each line.

centre-spread the middle two pages of a SADDLE-STITCHED magazine.

chapel a branch of the National Union of Journalists based on a single magazine house.

circulation a mailing list.

classifieds small advertisements grouped together.

clip art pictures not subject to COPYRIGHT restrictions, usually obtained in digitised form.

close to send an issue to the printers: 'The issue is closed.'

CMS content management system: software that allows you to publish and manage content to print, web, mobile or other platforms.

collate to assemble the pages of a magazine into the right order.

colour (a) printed using the FOUR-COLOUR PROCESS; (b) descriptive writing.

colour house where photographs are SCANNED and united with electronically generated pages and type to produce the FILM required to make printing PLATES.

colour separations the four separate pieces of FILM created when full-colour material is put through the FOUR-COLOUR PROCESS.

column (a) regular article; (b) a section of type set across a fixed MEASURE and running vertically down the page.

column rule a vertical line separating COLUMNS.

commission a contract asking a FREELANCE writer or photographer to produce a piece of work.

computer to plate sending finished pages from the editorial layout system to create a printing PLATE, with no interim FILM stage. Also known as 'straight to plate'.

contact sheet a sheet of photographs made by pressing the negatives directly against the photographic paper. The prints are the same size as the original negatives.

contacts journalistic sources.

contacts book a book of sources' telephone numbers.

contempt of court illegal interference with the course of justice.

content management system see CMS.

contract publishing a form of publishing in which professional publishers produce magazines on behalf of other commercial organisations.

controlled circulation a form of free distribution in which copies are sent to readers on a mailing list.

copy all written material.

copy edit to sub-edit written material for consistency, accuracy, grammar, spelling and house style.

copy-fit to ensure edited material fits the allocated space.

copy-flow the movement of journalistic material during the editing and production process.

copyright the right to reproduce a piece of creative work, initially held by its creator.

cover the first page of a magazine.

cover-line words used on the COVER to entice readers.

cover-mount a free gift attached to the COVER.

CPA cost per action: a method of costing online advertising – the advertiser pays a set amount every time a user performs a particular action as a result of their advert, e.g. ordering a brochure, setting up a user account, etc.

CPC cost per click: a method of costing online advertising – the advertiser pays a set amount for every time a user clicks on their advert.

CPM cost per thousand: a method of costing online advertising – the advertiser pays a set amount for every thousand users who see their advert.

credits details of photographers, authors, stylists, providers of clothes, etc., to go alongside photographs.

crop to alter the size and shape of a photograph.

crosshead a small HEADLINE in the body of the text.

cross-platform involving publication across more than one medium, e.g. print and mobile; web and tablet.

cross-reference a reminder to readers that further information on a subject is to be found elsewhere in an issue.

crowdfunding funding a project by raising money from a wide range of people, typically via online donations.

customer magazines magazines published by or for organisations to give or sell to their customers.

cut to delete a section of text.

cut-out a photograph in which the subject has been 'cut out' and the background discarded.

cuttings previously published articles, either a writer's own or other people's.

cuttings job disparaging name for a FEATURE or PROFILE written without extensive new research or interviewing.

database information organised and stored in a computer.

date-tied only relevant if published at a specific time.

deadline the time by which a journalistic task is expected to be completed.

deck technically, one complete HEADLINE, no matter how many lines it occupies. A subheading beneath it in a different font or size would be a second deck. Often used, erroneously, to mean a single line of headline type: a two-line headline is thus called a two-deck headline.

defendant a person or organisation subject to a legal action.

delete to cut a character, word or line.

departments   a useful American term for the regular elements found in each issue of a magazine: EDITOR'S LETTER, news, products, etc.

descender   the tail of certain LOWER CASE letters (p, q, y, etc.) which descends below the BASELINE.

desk   a department of a magazine, e.g. features desk, news desk, sub-editor's desk.

desktop publishing   computer hardware and software to permit the typesetting and publishing make-up of pages, complete with photographs, on-screen.

diary   the routine events covered by a magazine's reporters. Hence 'off-diary' stories are those that are out of the ordinary.

diary column   (a) a gossip column; (b) an account of someone's week.

digitisation   converting physical content – e.g. print – into digital content – e.g. a website.

dingbat   a typographic symbol available from the keyboard.

display ad   an advertisement that uses more than simple type and appears outside the CLASSIFIED section.

display type   large type used for HEADINGS etc.

domain   a fundamental part of the address of a computer within the INTERNET.

double-page spread   two pages opposite one another, whether used for a single advertisement or a single EDITORIAL item.

DPS   see DOUBLE-PAGE SPREAD.

drop cap   a large letter at the beginning of a paragraph, usually at least as deep as two lines of BODY TYPE.

dropout   a fault in camerawork or PLATE-making meaning light areas of a picture lose all detail.

DTP   see DESKTOP PUBLISHING.

dummy   (a) a mock-up of a new publication; (b) a complete set of PROOFS in correct order; (c) a reduced-size, plain paper mock-up of the current issue showing the location of display advertising etc.

duotone   a black and white picture reproduced by printing in black and one other colour.

e-commerce   selling goods or services online.

edit   (a) to cut, check, rewrite and otherwise improve an article; (b) to be an editor, either of a whole magazine or of a section.

editor's letter   introductory remarks by the editor.

editorial   (a) the journalistic content of a magazine; (b) the EDITOR'S LETTER or leader column.

em   (a) a unit of measurement, becoming archaic. An em, properly called a pica em, is 12 POINTS. It represents the space occupied by an upper case M in 12-pt type; (b) Historically, an em in any type size is the width of an upper case M in that size. Thus a 9-pt em is 9 pts wide, an 8-pt em is 8 pts wide and so on.

embargo   a ban on publication before a specified date.

en   half the width of an EM in any type size. Typesetting jobs were measured in ens, the en being the average width of a lower case character in any type size.

end symbol a typographic device (usually a black square or BULLET) used in magazine pages to indicate that a piece has finished.

ends written at the end of a piece of original COPY to indicate that it has ended.

exclusive a story or interview that is unique to a particular magazine.

expenses costs incurred.

facing matter an advertisement that is placed opposite EDITORIAL.

fair comment a defence to certain LIBEL actions.

fair dealing the permitted use of COPYRIGHT material.

feature a piece of writing that is longer, more discursive and contains more 'colour' than a news story.

fifth colour an extra colour, often day-glo or metallic, used to create a striking effect beyond the means of the normal FOUR-COLOUR PROCESS. Often used on COVERS.

file any document created on a computer.

file name the name given to a computer document.

fill to rewrite a piece of type, whether a HEADING, STANDFIRST, CAPTION or BODY TEXT, to fit a given space.

film material produced by image-setting machines and colour separation equipment and used to make printing PLATES.

first rights or first British serial rights the right to publish an article once in the UK. This is the standard commission, unless the writer agrees otherwise.

fit to CUT a piece of writing to match a fixed space.

fixed direct costs costs incurred in production but not proportionate to the volume of production.

flash a design device for drawing attention.

Flash ubiquitous proprietary software used to produce animation etc. in web pages.

flat-plan a plan of the magazine, indicating where every advertisement and every piece of EDITORIAL will appear.

focus concentration on the identity of a magazine.

focus feature a label sometimes used for AD-GET FEATURES.

focus group a small group of readers and potential readers assembled for research purposes.

folio page number.

follow-up a return to a story to encompass new developments.

footer a line, often including the magazine's name, that appears at the bottom of every page.

format (a) the size and shape of a page, e.g. A4; (b) to format text is to apply to it all the typographic specifications laid down in a magazine's design. This should happen automatically when text is transferred into a LAYOUT program.

forum Internet discussion area.

fount or font traditionally, a set of characters in one TYPEFACE and one size. Today it tends to mean a typeface in its complete range of sizes and italic and bold variants.

four-colour process   a printing technique that uses four colours of ink (cyan, magenta, yellow, black) to simulate full colour.

freelance   a self-employed journalist, either writing at home or working as a casual sub-editor.

furniture   (a) design elements common to every page of a magazine; (b) regular features and fixed items in the magazine as a whole.

galley proof   a proof produced as a single column of type, before page make up.

gatefold   a page, usually the inside front COVER, which folds out to accommodate a large advertisement. Occasionally used for editorial.

gone to bed   the magazine is at the printers and cannot be changed.

graduated tint   a TINT which changes in density or hue from top to bottom or from side to side.

grid   the underlying design structure of the magazine, determining COLUMN widths and image area. Now usually exists only in computer form.

gutter   the gap between two COLUMNS or two adjoining pages.

h&j   HYPHENATION and JUSTIFICATION. Now usually encountered as rules built into DESKTOP PUBLISHING programs.

half-tone   an illustration or photograph after it has been broken into dots for printing.

hard copy   words on paper rather than on the computer screen.

header   a line of type that appears at the top of every page.

heading or headline   an area of DISPLAY TYPE that draws the reader's interest to a feature. Need not be at the top of the page.

hold over   to keep an item for the next issue or some future date.

house ad   an advertisement placed in a magazine by its own publisher.

house journal   a magazine produced for employees of an organisation.

house style   a set of rules about disputed spellings, matters of punctuation, capitalisation, use of numerals, etc.

HTML   HyperText Mark-up Language, a computer language used for the creation of WORLD WIDE WEB pages.

human interest   a type of story or feature concentrating on emotional aspects of individual lives.

hypertext   text on a computer screen that can be clicked on to allow the reader to navigate around a page, document or site.

hyphenation   the insertion of a hyphen into a word as it breaks at the end of a line. Controlled by dictionaries built into DESKTOP PUBLISHING programs but subject to manual override.

icon   a drawing on a computer screen used to indicate and manipulate files, disc drives, etc. By extension, similar drawings used as illustrations and graphics in page design.

image area   the part of a page which is normally inked.

imprint   the names and addresses of the publisher and printer and any other legally required information.

indentation   (abbreviated to 'indent') a shorter line than usual, leaving a white space at the beginning or end. Used to mark paragraphs.

injunction   a court order used to prevent publication of material based on breaches of confidence.

insert   a loose advertisement or announcement that is inserted between a magazine's pages.

interim   a court order banning publication in advance of a court hearing.

intro   abbreviation for 'introduction': the author's opening paragraph. Not to be confused with the STANDFIRST or SELL, which are written by editors and sub-editors.

italic   sloping type used for emphasis, book titles, etc.

justification   (a) adjustment of the spacing between words and characters. 'Justified' type is set so that lines are full out at both ends; (b) Proving the truth of an allegation when defending a libel action.

justified   see JUSTIFICATION.

kern   to reduce space between two letters to make them fit neatly. Computer systems do this automatically, but it can be adjusted manually.

kicker   an introductory HEADING in small type above the main headline.

kill   to drop a story or FEATURE.

kill fee   a payment in respect of a story that has been dropped at an early stage.

landscape   a picture with a horizontal emphasis.

layout   designs for pages, SPREADS and features; printed versions of those designs.

lead   (pronounced 'leed') the most important and prominent story on a news page.

leading   (pronounced 'ledding') the vertical space between lines of type. Measured in POINTS.

legal   a potential legal problem or query: 'We've got a legal on this story.'

letterspacing   adjustment of the space between a group of letters to improve appearance.

libel   a defamatory publication or statement.

licence   an agreement to use COPYRIGHT material within negotiated restrictions.

lift   to acquire writing or pictures from some other published source without paying for them.

line drawing   an illustration that uses lines rather than areas of continuous tone.

linkblogs   blogs consisting entirely of links to interesting material on the web, sometimes with a brief comment, quote or description.

listings   details of events, entertainment, etc.

literal   a typographical error.

logo   abbreviation for 'logotype': the magazine's name, in the typographic style used on the cover.

lower case   small letters, as opposed to capitals.

manuscript   original COPY on paper.

masthead   the panel that includes the magazine's name, address and telephone numbers and often its staff box. Incorrectly used to mean TITLE-PIECE.

measure   the width of a column. Often measured in PICA EMS.

media pack   details of a magazine's circulation, readership and technical specifications. Used to attract advertisers.

metadata   information about a particular piece of content, for example its author, publisher, and date of publication; individuals, places and organisations referred to, etc.

mf   abbreviation for 'more follows'. Written at the end of individual pages of COPY.

model release form   a form to be signed by a photographic model, indemnifying the magazine against various legal claims.

mono   black and white.

mug-shot   simple identifying picture of an individual person.

multimedia   bringing together words, images, sounds and moving pictures to be accessed on a computer.

newsgroup   Internet discussion group, usually containing gossip but little real news.

newsletter   a magazine with minimal production values distributed by subscription.

next week/month box   a BOX or PANEL indicating what the magazine's next issue will contain.

nib   news in brief: a one-paragraph news story.

off the record   a statement made subject to restrictions as to how it is reported.

offline   an electronic medium that does not require a connection to a remote computer.

on spec   a feature offered for the editor's perusal, without obligation.

on the record   a statement made without restrictions as to how it is reported.

online   an electronic medium that requires connection to a remote computer.

online service   a commercial organisation selling information to those connecting to its remote computers.

orphan   the short line at the beginning or end of a paragraph appearing at the bottom of a COLUMN. Best avoided.

outs   photographs submitted for a LAYOUT but not used.

overheads   costs not directly related to a magazine's production.

overmatter   type in excess of the space allowed for it.

overs   see OUTS.

ozalid   a type of PROOF.

page rate   (a) the price of a page of advertising; (b) the sum an editor can spend on a page of EDITORIAL.

page traffic   measurement of how well a given page is read.

pagination   the number of pages.

panel   an area of type enclosed by RULES and often backed by a TINT.

Pantone   a proprietary colour-matching system. Fifth colours are sometimes called 'Pantone colours' because this is the system used to define them.

par/para   abbreviation for 'paragraph'.

paste up   to create pages from BROMIDES of type and HALF-TONES, ready to go before the camera. Effectively replaced by DESKTOP PUBLISHING programs.

pdf   a computer file in Adobe's portable document format, commonly used for final output of editorial pages.

peg   the event to which a story or feature has to be tied to make it topical: 'The peg for this is the new school term.'

perfect bound   a method of BINDING, using glue, that creates a magazine with a hard, square spine.

photomontage   a photograph assembled out of several originals or extensively retouched.

pica   12-pt type. A pica EM is a 12-pt em. The pica em is used as a unit of typographical measurement.

picture by-line   a BY-LINE incorporating a photograph of the author.

pingback   a notification that another web page has linked to yours, typically sent by email and displayed beneath the page that has been linked to.

pixelate   to treat a picture electronically so that the subject is unrecognisable. Used to protect anonymity in stories where this is legally necessary, and in imitation of television practice.

pixelated   used to describe an image or video which or is blocky and jagged in appearance. This happens when the image or video has low resolution as a result of, for example, being enlarged beyond its original size, or the file size being reduced for web publishing.

plaintiff   a person or organisation bringing a legal action, now officially called a 'claimant'.

planning meeting   a meeting dedicated to future issues.

plate   an ink-bearing surface used in the lithographic printing process.

point   the fundamental unit of typographical measurement. There are 72 pts to the inch and 28.35 to the centimetre.

portfolio   (a) group of magazines owned by a single company; (b) a folder showing examples of a designer's work.

portrait   a picture with vertical emphasis.

post-mortem   a meeting to discuss the previous issue or issues.

pre-plan   a meeting to discuss future features.

pre-press   print planning, FILM assembly, PLATE-making and other activities required before printing.

preprint   a section of a magazine printed in advance and then inserted into the issue.

print run   the total number of issues printed.

prior restraint   legal action preventing publication.

privilege   a defence to some LIBEL actions.

profile   a portrait in words, usually of a person but occasionally of an organisation, a place or an object.

proof   a printed copy of work in progress, for checking purposes.

pull quote   a quote extracted from a FEATURE or news story and given visual emphasis by typography.

qualitative research   research dealing with readers' opinions, aspirations and feelings.

quantitative research   research based on demographic and statistical aspects of the readership.

ragged right   type that is not JUSTIFIED, but is 'flush left' or RANGED LEFT. Each line may be of a different length, giving a 'ragged' appearance.

ranged left   type that is not JUSTIFIED but is lined up on the left.

ranged right   type that is not JUSTIFIED but is lined up on the right.

readership   the total number of people reading a magazine, based on research into how many people see each copy.

register   the correct alignment of all four colours of ink. Printing can be 'in register' or 'out of register'.

regulars   the repeated elements in a magazine: contents page, EDITOR'S LETTER, news, letters, etc.

repertoire   readers who choose from a range of magazines.

reportage   term used for 'gritty' investigative news features, with appropriate photography.

repro   abbreviation for 'reproduction', meaning high-level SCANNING of colour pictures and their reuniting with type and page LAYOUTS to make the FOUR-COLOUR FILMS required for colour printing.

repro house   also known as COLOUR HOUSE. Facility specialising in reproduction and colour work.

retouch   to improve or alter a photograph. Now done electronically.

revenue   income.

reverse out   typically, to show white type emerging from a black background. Sometimes known as a 'wob', for 'white on black'.

right of reply   procedure for correcting published errors.

ring-round   news story or FEATURE based on telephone calls seeking instant reactions to events.

river   white space forming an ugly river-like pattern through a column of type.

roman   the standard upright style of type.

rough   a designer's sketch leading to a finished layout or giving guidance to a photographer.

RSI   repetitive strain injury, a crippling condition affecting some of those who work on-screen.

RSS   a web-based technology that allows content to be cross-published between sites, or from websites to users of 'RSS reader' software.

RSS feed   a specific 'feed' of content from a website or web service. Typical RSS feeds might include the latest headlines from a news or magazine website, a section of that, or by a particular author; full or partial blog posts; updates from social media accounts; and the latest search results on a particular term.

RSS reader   a piece of software that can be used to follow RSS feeds from multiple sources, collecting them in a single place.

rule   any line appearing in printed matter.

runaround   type which is set to run around a photograph or graphic element.

running turn   ensuring that sentences carry on from one COLUMN to the next and from one page to the next, to discourage the reader from breaking off.

s/s   abbreviation for 'same size'.

saddle-stitching a method of BINDING magazines by folding pages at the seam and stapling.

scanner an electronic or computer device used for converting photographs, artwork and typewritten COPY into digital form.

scanning the process of converting photographs, artwork and typewritten copy into digital form.

schedule a timetable of production events from the commissioning of material to printing.

screamer an exclamation mark.

search engine optimisation see SEO.

section a part of a magazine formed from a single sheet of paper before being stitched and trimmed.

sell see STANDFIRST.

SEO search engine optimisation: the skill of improving the position of a web page in search engine rankings through writing, coding and/or attracting links.

separations see COLOUR SEPARATIONS.

server a computer used for storing large volumes of material, either in the office or as part of the INTERNET.

shoot a photographic session.

shovelware websites containing content produced for another medium that has not been re-edited for the web. Also known as 'brochureware'.

sidebar additional material enhancing a FEATURE, often placed in a PANEL or BOX to one side of BODY COPY.

sidehead a small HEADING in the text, flush with the left of the COLUMN of type.

slander spoken defamation.

slug a small HEADING at the top of a page used to define the type of material on the page beneath: 'news', 'personal view', 'industry focus', etc.

SMO social media optimisation: the practice of ensuring content is likely to be distributed by users through social media, either through the choice of content itself, engagement with users, or publication on social media platforms.

social bookmarking the process of 'bookmarking' a web page using online tools that allow those bookmarks to be seen by other people

social media optimisation see SMO.

solus ad the only advertisement on a SPREAD.

solus reader a reader who is loyal to a single magazine.

special feature often an AD-GET FEATURE.

spike a metal spike used for holding discarded copy. Now banned for safety reasons but sometimes replaced by a similarly named area in a computer system.

splash the front-page lead story in a newspaper-format magazine.

sponsorship generating revenue by selling one or more advertisers the right to associate themselves with some EDITORIAL area or event.

spot colour single colour (in addition to black).

spread see DOUBLE-PAGE SPREAD.

standfirst the introductory material to a FEATURE, written by editors or sub-editors.

standing artwork   graphic material used in every issue.

standing matter   text elements used in every issue.

stet   Latin for 'let it stand': an instruction to reinstate something shown as deleted on the HARD COPY or PROOF.

sting   the central and most damaging allegation in a LIBEL case.

strap or strapline   an additional HEADING above or below the main heading and in smaller type.

strict liability   a type of CONTEMPT OF COURT that can be committed accidentally.

style   see HOUSE STYLE.

style book   the repository of HOUSE STYLE.

style sheet   (a) a shorter version of a style book; (b) in DESKTOP PUBLISHING programs, a stored set of type specifications to which incoming text can be made to conform.

stylist   the person responsible for organising a photographic shoot, especially if models are involved.

sub   sub-editor (sometimes known as copy editor).

subhead   a subsidiary HEADING in small type beneath the main heading.

SWOT   Strengths, Weaknesses, Opportunities, Threats: a fashionable way of analysing a magazine's position in the market.

synopsis   a brief summary of an article.

Teeline   a shorthand system favoured by journalists.

think piece   a ruminative FEATURE.

thumbnail   a miniature print-out or drawing of a page.

TIFF   (Tagged Image File Format) a format for storing images in digital form.

tint   a printed area covered with dots to simulate light colour or grey.

title-piece   the magazine's title in the typographical form used on the COVER.

TOT   Triumph Over Tragedy: an emotional story built on human suffering but with a happy ending.

tracking   see LETTERSPACING.

transparency   a single frame of positive photographic film.

transpose   to reorder characters, words or paragraphs.

trim lines   lines indicating the printing area in DESKTOP PUBLISHING software.

turn arrow   a symbol at the end of a page of type telling the reader to turn the page.

typeface   a complete alphabet in a particular design.

typo   abbreviation for 'typographical error'.

UGC   user-generated content: any content created by users of your website, or content that is published on other websites and which your journalists use in their work.

unfair dismissal   any dismissal that is not in accordance with employment law.

unjustified   type which has not been made flush at both ends of a line.

upper and lower   a HEADLINE regime in which UPPER CASE and LOWER CASE letters are used as sense requires, as opposed to 'all capitals' or 'initial capitals'.

upper case   capital letters.

Usenet also known as NEWSGROUPS: an unmoderated INTERNET discussion area that has nothing much to do with news.

variable direct costs costs which increase with the PRINT RUN and PAGINATION.

variance departure from an agreed budget.

vignette a photograph that fades away to nothing at the edges.

viral content that is likely to be – or has been – passed on by a lot of people online.

virus a computer program designed to spread and damage either hardware or software.

vox pop a FEATURE or story based on short interviews and MUG-SHOTS of members of the public.

web browser a computer program for reading WORLD WIDE WEB pages.

web editor a computer program used to create WEB PAGES.

web page an individual document in WORLD WIDE WEB format. Will include words, photographs and graphics. May also include sound, moving pictures and animation.

website a group of related WORLD WIDE WEB pages.

white space unprinted areas used by a designer to direct the eye.

widow the last line of a paragraph appearing at the top of a column. Best avoided.

wing copy additional matter enhancing a FEATURE, appearing in a BOX or PANEL to one side: see SIDEBARS.

word rate the fee for freelance contributions.

word spacing the amount of space between words. Controlled by software.

World Wide Web a network of computer files stored according to an agreed format

wrongful dismissal a dismissal without proper notice or contrary to correct disciplinary procedures.

x-height the height of ordinary lower case letters without ASCENDERS or DESCENDERS (a, c, e, etc.). Determines how large a typeface of a given size actually appears.

Notes

Introduction

1 http://www.pbs.org/mediashift/2010/12/ipads-print-on-demand-slowly-transform-magazines-in-2010357.html

1 How magazines work

1 Quoted in 'The Renegade and the Rules' by Patricia Prijatel and Sammye Johnson, in *Journal of Magazine and New Media Research*, Fall 1999, Vol. 1, No. 2. White was editor of the *Emporia Gazette of Kansas*.
2 'Art for Industry's Sake: Halftone Technology, Mass Photography and the Social Transformation of American Print Culture, 1880–1920' dissertation by David Clayton Phillips, Yale University, 1996. Published online at http://dphillips.web.wesleyan.edu/halftone
3 Source: PPA *Magazines Handbook*.
4 From Wood, *Curtis Magazines*, quoted in Phillips, op. cit.
5 Quoted in *Media Week*, 4 July 2002. Published online at http://www.mediaweek.co.uk/news/508882/Skys-not-limit-contract-mags/?DCMP=ILC-SEARCH
6 http://www.brandrepublic.com/go/news/article/1050694/bbc-magazines-launches-good-food-magazine-ipad-app/

2 Editorial strategy

1 'Communicating Effectively', by Pat Robert Cairns, then editor of *House Beautiful*, paper presented at PPA Seminar 'Effective Advertising with Magazines', 21 September 1995.
2 http://www.qzwhw.com/media/april-2002.html
3 The first is from *Marie Claire Australia*, the second from the US version, and the third is from *Marie Claire* in the UK.
4 WCRS Media Research Department, 1989.

3 Leader and manager

1 See anything by Dr Gerard Blair, particularly these pages created with his students as part of his Edinburgh University mechanical engineering course: http://www.ee.ed.ac.uk/~gerard/MENG/ME96/
2 From *101 Ways to Boost Your Performance* (Management Books 2000 Ltd, 1999).
3 Casey Stengel was the celebrated manager of the New York Yankees baseball team.

4 http://www.bis.gov.uk/policies/employment-matters
5 http://www.acas.org.uk/index.aspx?articleid=2179
6 This idea is explored in detail in *The Rise of the Player Manager*, by Philip Augar and Joy Palmer (Penguin, 2002).
7 There is also lots of useful information on the web, including the Free Management Library available online at http://managementhelp.org/
8 See the NUJ's web page 'On Negotiating' available online at: http://media.gn.apc.org/rates/negotiat.html. Or this article from the union's *Freelance* newsletter: http://media.gn.apc.org/fl/9605barg.html.
9 http://www.acas.org.uk/index.aspx?articleid=2179
10 http://www.ppa.co.uk/training/magazine-journalism-courses/
11 Try the RSI UK mailing list, available online at http://www.rsi-uk.org.uk/
12 http://www.hse.gov.uk/risk/fivesteps.htm

4 Money matters

1 Conclusions of 'Advertorials: Qualitative Research', published by the SouthBank Publishing Group of IPC Magazines, 1996. Reported in *How Magazine Advertising Works*, by Guy Consterdine (PPA, London, 1999).

5 The right words

1 Author of *Writing at Work: Do's, Don'ts and How Tos* and *On-The-Job Communications for Business, the Professions, Government and Industry*, sadly both out of print
2 The term hyperlocal is a vague one. In the US, where it originated, it can refer to areas that would support a local paper in the UK. Typically it refers to an area more local than previously covered by local media.
3 http://tpmlivewire.talkingpointsmemo.com/2010/06/how-rolling-stone-won-the-news-cycle-and-lost-the-story.php
4 http://www.niemanlab.org/2010/06/rolling-stones-late-start-on-mcchrystal-costs-it-comments/
5 http://www.pressgazette.co.uk/story.asp?storycode=39944
6 Library of Congress Interview, June 30, 1948. Transcribed by John Webb and available online at http://www.io.com/gibbonsb/mencken/megaquotes.html (accessed 6 December 2002)

6 Pictures and design

1 *Editing by Design* (Bowker, 1982).
2 http://www.alistapart.com/articles/a-simpler-page/
3 Quoted in *Nine Pioneers in American Graphic Design* by Roger Remington and Barbara Hodik (MIT Press, 1989).
4 From 'Choosing the Cover: Art or Science?', a presentation to the Periodical Publishers Association 2001 Conference.

8 Where the buck stops

1 The most recently updated book on the law as it affects magazines is *Publishing Law* (4th edition), by Hugh Jones and Christopher Benson (Routledge, 2011).
2 http://www.editorscode.org.uk/downloads/codebook/codebook.pdf

Bibliography

Books

Adobe Creative Team (2010) *Adobe InDesign CS5 Classroom in a Book*, San Jose, CA: Adobe Systems, Inc.

Banks, David and Hanna, Mark (2009) *McNae's Essential Law for Journalists*, Oxford: Oxford University Press.

Battelle, John (2005) *The Search*, London: Nicholas Brealey Publishing.

Blair, Gerard M. (1996) *Starting to Manage: The Essential Skills*, Piscataway, NJ: IEEE.

Blastland, Michael and Dilnot, Andrew (2007) *The Tiger That Isn't*, London: Profile Books

Bowman, S. and Willis, C. (2003) *We Media: How Audiences are Shaping the Future of News and Information*, Washington, DC: The Media Center at the American Press Institute.

Connor, Angela (2009) *18 Rules of Community Engagement*. Cupertino, CA: Happy About Publishing

Croner's Reference Book for Employers, Kingston-upon-Thames: Croner CCH.

Cutts, Martin (1995) *Plain English Guide*, Oxford: Oxford University Press.

Davis, Anthony (1988) *Magazine Journalism Today*, Oxford: Heinemann.

Evans, Harold (2000) *Essential English for Journalists, Editors and Writers*, London: Pimlico.

Gillmor, Dan (2004) *We the Media: Grassroots Journalism by the People, for the People*, Sebastopol, CA: O'Reilly Media.

Hennessy, Brendan (2005) *Writing Feature Articles*, Oxford: Focal.

Hicks, Wynford (2006) *English for Journalists*, London: Routledge.

Hicks, Wynford (2008) *Writing for Journalists*, London: Routledge.

Hicks, Wynford and Holmes, Tim (2002) *Subediting for Journalists*, London: Routledge.

Jones, Hugh and Benson, Christopher (2011) *Publishing Law*, Fourth Edition, London: Routledge.

Keeble, Richard (2012) *The Newspapers Handbook*, London: Routledge.

Kelly, John (2009) *Red Kayaks and Hidden Gold: The Rise, Challenges and Value of Citizen Journalism*, Oxford: Reuters Institute.

Leslie, Jeremy (2003) *Magculture: New Magazine Design*, London: Laurence King.

Leslie, Jeremy and Blackwell, Lewis (2001) *Issues: New Magazine Design*, Corte Madera, CA: Gingko.

Lewis, David and Sargeant, Malcolm (2009) *Essentials of Employment Law*, London: CIPD.

Mason, Peter and Smith, Derrick (1998) *Magazine Law*, London: Routledge.

McKay, Jenny (2005) *The Magazines Handbook*, London: Routledge.

Moser, Horst (2011) *The Art Directors' Handbook of Professional Magazine Design: Classic Techniques and Inspirational Approaches*, London: Thames & Hudson.

Nielsen, Jakob (2000) *Designing Web Usability*, New York: New Riders.
Powell, Gabriel (2007) *Instant InDesign: Designing Templates for Fast and Efficient Page Layout*, San Jose, CA: Adobe Systems, Inc.
Ritter, R.M. (ed.) (2000) *The Oxford Dictionary for Writers & Editors*, Oxford: Oxford University Press.
Ritter, R.M. (ed.) (2002) *The Oxford Guide to Style*, Oxford: Oxford University Press.
Ritter, R.M. (ed.) (2005) *New Hart's Riules: The Handbook of Style from Editors and Writers*, Oxford: Oxford University Press.
Tancer, Bill (2008) *Click*, New York: Hyperion.
Trippenbach, Philip (2009) 'Video Games: a New Medium for Journalism', in *The Future of Journalism*, Charles Miller (ed.), London: BBC College of Journalism.
Ward, Mike (2002) *Journalism Online*, Oxford: Focal Press.
Waterhouse, Keith (2010) *Waterhouse on Newspaper Style*, London: Revel Barker.
Wharton, John (1992) *Managing Magazine Publishing*, London: Blueprint.
White, Jan V. (2003) *Designing for Magazines*, New York: Allworth Press.
White, Jan V. (2003) *Editing By Design*, New York: Allworth Press.

Online resources and articles

Advisory, Conciliation and Arbitration Service (2009) 'Code of Practice on Disciplinary and Grievance Procedures', London: HMSO: http://www.acas.org.uk/index.aspx ?articleid=2175 (accessed 19 August 2011)
Bernoff, Josh. 'The POST Method: A systematic approach to social strategy', Groundswell, 11 December 2007. http://blogs.forrester.com/groundswell/2007/12/the-post-method. html (accessed 19 August 2011).
Blair, Gerard M (1991–3) 'Basic Management Skills': http://www.see.ed.ac.uk/~gerard/ Management (accessed 19 August 2011)
Blood, Rebecca. 'Weblogs: A History and Perspective', Rebecca's Pocket. 07 September 2000. 25 October 2006: http://www.rebeccablood.net/essays/weblog_history.html (accessed 19 August 2011).
Cellan-Jones, Rory. Seismic Shock: When blogging meets policing, dot.Rory, BBC News, 26 January 2010 http://www.bbc.co.uk/blogs/thereporters/rorycellanjones/2010/01/ seismic_shock_when_blogging_me.html (accessed 19 August 2011).
Claesens, Amanda and King, Kate. 'Optimising Your Market' Research, Slidefinder, 19th June 2008, http://www.slidefinder.net/n/nsm_research/431380 (accessed 19 August 2011)
Consterdine, Guy. 'How Magazine Advertising Works', Consterdine.com, July 2005, http:// www.consterdine.com/articlefiles/42/HMAW5.pdf (accessed 19 August 2011).
Department for Business Innovation and Skills. 'Employment Matters', undated: http:// www.bis.gov.uk/employment (accessed 19 August 2011).
Department for Culture, Media and Sport. Gambling Act 2005, undated: http://www. culture.gov.uk/what_we_do/gambling_and_racing/3305.aspx (accessed 19 August 2011).
Free Management Library 'Problem Solving, Delegating to Employees, Organizing Yourself, Decision Making, Time Management': http:// www.managementhelp.org (accessed 19 August 2011).
Grow, Gerald (2002) 'Magazine Covers and Cover Lines: An Illustrated History. History', Journal of Magazine and New Media Research: http://longleaf.net/coverlines/ (accessed 19 August 2011).

Hanson, Nigel. Newspaper wins and loses in new privilege ruling, *Hold The Front Page*, 3 November 2009: http://www.holdthefrontpage.co.uk/law/091103reynolds.shtml (accessed 19 August 2011)

Health and Safety Executive (2011) 'Five Steps to Risk Assessment': http://www.hse.gov.uk/risk/fivesteps.htm (accessed 19 August 2011).

Higgerson, David. 'Running a group on flickr: tips on how to keep everyone happy' 11 November 2009: http://davidhiggerson.wordpress.com/2009/11/11/running-a-group-on-flickr-tips-on-how-to-keep-everyone-happy/ (accessed 19 August 2011).

Karp, Scott. 'Drudge Report: News Site That Sends Readers Away With Links Has Highest Engagement', Publishing 2.0, 15 September 2008: http://publishing2.com/2008/09/15/drudge-report-news-site-that-sends-readers-away-with-links-has-highest-engagement/ (accessed 19 August 2011).

Lasica, JD 'What is Participatory Journalism?' *Online Journalism Review*, 7 August 7 2003 http://www.ojr.org/ojr/workplace/1060217106.php (accessed 19 August 2011)

Professional Publishers Association (2011). 'Marketing': http://www.ppa.co.uk/marketing/ (accessed 19 August 2011).

Phillips, Gill. 'Fair comment is dead. Long live honest comment', *The Guardian*, 1 December 2010: http://www.guardian.co.uk/law/2010/dec/01/libel-reform-medialaw (accessed 19 August 2011).

Ponsford, Dominic. 'Libel landmark: Fair comment now 'honest comment'', *Press Gazette*, 1 December 2010: http://www.pressgazette.co.uk/story.asp?c=1&sectioncode=1&storycode=46378 (accessed 19 August 2011).

Press Complaints Commission 'Code of Practice', London: PCC: http://www.pcc.org.uk/cop/practice.html (accessed 19 August 2011)

Ruel, Laura and Paul, Nora. 'Multimedia storytelling: when is it worth it?', *Online Journalism Review*, 12 February 2007: http://www.ojr.org/ojr/stories/070210ruel/ (accessed 19 August 2011).

Ruel, Laurs and Outing, Steve. 'Recall of Information Presented in Text vs. Multimedia Format', September 2004: http://www.poynterextra.org/EYETRACK2004/multimedia recall.htm (accessed 19 August 2011)

Rusbridger, Alan. 'The Trafigura fiasco tears up the textbook', *The Guardian*, 14 October 2009: http://www.guardian.co.uk/commentisfree/libertycentral/2009/oct/14/trafigura-fiasco-tears-up-textbook (accessed 19 August 2011).

Salopek, Jennifer (2001) 'The Editorial High Wire', in *The Westbound Loupe*, Alexandria, VA: Westbound Communications: http://www.westboundl.com/loupe/00wa056sl.html (accessed 19 August 2011).

Shirky, Clay. 'Broadcast Institutions, Community Values', Shirky.com, 9 September 2002. http://shirky.com/writings/broadcast_and_community.html (accessed 19 August 2011).

The Teenage Magazine Arbitration Panel 'Guidelines': http://www.tmap.org.uk/public/downloads/tmap_guidelines.pdf (accessed 19 August 2011).

Walsh, Jason (2007) 'Build the perfect web community'. *.net Magazine*, no.165, pp39–43, August: http://www.netmag.co.uk/zine/podcast/episode-12 (accessed 19 August 2011).

Wardle, Claire and Williams, Andrew (2009) ugc@thebbc: 'Understanding its impact upon contributors, non-contributors and BBC News'. BBC Knowledge Exchange: http://www.bbc.co.uk/blogs/knowledgeexchange/cardiffone.pdf (accessed 19 August 2011).

Wertheim, E (1996) 'Negotiations and Resolving Conflicts: An Overview': http://www.iiasa.ac.at/Research/DAS/interneg/training/conflict_overview.html (accessed 19 August 2011)

Magazines and blogs

British Journalism Review, SAGE Publications, 1 Oliver's Yard, 55 City Road, London EC1Y 1SP: http://www.bjr.org.uk.

InPublishing, InPublishing Ltd, Hawthorns, Station Road, Eynsford, Dartford, Kent DA4 0EJ: http://www.inpublishing.co.uk/Journalism.co.uk, http://www.journalism.co.uk/

Media Week, Griffin House, 161 Hammersmith Road, London W6 8SD. http://www.mediaweek.co.uk.

Press Gazette, John Carpenter House, John Carpenter Street, London EC4Y 0AN. http://www.pressgazette.com.

B2B Memes: http://www.b2bmemes.com/

David Hepworth's blog: http://whatsheonaboutnow.blogspot.com/

Digital Magazines: http://digitalmags.blogspot.com/

FIPP – the worldwide magazine media association: http://www.fipp.com/News

FOLIO magazine publishing: http://www.foliomag.com/

magCulture.com: http://magculture.com/blog/

The Media Briefing: http://www.themediabriefing.com/

One Man And His Blog: http://www.onemanandhisblog.com/

Online Journalism Blog (magazines category): http://onlinejournalismblog.com/category/magazines/

Society of Publication Designers: http://www.spd.org/

You can find a 'bundle' of updates from around 30 blogs covering the magazines industry at http://www.google.com/reader/bundle/user%2F12323076578145270806%2Fbundle%2FMagsOJ

Index